SYRIA: ANATOMY OF REGIME CHANGE

SYRIA: ANATOMY
OF REGIME CHANGE

Jeremy Kuzmarov and Dan Kovalik

Baraka
Books

Montréal

ISBN 978-1-77186-396-4 pbk.
ISBN 978-1-77186-413-8 epub
ISBN 978-1-77186-414-5 pdf

Cover by Leila Marshy
Book Design by Folio Infographie
Editing: Robin Philpot
Proofreading: Anne Marie Marko

Legal Deposit, 4th quarter 2025

Bibliothèque et Archives nationales du Québec
Library and Archives Canada

Published by Baraka Books of Montreal

TRADE DISTRIBUTION & RETURNS

Canada
UTPdistribution.com

United States
Independent Publishers Group: IPGbook.com

We acknowledge the support from the Société de développement des
entreprises culturelles (SODEC) and the Government of Quebec tax credit
for book publishing administered by SODEC.

Société
de développement
des entreprises
culturelles
Québec

Financé par le gouvernement du Canada
Funded by the Government of Canada | Canada

PUBLISHED &
PRINTED IN
CANADA

Contents

Contents

Foreword by Oliver Stone

Another nation has fallen to the predations of Western interventionism. This time, it is Syria, a once beautiful and prosperous country, which has been home to peoples of different religions and ethnicities who lived together peacefully for centuries. That peaceful coexistence was purposefully destroyed by the U.S. and its allies who decided to effectuate regime change by inciting sectarian violence and supporting terrorist groups whose explicit plan was to set up an extremist religious Caliphate intolerant of all other religions.

Quite tragically, the terrorist group Al Qaeda, now named HTS, has taken over Syria and is now in the process of setting up such a Caliphate. Part of this process entails the mass slaughter of religious minorities, such as Alawites and Christians, and the kidnapping of young women from these groups who are raped and enslaved.

It would be shocking to know that this is all happening with the full connivance of modern, Western nations, except for the fact that we have seen this all before—most notably, in Afghanistan where the U.S. supported religious extremists to overthrow a secular, socialist government and to lure the USSR into the "Afghan trap," in the words of Zbigniew Brzezinski. Years later, the Soviet Union is gone, Afghanistan is now being ruled by the Taliban, and the offspring of the terrorist groups the U.S. supported in Afghanistan—namely, Osama bin Laden's Al Qaeda—is now flourishing more than ever as the ruling group of a major country.

For years, there have been some of us who, like voices in the wilderness, have warned of what was happening in Syria and of the U.S.'s role in supporting terrorists there. In response, we were maligned as Assadists, apologists of dictatorship and Putin dupes. We were also called "conspiracy theorists" for daring to point out the obvious fact that the U.S. had aligned with the very groups in Syria that it claimed to be fighting after 9/11. Now, of course, what we warned would happen has come to pass, and the Syrian people are paying the price. Meanwhile, the mainstream press which did its best to gin up support for the U.S.'s regime-change operations in Syria has lost interest in that country now that those operations have been successful. And so, the new regime is able to carry out mass atrocities with little to no scrutiny.

Of course, it was not just dissident voices who warned about the fate of countries like Syria. Years ago, shortly after 9/11, General Wesley Clark told the world exactly what the plan was; that the U.S. had decided to overthrow seven sovereign nations in five years, "starting with Iraq, and then Syria, Lebanon, Libya, Somalia, Sudan and, finishing off, Iran." While the order was somewhat changed by circumstances, and while it has taken a bit longer than planned, the U.S. is well under way in accomplishing this deadly project, with Iran now being the last of these listed countries in its sights.

The toll of this mad plan has been extraordinary but rarely discussed. According to Brown University's Watson Institute for International and Public Affairs, as of October, 2024, between 4.5 and 4.7 million people in the Middle East and Northern Africa have been killed in the U.S.'s post-9/11 wars, with 7.6 million children still suffering acute malnutrition from these conflicts. And these numbers continue to mount. Meanwhile, the U.S. has spent trillions of dollars on these wars—an expenditure which has driven the U.S. into a debt it can never pay; which threatens the global economy; and which, most importantly, could have been used on alleviating human suffering rather than causing it.

The great lie, of course, has been that this was all done to fight terrorism, when in fact the U.S. was all the while supporting ter-rorists to effectuate its regime-change plans. At the same time, the targets of U.S. regime change have almost invariably been governments (such as the ones in Iraq, Libya, Syria) which were actively opposed to terrorism, and especially to Al Qaeda. Iran, the final target of the U.S.'s regime-change plan, actually assisted the U.S. in fighting terrorism after 9/11, and it has been rewarded for these efforts with scorn and maximum sanctions. It is hard to think of a greater travesty, and a greater betrayal of the public trust. Indeed, all of this belies any claim the U.S. has to being a functioning democracy or a force for good in the world.

As I write these words, the U.S. government seems hell-bent on carrying out its regime-change plans against the big prize, Iran—a country of around ninety million people. Iran is one of the oldest nations in the world, with an incredible history of art, architecture, scientific thinking and culture. The U.S. is now threatening to shatter all of that as it has in so many other countries. The costs of such an intervention will be colossal in terms of blood and treasure, as if enough of this has not been lost already.

This book by Jeremy Kuzmarov and Dan Kovalik is a warning and a call to action. It is a warning against what regime change means for the people living in the nations targeted, and a call to organize to prevent the regime-change war.

While we are sold on interventions in such countries as Syria with claims that we are bringing them democracy and freedom and stability, the very opposite is true. Indeed, after years of war and economic sanctions imposed upon it by the West, Syria is no more. This once-proud nation is now being carved up by neo-colonial powers such as the U.S., Israel, Turkey, and France. And in the place of a modern nation-state, Syria is being brought back to the Middle Ages by a fanatical government, which is imposing its own brand of extremist Sharia law, and is threatening to kill, jail, or expel anyone who refuses to go along with this.

A similar fate awaits Iran if the U.S. decides to wage war against that country. And this is why we must do all we can to stop this next war before it is too late.

Introduction

> "America is a god and a thousand cowards kneel at its feet."
> —Nizar Qabbani, Syrian poet.[1]

On December 8, 2024, Syria's longstanding President Bashar al-Assad departed to Russia after being deposed by Sunni militia forces in what *New York Times* columnist Thomas L. Friedman called the "biggest, potentially most positive, game-changing event in the Middle East in the last 45 years."[2] Friedman was enthusiastic about the regime change, though Syria's new head of state, Abu Mohammed Al-Jolani (aka Ahmed Hussein al-Sharaa), had a $10 million bounty placed on his head by the U.S. State Department in 2017 as a wanted terrorist.[3]

The "blazer wearing revolutionary," as *CNN* called him,[4] had been imprisoned from 2006-2011 at Abu Ghraib and other U.S. military prisons for supporting Al Qaeda in Iraq. Conveniently, Al-Jolani was released on the eve of the 2011 U.S.-backed uprising against Al-Assad, fueling suspicion that he had somehow been turned and transformed into a CIA/MI6/Mossad agent while in custody.[5] Claiming to "love Israel" and that he wanted to build a Trump tower in Damascus and open up Syria's oil and gas industry to U.S. corporations, Al-Jolani headed an Al Qaeda affiliate, Tahrir al-Sham, backed by Turkey, Qatar, Israel, Saudi Arabia, the UK, France, Canada, and the U.S.[6] Amazingly given this latter support, White House spokesman John Kirby said on December 2, 2024 that Tahrir al-Sham "are not good folks."[7]

A Shia Alawite who succeeded his father, Hafez (1970-2000), Bashar al-Assad was supported by Iran and Russia in the war on

Syria, which claimed around half a million lives. President Joe Biden stated on December 8, 2024 that Syria now faced a "historic opportunity for peace" and "the establishment of a new Syrian state . . . at long last the Assad regime has fallen."[8] U.S. media echoed Biden's triumphalism and became filled with stories about ghastly atrocities allegedly carried out by Assad and the gaudy riches that his family had supposedly accumulated through illicit means, inlcuding by presiding over a drug empire.[9] Suppressed were reports about field executions by Syria's new Islamist rulers, desecration of ancient shrines, and house-to-house searches of Assad supporters susceptible to revenge attacks as well as death squad operations targeting Alawites and other members of Syria's minority groups.[10] The Al-Nusra Front and Tahrir al-Sham under Jolani's leadership had perpetrated suicide bombing and sectarian cleansing massacres against Shia Muslims, Druze, and Alawites during the 2012-2017 phases of the Syrian civil war, which were also not discussed.[11]

A *New York Times* article by Neil McFarquhar, characteristically entitled "The Assad Family's Legacy is One of Savage Oppression," compared the Assads to the mafia Corleone family and quoted from a senior fellow at the Washington Institute for Near East Policy, Andrew J. Tabler, who stated that the Assads "cared nothing about the Syrian people. They launched Scud missiles against their own people—who does that?—while the chemical weapons were a sign of just how far they would go to hold on to power." The article further quoted from a former college friend of Assad who joined the opposition out of disgust over the lack of reform, and who said that "they were not running a country with a history of 5,000 years of civilization. They were running it like the Mafia, as if it was a private estate, the whole country was their backyard inherited from their father."[12]

Reappropriating Orientalist stereotypes of Western Asian rulers as despotic and savage, McFarquhar's piece advanced disinformation about chemical weapons attacks that had been disproven by MIT scientist Theodore Postol, a weapons adviser to the U.S. Navy's Chief of Operations, and journalists Seymour Hersh and Robert Fisk among others.[13] The *Times* article further obscures the factors underlying the Assad dynasty's durability, though does acknowledge that Syria was "known as the most unstable country in the Middle East after War II" with "at least eight coups carried out right before Hafez al-Assad took power in 1970."[14]

The *Wall Street Journal* published an op-ed in the wake of Assad's downfall by star reporter Sune Engel Rasmussen that celebrated the "Syrian revolution" for "dealing a historic blow to Iran." Rasmussen wrote that Iran had "spent decades and billions of dollars building a network of militias and governments that allowed it to exercise political and military influence across the Middle East," however, in a "matter of weeks, the pillars of that alliance came crashing down, with the fall of Bashar al-Assad serving as Iran's latest strategic catastrophe."[15] Rasmussen continued to note that Syria under Assad's leadership had provided Iran with land access to Hezbollah, the centerpiece of its self-labeled "axis of resistance," which, thanks to Tehran's support, became the world's best-armed nonstate actor but was now effectively dismantled. In Rasmussen's assessment, Israeli policy since October 7 could now be considered a great success as "in more than a year of attacks, Israel has devastated Hamas, Iran's main Palestinian ally . . . killed most of the leadership of Hezbollah, the Lebanese militia that is Iran's most powerful ally, and sent its surviving top commanders into hiding. Assad's toppling [further] destroys the entire front line of Iran's so-called 'forward defense.'"

Rasmussen's triumphalist account amazingly attempted to rebrand Israeli military aggression and crimes that have resulted in the deaths of tens of thousands of people as a "strategic success." Rasmussen pays no heed at all to the historical factors that fueled the rise of Hamas and Hezbollah or to the massive human suffering Israeli policies have resulted in. Nor to the U.S. empowerment of Al Qaeda-linked jihadists in Syria or the danger of a war with Iran. The callous disregard for human welfare extends to Syria itself, whose population has suffered from biblical scale calamities engendered by a civil war triggered by outsiders and as a result of the imposition of draconian sanctions designed to devastate Syria's economy so that they would turn against the Assad government.[16]

Most revealingly absent in U.S. media accounts was the fact that the U.S. had engaged in a thirteen-year regime-change operation that started with the "Arab Spring" and continued with the launching of Operation Timber Sycamore by the Obama administration—the largest covert operations since the CIA's support for the Afghan mujahidin in the 1980s. *The New York Times, Wall Street Journal,* and even alternative media outlets like *Democracy Now* made it seem like Assad had fallen suddenly and organically in December 2024 as a result of a popular rebellion and that this was cause for celebration.[17] Blogger Caitlin Johnstone wrote, "we're all meant to pretend this was a 100 percent organic uprising driven solely and exclusively by the people of Syria despite years and years of evidence to the contrary" and the fact that the "U.S. power alliance" [encompassing Israel, Turkey, Saudi Arabia, and Qatar] crushed Syria using proxy warfare, starvation sanctions, constant bombing operations, and a [U.S.] military occupation explicitly designed to cut Syria off from oil and wheat in order to prevent its reconstruction after the western-backed civil war."[18]

The U.S. State Department actually took credit for Assad's overthrow. Spokesman Matthew Miller stated on December 9, 2024 that U.S. policy had "led to the situation we're in today." It "developed during the latter stages of the Obama administration" and "has largely carried through to this day."[19] The regime-change operation in Syria was openly advertised even earlier, when General Wesley Clark was told during a visit at the Pentagon after 9/11 that "we're going to attack and destroy the governments in seven countries in five years—we're going to start with Iraq, and then we're going to move to Syria, Lebanon, Libya, Somalia, Sudan and Iran."[20]

The methods that were utilized to oust Assad fit a long-standing regime-change playbook that had been applied in many of the countries listed by Clark. This playbook involves:

a) a protracted demonization campaign that spotlights the dastardly human rights abuses allegedly committed by the target of U.S. regime change. This demonization campaign enlists journalists and academics and highlights the viewpoint of pro-Western dissidents while maligning politicians, journalists or academics who voice criticism of U.S. foreign policy or who are against the regime-change operation (the latter being derided as "dictator lovers" or "apologists").[21]

b) National Endowment for Democracy (NED) and United States Agency of international Development (USAID) funding of civil society and opposition groups and opposition media with the aim of mobilizing support of students and young people against the government.

c) a program of economic warfare designed to weaken the economy and facilitate hardship for the population that will push them to turn against their leader.

d) CIA financing of rebel groups and fomenting of protests or an uprising that aims to elicit a heavy-handed government response that can be used to further turn domestic and world opinion against the government.

e) a false flag is often necessary in which paid snipers dressed up in army or police uniforms fire on protesters. Blame is cast on the targeted government when it urges restraint. Chemical or biological warfare attacks are also staged in order to rally Western opinion in support of "humanitarian" military intervention.

f) drone warfare, bombing, and clandestine Special Forces operations using Navy Seals and private mercenaries. The light U.S. footprint approach will avert antiwar dissent at home.

g) enlisting third country nationals and proxy forces to carry out a lot of the heavy lifting and many of the military or bombing operations to ensure plausible deniability.

h) enlistment of disaffected minority groups who are paid to fight against government forces.

i) whitewashing of the background of rebel forces who are presented in the media as "freedom fighters" or "moderate rebels" and not the terrorists and Islamic extremists or fascists that they usually are.

j) accusing the government of enlisting foreigners to put down the rebellion when the rebellion itself has been triggered by foreign mercenaries financed by MI6/CIA/Mossad.

The targets for U.S. regime change are inevitably leaders who are independent nationalists intent on resisting U.S. corporate penetration of their countries and challenging U.S. global hegemony. Bashar al-Assad fit the bill for the latter because he backed Palestinian resistance groups and stood up to Israel, aligned closely with Iran and Russia, and adopted nationalistic economic policies.[22] Assad was also growing economic relations with China and refused to construct the Trans-Arabian Qatari pipeline through Syria, endorsing instead a Russian approved "Islamic" pipeline running from Iran's side of the gas field through Syria and to the ports of Lebanon. According to Robert F. Kennedy Jr., this latter pipeline would make "Shiite Iran, not Sunni Qatar, the principal supplier to the European energy market" and "dramatically increase Iran's influence in the Middle East and world"—which the U.S. and Israel would not allow.[23]

The success of the U.S. regime change in Syria was a defeat for all humanity. The country is now under the rule of Sunni extremists backed by foreign interests intent on weakening and carving up Syria for their own designs. British journalist Vanessa Beeley described post-Assad Syria as "a toothless melting pot of foreign interests, resource looting and expanding Zionist land grab"[24]— which is exactly what the architects of Assad's toppling wanted. In the two days following the collapse of the Assad government, Israel conducted about 480 strikes across Syria, and destroyed the Syrian fleet in Latakia. Pursuing his expansionist agenda,

Israeli Prime Minister Benjamin Netanyahu illegally claimed control over the demilitarized buffer zone in the Golan Heights and declared that the Golan Heights will be a part of the State of Israel "for eternity."[25]

Syria: Anatomy of Regime Change is the first book that offers an overview and analysis of the U.S. regime-change operation that started well before the "Arab Spring" and culminated with the toppling of the Assad government in December 2024. It can be read as a primer on regime-change operations and how they are carried out. The first chapter looks at the precursors to the anti-Assad operation in a little-known CIA regime-change operation in the 1940s, which removed another nationalist leader, Shukri al-Quwatli, who came back to win presidential elections in 1955 (the CIA then again tried to overthrow him but failed). The second chapter examines U.S. regime-change efforts targeting Hafez al-Assad in the 1980s and how they set the groundwork for the twenty-first century. Chapter three looks at the "Arab Spring" and Syrian revolution and U.S. attempts to trigger and manipulate it. Chapter four examines the Syrian conflict from the perspective of Syrians. Chapter five looks at the logistics of the Operation Timber Sycamore and other covert meddling in Syria by the NED and USAID that contributed to the regime-change operation along with Special Forces operations in Syria.

Chapter six looks at the international dimension of the Syrian conflict and involvement of Turkey, Saudi Araba, Israel, and Qatar. Chapter seven examines the chemical weapons hoax and how this was used to engender public support for bombing operations and expanded U.S. interference in Syria. Chapter eight looks at the White Helmets and how they were part of a psychological warfare operation. Chapter nine looks at the U.S. sanctions and their significance in wearing the population down and undercutting their capacity to resist outside invasion. Chapter ten looks at the media and intellectuals' role in manufacturing consent for regime change. The final chapter looks at the fall of the Assad government and prospects for Syria today.

Overall, Syria was seen as a great success by U.S. policy-makers because the U.S. achieved its geostrategic goals at minimal economic and political cost. The U.S. was able to obtain plausible deniability and avoid large-scale protests among Americans because it kept its involvement largely hidden and worked through intermediaries like Israel, Saudi Arabia, Jordan, Qatar, and Turkey, along with France, the former colonial power, Britain, and other European Union countries, who had their own geopolitical ambitions. Additionally, the U.S. government proved very effective in winning the informational war by conditioning the public to believe that Assad was a brutal tyrant who adopted chemical warfare attacks against his own people.

The spectacular success of the propaganda was evident in the fact that anti-genocide protesters on college campuses did not display the same outrage at U.S. or Israeli policy in Syria as they did with the genocide in Gaza, even though it was the same people behind both, resulted also in a terrible humanitarian crisis, and led to the removal of a key ally of the Palestinian people. For years, what passes for the antiwar left in the U.S. was largely silent about Syria. Many traditional leftists in the U.S. and other Western countries, who opposed the Vietnam and Iraq Wars rebuked Donald Trump when he threatened to remove U.S. troops from Syria, claiming it would result in Turkish ethnic cleansing of Syria's Kurds.[26] The U.S. left also largely distanced itself from Tulsi Gabbard, who defected from the Democratic Party after being attacked by party leaders as "an Assad lover" because she met with Assad in the attempt to initiate a peace process.[27]

The foreign policy elite in Washington will surely look upon Syria as a model that can provide a blueprint for similar regime-change operations in other countries—no matter how long it took to consummate and how cataclysmic it was for the Syrian people. Two generations ago, Laos provided a similar such model because the U.S. was able to fight a secret war through reliance on a CIA mercenary army combined with heavy application of U.S. airpower that was kept invisible to the American public.[28]

Syria is even better for the U.S. policy elites because a lot of the bombing was carried out by the Israelis, who can easily be blamed if the atrocities start to generate public outrage or if things don't go quite as planned. The Syria regime change additionally set the groundwork for a joint U.S.-Israeli military attack on Iran, which neoconservatives had long planned for.

CHAPTER 1

The First U.S. Regime Change in Syria—The Early Cold War

The 21st century U.S. regime-change operations targeting Bashar al-Assad fit with a long history of U.S. covert meddling in Syria dating back to the 1940s. In 1999, historian Douglas Little published an article in *Middle East Journal* entitled "Cold War and Covert Action: The U.S. and Syria, 1945-1958," which noted that, "as early as 1949, Syria had become an important staging ground for the CIA's earliest experiments in covert action."[1] The experiment included the staging of a coup d'état in March 1949 against Syrian President Shukri Al-Quwatli by right-wing military officers led by Hosni Al-Zaim, who had been jailed at the end of World War II for receiving illegal funds from France's pro-Nazi Vichy regime.[2]

A member of a secret anti-Ottoman-empire organization who had opposed a U.S. mandate in Syria at the end of World War I, Al-Quwatli had forged very good relations with President Franklin D. Roosevelt and had reached out to the U.S. for financial support at the end of World War II.[3] The Truman administration, however, wanted to maintain colonial control over countries in the Global South and saw Syria as being too independent under Al-Quwatli's leadership. Historian Patrick Donovan Higgins wrote in his article, "Gunning for Damascus: The U.S. War on the Syrian Republic," that the U.S. swooped into West Asia to take over colonial rule from Britain and France who had Balkanized and divided up control over this region through the Sykes-Picot Agreement of 1916.[4] A key U.S. goal was to make sure that trade and economic relations would be structured in a way to allow U.S. corporations maximum exploitation of the region's labor and resources, notably oil—something Al-Quwatli was not keen to allow. Truman's Cabinet included figures such as Defense Secretary James Forrestal who had deep ties to Wall Street and the oil industry.[5] Al-Quwatli's unwillingness to crack down on Syria's left-wing movements and Communist Party and forging of good relations with Soviet leaders prompted Secretary of State George C. Marshall to warn of the "encroaching specter of Syrian-USSR rapprochement."[6]

An additional key impetus for the 1949 coup—called by CIA operative Miles Copeland Jr. a "pilot project"—was the goal of establishing an oil pipeline built by the Arabian American Oil Company (ARAMCO) carrying Persian Gulf Oil from the Dhahran oil fields in Saudi Arabia through Syria to the Mediterranean. Europe's economic recovery depended on oil, and the ARAMCO Trans-Arabian pipeline would have helped provide it with cheap oil from the Middle East. Al-Quwatli, however, refused to go forward with negotiations for the Trans-Arabian pipeline, which was to be built by the San Francisco-based Bechtel Corporation. Al-Quwatli had feared that the pipeline would upset the Iraqi Petroleum Company (IPC) and the British, who helped Syria obtain independence, and recognized that Syrian public opinion saw it as a new form of indirect economic control.[7]

The other threat Al-Quwatli posed to the colonial aims of the U.S. was his support for Arab anti-colonial struggles—notably the Algerians against the French and the Palestinians against the creation of Israel. During the 1948-49 Israeli independence war, Al-Quwatli organized the creation of the Arab Liberation Army (ALA) that tried to defend Palestinians displaced in the Nakba.[8] As we will see later, Syria's ongoing support for the Palestinians continued to be a big motivating factor in the U.S.'s relentless campaign to overthrow the Assad governments that was to follow.

Douglas Little wrote that the 1949 CIA-backed coup in Syria "helped reverse a century of friendship [between the U.S. and Syria] that began with the American missionaries who flocked to the Levant after 1820 and encouraged the Arabs to overthrow the Ottoman yoke."[9] The coup additionally provided a model for the 1953 Iranian coup that ousted secular nationalist Mohammed Mossadegh and poisoned U.S.-Iranian relations irrevocably.[10] CIA operatives Miles Copeland Jr. and Stephen Meade, who had served in the elite U.S. Army Rangers Battalion ("Darby's Raiders") in North Africa during World War II, were dispatched to Syria to engineer the March 1949 coup. Described by historian Hugh Wilford as a "tough-looking, muscular, James Bond kind of character," Meade met secretly at least six times with Colonel Zaim to discuss the possibility of an army-supported dictatorship that would replace Al-Quwatli.[11]

In the days leading up to the coup, Assistant Secretary of State for Near Eastern Affairs, George McGhee, a wealthy oilman from Waco, Texas, visited Damascus and is alleged to have sanctioned the coup plot. According to Little, U.S. officials recognized that Zaim was a "banana republic dictator type" who "did not have the competence of a French Corporal." They supported him because of his "strong anti-Soviet attitude, willingness to talk peace with Israel [which the Truman administration chose to support] and his desire for American military assistance."[12]

The Soviet newspaper *Pravda* reported that Zaim's coup had been organized "by the Anglo-American rivals for the oil resources and strategic bases in that area."[13] A 1950 article in the *Middle East Journal* emphasized Zaim's use of Circassian and Kurdish units to carry out the coup, foreshadowing the importance of Kurds and other minority groups in twenty-first century regime-change operations.[14] Described by Robert F. Kennedy Jr. as a "convicted swindler" and by historian Sami Moubayed as a "military officer who looked and acted like Benito Mussolini," Zaim was very close to France, which became his primary arms supplier.[15] Before he took power, Zaim had requested that

U.S. agents "provoke and abet internal disturbances, which are essential for coup d'état" or that "U.S. funds be given for this purpose as soon as possible."

Stephen Meade reported favorably on April 15, after Zaim had taken power and Al-Quwatli had been placed under arrest, that "over 400 Commies [in] all parts of Syria have been arrested," and that Zaim was "prepared to ratify TAPLINE [ARAMCO oil pipeline]." A month later, Zaim approved the long delayed TAPLINE concession, removing the final obstacle to ARAMCO's plan to pipe Saudi oil to the Mediterranean. Zaim also broadened his anti-Soviet campaign by fully banning the Communist Party and jailing left-wing dissidents. Additionally, he withdrew all Syrian claims against Turkey (staunch U.S. ally) and signed an armistice with Israel.[16] As we shall see later, the new HTS government in Syria, after the ouster of Bashar Al-Assad, would swiftly follow Zaim's example by outlawing the communist parties in Syria, making concessions to both Turkey and Israel and vowing to sell off Syria's oil and gas industry to U.S. corporations.

Zaim's love of pomp and personal aggrandizement and indulgence in personal luxuries earned him the enmity of most Syrians not long after he had taken power.[17] With no protestation from the Americans, Zaim abolished Syria's constitution, shut down parliament, closed newspapers, and outlawed all political parties, enforcing martial law and arresting anyone who uttered the slightest opposition to his regime.[18] British journalist Patrick Seale wrote that Zaim's "extravagant regime lay somewhere between political gangsterism and musical comedy."[19]

On August 2, 1949, Zaim was overthrown and executed after a coup by Colonel Sami al-Hinnawi and other army officers unhappy with Zaim's personalistic rule and friendly policies towards Israel (which defeated Syria in the 1948 Israeli independence war). The Truman administration recognized the new government. However, U.S. military intelligence warned that "commies were attempting to assume increasing influence in the new parliament by offering to support numerous non-commie candidates throughout the country." When Hinnawi's party announced plans for a Syrian union with Iraq's Hashemite dynasty, Hinnawi was ousted in Syria's third coup in nine months. The coup was led by Colonel Adib Shishakli, whom historian Sami Moubayed calls an "advanced version of Al-Zaim." Miles Copeland Jr. and others in the U.S. embassy in Damascus knew of Shishakli's coup plans in advance and gave them the green light.[20]

Scuttling plans for a Syria-Iraqi federation, Shishakli renewed the TAPLINE concession on terms favorable to ARAMCO and expressed willingness to conclude a peace treaty with Israel. At the same time, he dissolved parliament and set up a military dictatorship. Patrick Seale presents Shishakli as a failed leader who "had no coherent social or economic philosophy" that could mobilize popular support for him or guide policies that would help improve Syria's economy.[21] Shishakli's political mentor, Anton Sadeh, was described by *The New York Times* as a "fascist oriented leader."[22] The party to which both belonged adopted Nazi-type salutes.[23] Though he had gained fame for his exploits fighting the French in the 1930s and Israelis in the late 1940s, Shishakli's brutality was evident when he deployed aircraft and tanks to help crush a Druze rebellion in Jabal al Arab, resulting in the death of around 200 civilians. Hostile to Baathists, socialists, and communists, Shishakli's regime also sent in the army to crush left-wing protestors in the southern Druze city of al Suwayda.[24]

The Eisenhower administration wanted Syria to join the Baghdad Pact, a pro-western alliance modeled after NATO, that would help isolate radical Arab states like Egypt under Gamal Abdel Nasser.[25] Colonel Adnan Maliki was a main opponent of the Baghdad Pact within the Syrian military. He was assassinated by a right-wing terrorist group supportive of Shishakli, the Syrian Social Nationalist Party (SSNP), that had long been rumored to have been close to the CIA.[26] In August 1955, after Al-Quwatli won elections, CIA Director Allen Dulles flew to London with Kermit Roosevelt—architect of the CIA's 1953 coup in Iran—to work out details for another Syrian coup with Britain's secret intelligence service (SIS).

Dulles' plan, Operation Straggle, called for Turkey to stage border incidents, for British operatives to stir up Syria's desert tribes with Iraq, and for American agents to mobilize SSNP guerrillas, all of which would trigger a pro-western coup that would bring Shishakli back into power.[27] Approved by Eisenhower and British Prime Minister Harold Macmillan, the coup would involve assassination of Syria's chief of intelligence, Abdul al-Hamid Sarraj, chief of the army general staff, Afif al-Bizri, and the head of the country's Communist Party, Khalid Bakdash.[28] The CIA and MI6 also planned to instigate internal uprisings by the Druze in the south, free political prisoners held in the Mezzeh prison, and stir up the Muslim Brotherhood in Damascus, which would be later called upon to assassinate officials the CIA or Britain's MI6 wanted taken out.[29]

In his 1980 memoir *Ropes of Sand: America's Failure in the Middle East*, CIA operative Wilbur Crane Eveland wrote about payoffs to a conservative politician, Mikhail Ilyan, and about CIA operative Art Close's almost comical efforts to smuggle Shishakli's chief of security, Colonel Ibrahim Al Husseini, who was as big as a moose, in the trunk of an embassy car back into Syria from across the border (Husseini had been serving as Syrian military attaché in Rome). Eveland describes his assignment in Syria as being "to stem the [country's] leftist drift."[30]

The key CIA point man in the coup plot, Archibald (Archie) Roosevelt, Kermit's brother and Theodore Roosevelt's grandson, possessed a deep hatred of communism synonymous with his class background. Later, he went on to organize Armenians, Kurds, Georgians, and other minority groups in Turkey to penetrate the Soviet Union.[31] A bookish boy who excelled in the study of history and the classics at Groton and Harvard, Archie ironically identified with "the losers of history, Carthage against Rome, the Moors of Spain against Castille, and the Byzantines against everyone," according to Hugh Wilford. Learning Arabic and

Hebrew, Archie also sympathized with Arab nationalist movements and at one point delivered a blistering critique of American complicity with French colonial rule in Tunisia where he served with the U.S. Army Psychological Warfare Branch (PWB) in World War II. Archie also supported the American Friends of the Middle East, a lobby group that opposed U.S. support for Israel out of fear of compromising the U.S. relationship with the Arab countries.

Despite adopting certain sensible positions, Archie was an Anglophile who hobnobbed with British imperial agents and fashioned himself in the mold of Lawrence of Arabia, who integrated into Arab culture and befriended Arab leaders so they could be coopted by the British.[32] Roosevelt similarly embraced Arab culture and ingratiated himself to Syrians in order to try to win them over to the American side. His forecast that the post-coup government there would "rely first upon repressive measures and arbitrary exercise of power" was not considered problematic so long as the targets were leftists and communists and the government moderated its course over the long term and upheld U.S. geostrategic ambitions in the Middle East.[33]

One of Roosevelt's key associates in carrying out the coup plot—which involved about $3 million in bribes—was Howard "Rocky" Stone, a political action specialist from Cincinnati who coordinated Syrian dissidents in Tehran and Khartoum.[34] A veteran with Kermit Roosevelt of Operation Ajax in Iran who later served with the CIA in Pakistan, Vietnam, and Nepal and was chief of operations of the Soviet bloc division from 1968 to 1971, Stone was expelled from Syria with Lt. Col Robert W. Molloy and Vice-Consul Francis Jeton, after Abdul Hamid Sarraj [Syria's intelligence chief] got wind of the coup plot. According to Eveland, the coup plotters walked into Sarraj's office, turned in their money, and named the CIA officers who had paid them. They then went on television to announce that they had received money from "the corrupt and sinister Americans in an attempt to overthrow the legitimate government of Syria."[35] The CIA's clumsy attempts to overthrow the Syrian government in 1957 would hardly mark its final attempt at doing so. In 1962, John F. Kennedy met with Harold Macmillan and according to a CIA report, formulated plans for "penetration and cultivation of disruptive elements in the Syrian armed forces . . . so that Syria can be guided by the West."[36] These efforts too ultimately failed.

Miles Copeland's Account

Miles Copeland Jr. revealed U.S. coup plotting in Syria in his 1989 memoir, *The Game Player: The Confessions of the CIA's Original Political Operative*.[37] Described by Archie Roosevelt, with whom he got along famously well, as a "brilliant extrovert from Alabama [Montgomery]," Copeland was a skilled jazz trumpeter and varsity boxer at the University of Alabama, Tuscaloosa, in the late 1930s, who became ensconced in the world of espionage and subversion while serving with the U.S. Army Counter Intelligence Corps (CIC) in World War II.[38] Influenced by the ideas of James Burnham, an original neoconservative and proponent of aggressive rollback operations in the Cold War, Copeland came to write numerous articles for the conservative *National Review*. In 1986 he gave an interview to *Rolling Stone* in which he stated: "unlike *The New York Times*, Victor Marchetti and Philip Agee, my complaint has been that the CIA isn't overthrowing enough anti-American governments or assassinating enough anti-American leaders, but I guess I'm getting old."[39]

Working as a military attaché at the U.S. embassy, Copeland recounts in *The Game Player* his arrival in Damascus in 1949 and coordination with a British MI6 man "on all sorts of projects" that combined the "best in American money and British brains." These projects included obtaining secret documents from the Syrian Defense Ministry after Copeland bribed two male secretaries and got them to steal documents from their employer's safe. Once it was decided that Zaim—whom he referred to as a "burly Kurd"— was the man to lead the coup against Al-Quwatli, Copeland says that he helped arrange for him to come to Damascus to serve as chief of police before making him commander-in-chief of the Syrian army. Though at times downplaying the U.S. role in the 1949 coup, Copeland also suggests that he and Steve Meade helped mastermind the coup.[40]

Before the coup took place, Meade took a ride with Zaim in a limousine through Damascus and pointed out targets to be seized during the coup, including the city's main radio station, power generators, and the central office of the telephone company. Copeland and Meade further assisted Zaim to develop a program of disinformation, and drafted a statement that he gave to the Syrian people after the coup was consummated. Copeland seems most proud about a devious scheme he concocted to trick one of Al-Quwatli's allies in the army, Fakhri al-Barudi, into raiding his home in order to make it look like Syria had become a police state.[41] When Copeland ordered an Air Force pilot named Dick Rule to confront al-Barudi's men, Rule tellingly replied: "Screw you. You go out there yourself cowboy. I'm not going to get my ass shot off in aid of one of your CIA pranks."[42]

Meade was particularly close with Zaim, and Copeland with Adib Shishakli, whom he characterized as a "likeable rogue" who drank too much, smoked pot, made false accusations, and had committed "blasphemy, murder, adultery and theft." Copeland admitted to buying Shishakli's loyalty through blackmail, having gained information about his "dabbling in homosexuality" during a stint in prison. The two became so close that Copeland gave his second son the middle name Adib—after he had assisted his pregnant wife before she went into labor.

Copeland felt that Shishakli was smarter than Zaim and would manipulate him once the new government was installed. Indeed, after Zaim came to power, the coup increasingly became Shishakli's. Later, when Shishakli mounted a failed coup, he had to flee Syria after being given a death sentence and went to Paris where Copeland visited him and paid his hotel bill.

Déjà Vu?

At the end of the chapter on Syria in *The Game Player*, Copeland suggests that the 1949 Syrian coup was studied at CIA training classes for the next two decades. This is ironic because in the 2010s the CIA mounted one of its largest covert operations in Syria since the anti-Soviet mujahidin in the 1980s—Operation Timber Sycamore. The target of Timber Sycamore, Bashar al-Assad, bears some resemblance to Shukri Al-Quwatli in that he refused to construct the Trans-Arabian pipeline through Syria, instead endorsing a Russian approved "Islamic" pipeline running from Iran's side of the gas field through Syria and to the ports of Lebanon—which Miles Copeland's heirs would never allow.[43]

Copeland interestingly drew the lesson from the 1949 coup that West Asian societies such as Syria were inherently prone to "chronic political instability" and "self-destructive emotionalism;" therefore the next time the U.S. set about the "business of interference in the internal affairs of sovereign nations," it would "need to find a stronger leader than Zaim," one capable "of building a durable power base and of surviving." In other words, the problem was "not one of bringing about a change of government, but of making the change stick."[44] Replete with Orientalist stereotypes, these comments are deeply ironic in light of the fact that the professed goal of CIA meddling in Syria and other countries around the world was to help engender democracy. When Copeland uses the word stronger, it really means dictatorial, which Zaim surely was. While it is unclear if they hold much historical consciousness, today's regime-change operators seem to think in a similar kind of way to Copeland. Their hubris makes it likely, in turn, that history will repeat itself—the U.S. imposed Jolani regime that overthrew Assad is clearly as brutal and unpopular as Zaim was in 1949, if not far more so, and hence may not last for very long.

CHAPTER 2

Back to the Future: Long-Term
U.S. Regime-Change Strategy

In 2010, the website Wikileaks began publishing leaked U.S. diplomatic cables that offered a window into covert U.S. plans and
strategies going back several decades. One of the more telling
documents was a December 2006 blueprint for regime change
in Syria written by William Roebuck, at the time the chargé
d'affaires at the U.S. embassy in Syria, which outlined a strategy
for destabilizing the Syrian government. In his summary of the
cable, Roebuck wrote:

> We believe Bashar's weaknesses are in how he chooses to react
> to looming issues, both perceived and real, such as the conflict
> between economic reform steps (however limited) and entrenched,
> corrupt forces, the Kurdish question, and the potential threat to
> the regime from the increasing presence of transiting Islamist
> extremists. This cable summarizes our assessment of these vulner-
> abilities and suggests that there may be actions, statements, and
> signals that the USG can send that will improve the likelihood of
> such opportunities arising.

A key takeaway was Roebuck's interest in exploiting Assad's
vulnerabilities to achieve regime change, including through the
recruitment of Kurdish minority groups and seizure on the disaffection of part of Syria's population with the slow pace of liberal
economic reform. At one point in the cable, Roebuck argued
that the U.S. should try to destabilize the Syrian government by

coordinating more closely with Egypt and Saudi Arabia to fan sectarian tensions between Sunni and Shia, including by promoting "exaggerated" fears of Shia proselytizing of Sunnis, and about "the spread of Iranian influence" in Syria in the form of mosque construction and business activity.[1]

In this chapter, we maintain that U.S. regime-change designs in Syria actually went back further than Wikileaks cables could disclose—back to the 1970s and 1980s when Hafez al-Assad, Bashar's father, was in power. In that respect, we see almost a continuous pattern since World War II by which the U.S. government sought to interfere and manipulate Syrian political affairs to its perceived advantage. The U.S. targeted Hafez al-Assad like his son because of his close ties to the Soviet Union and the Iranian revolutionary regime, because he was a Syrian nationalist who tried to stand up to Israel, and because he was a leader in the Pan-Arab movement, which sought to unify the Arab states under socialism so they could control their own natural resources and present a strong front vis-à-vis the West.

Though the regime-change operation targeting Hafez al-Assad ultimately failed, it was nevertheless significant in setting the groundwork for later regime-change operations, particularly through the spread of propaganda that depicted Assad as "the bad boy of the Middle East," as Ronald Reagan called him, and Syria as a "state sponsor of terrorism."[2] Through such designations, the U.S. public was conditioned to view the Assads in a very negative light and to sanction their overthrow as a positive step for the advancement of human rights.

An Arab De Gaulle

Hafez al-Assad was a Baath Party activist from the time of his youth who served as Syrian Defense Minister in the mid-1960s following the country's Baathist coup, and then President from 1970 until his death in 2000. Born in Querdaha, a small Alawite village outside Latakia, Assad was among the first in his family to receive formal schooling and gained power after being elected president of the nationwide union of Syrian students in 1951 and then rising through the ranks of the Syrian military. Assad's grandfather, Ahmed Ibn Sulayman, and father, Ali Sulayman, were known for their exceptional strength and courage and it was a family tradition to mediate quarrels and give protection to the weak.[3] According to one biographer, Ali Sulayman's reputation for "defending the rights of his fellow peasants against the venal claims of the big Sunni landowners," is what led him to change the family name from Wahhish to Assad, which means "lion."[4]

Like many of his generation, Hafez grew up to hate the Sykes-Picot Agreement that resulted in the French colonization of Syria in the early 1920s. As a young Baath Party activist, Hafez was known for helping to expand the party's influence in Alawite mountain villages and helping to raise money for kids whose parents had fallen behind on their school fees. The Baath party adopted a leftist and Arab nationalist philosophy and its purpose was to help facilitate an Arab renaissance following a period of humiliation bred by Western colonialism. The Muslim Brotherhood was a natural enemy of the Baath and Assad whom they had knifed in the back and tried to beat up when he was a Baath Party student leader in the 1940s.[5] The popularity of the Baath party was in part a response to the ineptitude and corruption of U.S.-backed military dictators who ruled Syria in the late 1940s and 1950s: figures like Colonel Husni al-Zaim and Adib Shishakli that were profiled in the first chapter.

When Assad took power in 1970, he was intent on "coup-proofing" the Syrian regime, which accounts for the elaborate surveillance networks and intelligence services that Assad helped to develop.[6] Assad's corrective movement moderated the revolutionary left-wing course adopted by his predecessors, Major General Salah Jadid and Dr. Nur al-Din Atari.[7] During his tenure, Assad maintained strong links with anti-colonial liberation movements. In 1971, Syria characteristically hosted the 10th executive meeting of the Afro-Asian Peoples' Solidarity Organization (AAPSO), a branch of the non-aligned movement, which prioritized the struggle of the Indochinese people against U.S. imperialist aggression, the struggle of the Arab people against American-Israeli aggression, and the struggle of the African people for liberation from colonialism.[8] The more liberalized climate in Damascus after Assad's accession was exemplified in the staging of a play in Damascus in 1971 by Saadallah Wannous that debunked the official Syrian version of the 1967 Six-Day War (a war in which Israel took control of the Golan Heights).[9] Assad further oversaw the establishment of popular organizations to widen political participation—including the General Union of Peasants, the General Federation of Trade Unions, General Women's Federation, and General Union of Students.[10]

The demonization of Assad in the West ignores the legacies of French colonialism and U.S. neocolonialism in shaping Syrian political evolution. It also glosses over the fact that the country was under constant threat of attack from Israel, a nuclear weapon-possessing country heavily armed by the U.S. that took over part of its territory (the Golan Heights), It also hides the fact that Assad had enemies from within that wanted Iran to fall and that worked with the CIA. Still, it is hard to defend the treason trial of Baath Party founder Michel Aflaq, and imprisonment of Salah Jadid until his death in 1993 and many of his supporters. Assad was also accused of sanctioning torture at Mezzeh prison in Damascus and having some political prisoners "disappeared."[11] The suppression of a Muslim Brotherhood rebellion in Hama in 1982 has been widely criticized for decades because of brutality allegedly committed by Assad's brother Rifaat, the chief of security. However, that rebellion was a violent one supported by outside powers including the U.S. Muslim Brotherhood terrorists—whom the CIA considered "right-wing extremists"—killed more than 500 of Assad's supporters and several Soviet advisers, set off car bombs, attacked a military academy, and almost succeeded in assassinating Assad.[12]

Accusations in the U.S. media that Hafez al-Assad and his son Bashar accumulated lavish riches are disproven by leading scholarship. British journalist Patrick Seale emphasized in a biography that Hafez's "lifestyle and tastes were restrained" and that he was a workaholic who "lived rather modestly in a residence in Damascus that was no more than the home of a successful professional man with none of the Arabian Nights splendor of the palaces of Kings and Presidents in other states of the region."[13] Echoing this assessment, *TIME* magazine reported in March 1983 that Assad and his wife "do not live lavishly—though one of their children, Basil, can be occasionally spotted tooling around Damascus in his Porsche."[14] Trinity University Professor David Lesch meanwhile wrote about Bashar: "There were no Wikileaks reports detailing the extravagant lifestyle of [Bashar] Assad—as there were with Tunisian President Ben Ali. Assad does not have an extravagant lifestyle."[15]

According to Seale, Hafez al-Assad's career should be placed in the context of the Baath Party's campaign for Arab revival. Assad sustained legitimacy by modernizing and strengthening Syria's economy and through his stature as a leading pan-Arabist in the mold of Egyptian leader Gamal Abdel Nasser—the "sole remaining barrier to Israel's regional hegemony."[16] Historian Reuven Avi-Ran wrote that "under the [Hafez al] Assad regime, Syria ceased being the object of Egyptian-Iraqi rivalry and became a state which in its own right could compete with them for leadership in the Arab world"—a major accomplishment.[17] *The New York Times* editorialized in 1984 that "although the world powers and the stronger of the regional governments often trifled with his predecessors, Assad has made Syria a force to be reckoned with."[18] The CIA National Assessment Center had reported six years earlier that Assad was "well thought of by the [Syrian] population, which appreciates the benefits stability has brought. By Syrian standards Assad is popular."[19]

Placing Syria's natural resources and public utilities under public ownership in Syria's 1973 constitution, Assad's popularity stemmed in part from his skill at wooing Syria's disaffected classes and minority groups and forging wide coalitions. Respecting

Syria's religious leaders, Assad won over many Sunni Muslims by making a pilgrimage to Mecca. Sunni Muslims were also appointed to important positions within his administration along with Alawites and Druze. Complete religious freedom was guaranteed and people had freedom of movement.[20] Even Syria's small Jewish community was treated equitably.[21] While not sugarcoating all aspects of his leadership, Seale depicts Assad quite favorably as "an Arab De Gaulle" who oversaw a "rapidly modernizing and reasonably prosperous society" that "performed rather better than most developing countries of the Third World."[22] Seale wrote that "quality of life was enhanced for the great majority of Syrians" under Assad's rule, especially "the once neglected peasants of the countryside."[23]

TIME magazine reported that per capita income increased from $200 per person in 1970 when Assad first gained power to $1,000 in 1983.[24] The literacy and primary school rate approached 100 percent at this time and infant mortality was in decline.[25] Investing heavily in construction projects in Damascus, Assad's administration built many roads, hospitals, universities and dams—including a large one on the Euphrates that helped virtually double the acreage of arable land in Syria. All Syrians became eligible for subsidized food, free education, and state medical care. After Assad took power, the price of basic foods was cut by 15 percent. Electrification and access to piped water was expanded and modern health care and reasonably good schooling was made accessible to people living in the countryside. In Assad's home province of Latakia, whereas only 15 percent of the people had access to piped water in 1970, more than 70 percent had access to it in 1985. Introducing management and accounting methods of private business into the public sector, Assad began a program of industrialization that resulted in the development of sulfur oil refineries and good quality light and crude oil production facilities along the Iraqi border.[26]

Continuity Under Bashar

The Syrian population continued to reap benefits under Bashar al-Assad (2000-2024), which explains why the majority supported him when the "Arab Spring" uprising broke out in 2011.[27] A six-country poll in 2009 put Assad as "the most popular Arab leader in the Middle East."[28] In April 2015, a World Health Organization document noted how pre-civil war Damascus "had one of the best-developed healthcare systems in the Arab world." A UN investigation pointed to the extension of "universal, free healthcare" to all Syrian citizens, who "enjoyed some of the highest levels of care in the region" under Bashar's rule. Education was likewise free, and before the conflict, "an estimated 97% of primary school-aged Syrian children were attending class and Syria's literacy rates were thought to be at over 90% for both men *and women*."[29] Life expectancy increased by seventeen years between the beginning of Hafez' rule in 1970 and 2009.[30] A UN Human Rights Council report noted prior to 2011, Syria "was the only country in the Middle East region to be self-sufficient in food production," its "thriving agricultural sector" contributing "about 21% to GDP 2006-2011." Daily caloric intake "was on par with many Western countries," with prices kept affordable via state subsidy. The country's economy was "one of the best performing in the region, with a growth rate averaging 4.6%" annually.[31] Assad constructed and restored over 10,000 mosques and 500 churches, built 8,000 schools and 40 universities, more than 6,000 hospitals and 600,000 houses/apartments for young people.[32]

In December 2010, the *LA Times* ran an article entitled, "Syria a Bright Star in the Middle East," which suggested that Assad had helped transform Syria into a rising destination for Western tourists. On their visit, these tourists could view a clay tablet with mankind's first recorded alphabet and landmark Umayyad Mosque, where some of the Arab world's great heroes were buried. The author of the article, Susan Spano, wrote: "Syria, in the ancient heart of the Middle East, used to be rough, insular, politically extreme and all but off the map for travelers. Now, with a more forward-looking government, tourism increasing by almost 50% a year and opulent new hotels opening by the score, the luster is back on the magic lamp, making Syria one of the world's most compelling destinations for 2011."[33] These remarks are deeply ironic in light of the "Arab Spring" revolts that broke out in that very same year accompanied by a sweeping media demonization campaign directed against the Assads that was behind the long U.S. regime-change operation in Syria.

Why the U.S. Hated Hafez al-Assad and Wanted Him Removed

As Noam Chomsky and Edward S. Herman detailed in *The Political Economy of Human Rights: The Washington Connection and Third World Fascism* (1979), the U.S.-supported tyrannical right-wing regimes across the developing world that were far worse than Syria under Assad in their record on human rights and economic development. Somoza, Pinochet, Marcos, Suharto, Diem, Thieu, and Mobutu were some of the bloody tyrants that Washington helped empower. In West Asia, the U.S.-favored conservative autocrats like the Saudi Royal family, which traded oil in U.S. dollars in exchange for U.S. security guarantees, and the Shah of Iran who ran a torture chamber at Evin Prison that is now a museum.[34]

The 1970s was a precarious time for American foreign policy planners. The triumph of the Islamic revolution in Iran (1979) resulted in the fall of the Shah. The revolution in Libya led by Muammar Gaddafi (1969) overthrew the pro-western King Idris and resulted in the removal of U.S. military bases from Libya and nationalization of the country's oil industry. The "loss of Syria" under Baathist rule following the failed 1957 U.S./UK coup attempt only compounded America's growing strategic weakness, although the U.S. government achieved a major geopolitical victory in its ability to draw Egypt into the Western camp after the

BACK TO THE FUTURE 41

fall of Gamal Abdel Nasser. Under Anwar Sadat (1970-1981) and
Hosni Mubarak (1981-2011), the U.S. was able to carry out military
exercises with Egypt and use Egyptian military facilities to project
U.S. military power—something it hoped ultimately to achieve
with Syria. During the 1980s, Egypt became a leading recipient of
U.S. military aid at over $1 billion per year even though Mubarak
became infamous for his repressive rule.[35]

The U.S. government targeted Hafez al-Assad for regime
change primarily because of his resistance to U.S. and Israeli
hegemonic designs and commitment to preserving Syria's political
and economic sovereignty. Washington did not like Assad's socialist leaning economic program and commitment to pan-Arabism.
The U.S. also objected to his support for Third World liberation
movements along with his ties to other radical Arab regime like
Libya's Arab Jamahiriya under Muammar Gaddafi and adoption
of independent foreign policy positions like support for admission
of the People's Republic of China (PRC) to the UN. U.S. leaders
hated Assad further because he bolstered Syria's military and economic relations with the Soviet Union and allowed the Soviets in
1971 to establish a naval base at Tartus. Soviet arms deliveries to
Syria constituted "the most sent to any of Moscow's Third World
clients" by 1974, according to U.S. analysts.[36]

Henry Kissinger wrote in the early 1970s that Syria under
Assad became "the ideological heartland of Arab nationalism,"
which Washington was committed to undermining.[37] Though rec-
ognizing that he had a "first class mind," Kissinger came to view
Hafez as the most militant of Israel's enemies.[38] When Hafez was
serving as Syria's Minister of Defense during the 1967 Six-Day war,
he mobilized Syrian infantry units in resistance to Israeli invaders,
resulting in their destruction of 160 Israeli tanks.[39] Subsequently,
Assad was accused of planning to reinvade Israel with Egypt
in the 1973 Yom Kippur War in an effort to reclaim Syrian and
Egyptian territory lost in 1967.[40] Assad also supported Palestinian
commandos (fedayeen) living in Syria that plotted raids into
Israel.[41] A 1972 CIA report lamented "the spirit of militancy" that

animated "forceful Syrian responses" to ongoing Israeli attempts, through "pre-emptive strikes," to destroy the "fedayeen bases" then residing in Syria.[42] A 1988 CIA report further lamented Assad's unwillingness to back any peace initiative with Israel that did not include the return of the [Israeli-occupied] Golan Heights, complete Israeli withdrawal from territories occupied in June 1967, and gave the Palestinians the right of return to their homes that had been destroyed in the 1948 Nakba.[43]

In 1975-76, Assad invaded and then maintained a long occupation of Lebanon, which Syrians felt had been made into a separate country by the French to create two weak states instead of a strong one.[44] In the 1980s, Syrian forces stationed in Lebanon directly confronted the Israelis in the Bekaa Valley and fought against the U.S.[45] Assad solidified his status as an enemy of the U.S. and Israel when he allowed Iranian dissidents to conduct anti-Shah activities from Syrian territory and firmly allied with the new Iranian government following the 1979 Iranian revolution that toppled the Shah. Iran supported Hezbollah, which emerged as the leading resistance force to Israeli aggression in Lebanon, and was accused with Syria of sponsoring terrorist attacks against the U.S.[46]

The acceleration of U.S. regime-change efforts in Syria during the 1980s fit with a growing U.S. imperialist presence in the Middle East that resulted in part from the growing anxiety of corporate elites about waning business competitiveness and the Arab oil embargo of the 1970s.[47] Under the late 1970s Carter Doctrine—pursuant to which the U.S. claimed the right to intervene militarily to protect its interests in the Persian Gulf—the U.S. embarked on an aggressive post-Vietnam military buildup in which arms sales were expanded along with the U.S. military base network in the Middle East. U.S. support for Israel as a strategic proxy was consolidated as Israel was increasingly dominated by right-wingers supportive of the goal of a Greater Israel. The Carter administration significantly established a Rapid Deployment Force (RDF) that would evolve into the U.S. Central Command (CENTCOM), a major Middle East military command.[48] Carter's

Defense Secretary Harold Brown touted the RDF as "one of four U.S. 'pillars of military power,'" along with nuclear weapons, NATO, and the U.S. Navy. Within the context of evolving U.S. foreign policies, Hafez al-Assad and his son Bashar were considered more and more a thorn in Washington's side that had to be removed.

Subversion, Propaganda, Military Attack, and Plans for Regime Change

In 1979, in the wake of Syrian support for the Iranian revolution, the U.S. State Department first put Syria on its list of "state sponsors of terror." This designation was accompanied by the imposition of export controls on certain goods, "miscellaneous financial and other restrictions" and restricted U.S. foreign assistance to Syria.[49] A cable from President Jimmy Carter's National Security Council adviser Zbigniew Brzezinski to Secretary of State Cyrus Vance urged a coordinated study of "identifying possible alternative regimes to the Syrian government led by Hafez-Al Assad." Brzezinski was considering "how to reduce the problems of ill-considered reaction" by Syria's ally, the Soviet Union, "to a change in regime in Damascus."[50]

In March 1980, Assad accused the CIA of "encouraging sabotage and subversion in Syria so as to bring the entire Arab world under joint U.S.-Israeli domination." Specifically, Assad said that his security services had discovered U.S. equipment in the hands of Muslim Brotherhood guerrillas who mounted a campaign of terrorism directed against the Syrian government from their stronghold in Hama. The equipment included sophisticated communications equipment of a kind Assad claimed could only be sold to a third party with U.S. government permission.[51] Syrian intelligence was convinced that an American manufacturer had, with the U.S. government's blessing, arranged for conspiracists to reach the guerrillas through Israel, Beirut, and Amman. Assad later recounted: "We told the Americans that we had proof and they asked us to produce it and we did. They denied giving the Muslim Brothers the equipment. 'All right then,' we said, 'here are the serial numbers. Perhaps you could tell us to whom you did sell it.' The Americans refused to say. Finally, I said to them, 'your involvement is clear and nothing can prove your innocence, but I'm prepared to let the matter rest.'"[52]

British journalist Patrick Seale reported that U.S. weapons were captured by Syrian army soldiers from the Muslim Brotherhood insurgents and that foreign backing of the insurgents came from several U.S. collaborators, notably King Hussein of Jordan, Lebanese Christian militias (the Israeli-aligned "Guardians of the Cedar") and Saddam Hussein in Iraq.[53] Former U.S. State Department official William Polk noted that more than 15,000 foreign-supplied machine guns were captured, along with prisoners including Jordanian- and CIA-trained paramilitary forces.[54]

In December 1983, the Reagan administration directly attacked Syrian forces in Lebanon after Syrian anti-aircraft batteries in Lebanon fired upon U.S. Navy F-14 reconnaissance planes that were part of a U.S. invasion force in support of Lebanon's government which was then aligned with pro-Israel Christian militias. Twenty-eight U.S. bombers engaged in retaliatory attacks that were a "military and political disaster for the U.S," according to Council on Foreign Relations fellow Micah Zenko. Two of the U.S. planes were shot down by Surface-to-Air Missiles (SAMs); one pilot was killed, another was captured by Syrian forces, and another parachuted safely into the Mediterranean Sea. (The hostage pilot, Lieutenant Robert Goodman Jr., was held and interrogated in a Syrian prison for thirty days until Reverend Jesse Jackson secured his release.) Although the Pentagon claimed that the airstrikes were "very successful and achieved our objective, which was to prevent . . . repetition of the attacks on our reconnaissance aircraft," Syrian forces continued to target the U.S. reconnaissance flights.[55]

Radio Damascus boasted afterwards that "The rout of the U.S. in Lebanon is a rout of historic significance for this is the first time that the U.S. has entered into a direct military confrontation in this area with the Arab liberation movement, represented by Syria . . . . It has been shown that a small country like Syria is capable of defending justice and peace and defeating a large country like the U.S."[56] Robert McFarlane of the National Security Council (NSC) visited Syria following the debacle with special envoy Donald Rumsfeld and authorized airstrikes directed against Syrian targets that aimed to "stun the Syrians and get them to stop causing trouble."[57] The *U.S.S. New Jersey*, which MacFarlane accused the Syrians of attacking in the Mediterranean Sea, subsequently shelled the Mtein mountains to the east of Beirut. Equipped with the first operational tomahawk missiles, the Vietnam vintage ship fired over 300 artillery rounds that knocked out 30 Druze and Syrian gun batteries along with a Druze military command post and killed the Syrian Commanding General there. To survive the attacks, residents had to barricade themselves in their homes.[58] Numerous shell strikes "missed [their] targets by very wide distances," according to the Pentagon, and "put holes into mountainsides."[59]

When militants detonated a bomb at the U.S. Marine barracks at the Beirut international airport in October 1983, the Reagan administration pointed a finger at both Iran and Syria, claiming that explosives that were used had passed through Syria.[60] The State Department at this time placed Syria on its list of nations that have "repeatedly provided support for acts of international terrorism."[61] The NSC in turn developed a plan to destabilize Syria and overthrow Assad. The blueprint for the plan read:

> When Assad challenges Israel and the Marines in Lebanon, he knows that if Israel attacks him it cannot occupy all of Syria. Assad feels he can always retreat to the North and set up a smaller state and with stronger Alawite control. However, if Turkey is brought into the calculations of Rifaat [Assad—considered the real power in Syria) and Hafez, their calculations will be totally different and would be impossible to add up without losing their power. If Syria is attacked by Turkey from the north the Alawite stronghold will

be gone at the start and Assad and his supporters will have to fall back on an ocean of hateful Sunni Moslems (sic) in the south where they will be eaten like lost sheep. Therefore the pressure on Syria should come from Turkey and not from the Marines and or Israel.[62]

Though not implemented at the time, this strategy provided a formula for the 2011-2024 regime-change operation with its emphasis on the use of Turkey as a mechanism for destabilizing Syria and weakening Assad. A 1983 report authored by CIA officer Graham Fuller, the former station chief in Kabul who helped create the anti-Soviet mujahidin, suggested that the U.S. should consider "sharply escalating the pressures against Assad" from three border states hostile to Syria—Iraq, Israel, and Turkey, which would force Assad to abandon his closure of the Trans-Arabian pipeline—a continued source of U.S. opposition to him. In Iraq, Fuller hoped that local troops then fighting against Iran could be diverted to invade Syria from its eastern border, thus undermining Damascus' ability to resist pressure on its fronts from Israel, the U.S., and internally from Islamist insurgents.[63]

CIA Director William Casey authorized another study around the same time mapping Syrian ports and military facilities that could be bombed.[64] A newly declassified CIA document from July 1986 entitled "Syria: Scenarios For Dramatic Political Change" analyzed the prospects of a revitalized Muslim Brotherhood uprising like the one that arose in Hama and had been crushed by Assad in 1982. Offering another blueprint for regime change, the document stated:

> Although we judge that fear of reprisals and organizational problems make a second Sunni challenge [Muslim Brotherhood uprising like in 1982] unlikely, an excessive government reaction to minor outbreaks of Sunni dissidence might trigger large-scale unrest. In most instances the regime would have the resources to crush a Sunni opposition movement, but we believe widespread violence among the populace could stimulate large numbers of Sunni officers and conscripts to desert or mutiny, setting the stage for civil war.

How the CIA would help provide the spark for the unrest was not mentioned but clearly part of the plan. According to former U.S. Marine Corps officer Brad Hoff, while downplaying the nationalist and pluralistic composition of the ruling Baath Party, the July 1986 CIA report envisioned a renewal and exploitation of sectarian fault lines pitting Syria's Sunni population against its Alawite leadership. Hoff quotes from another passage in the document which stated:

"Sunnis make up 60% of the Syrian officer corps but are concentrated in junior officer ranks; enlisted men are predominantly Sunni conscripts. We believe that a renewal of communal violence between Alawis and Sunnis could inspire Sunnis in the military to turn against the regime." The ultimate goal was establishment of a "pliant Sunni regime" to replace the one led by Assad that would "serve U.S. economic interests."

The document concluded: "In our view, US interests would be best served by a Sunni regime controlled by business-oriented moderates. Business moderates would see a strong need for Western aid and investment to build Syria's private economy, thus opening the way for stronger ties to Western governments."[65] This is exactly the kind of regime that the U.S. helped to install in December 2024. The CIA may refer to them as moderates, however, it has long preferred Islamist, pro-capitalist political factions to secular nationalist and left-leaning ones.[66] The CIA report in fact acknowledged that the collapse of the Baathist state could help to empower "religious zealots" seeking to establish "an Islamic Republic."[67] But this was a risk that Washington was willing to take, just as it had in Afghanistan where it supported the mujahidin to draw the Soviet Union into a war there whose result was the take-over of that country by the Taliban.[68]

To help condition public opinion in support of U.S. foreign policy objectives, the Reagan administration played up Syria's alleged connection to terrorism that was said to have been supported by the Soviet Union. Leaked intelligence reports associated Syrian intelligence with the Italian Red Brigades and other extreme left-wing groups in Europe that carried out terrorist attacks—many of which resulted actually from the presence of agents provocateurs or were set up under the CIA/NATO's Operation Gladio.[69] Syria was said to have housed 7,000 Soviet advisers and technicians who manned a massive amount of Soviet weaponry, including SS-21 ground-to-ground missiles capable of reaching vital areas of Israel. The goal of such proclamations was to scare the public and support the vast arms buildup of the 1980s and regime-change operations targeting both Assad and the Soviet Union.[70]

A key propaganda tract of the 1980s was Claire Sterling's book, *The Terror Network* (1982). CIA analysts assigned to the task of checking Sterling's sources found that "virtually all of them were CIA disinformation—articles planted by covert operators in various media."[71] Endorsed by Secretary of State Alexander Haig, Sterling's book accused the Soviet Union of supporting terrorist training camps in the Middle East as part of its effort to undermine the West.[72] On page 236, Sterling wrote about a platoon of Cuban terrorist instructors who had allegedly been invited by Assad to come to Syria to provide training to Syrian army officers and the Palestinian Liberation Organization (PLO) in guerrilla training camps that Assad had set up. Sterling wrote that "the first of these camps were spotted in 1976. According to U.S. Defense Secretary Melvin Laird, they were training Japanese, German and Iranian terrorists as well as Arabs."[73]

The Reagan administration's War on Terror provided a pretext to validate the expansion of U.S. military forces in the Middle East, and establishment of a slew of new air and naval bases from the Persian Gulf to the Horn of Africa, which provided a platform to access Middle East oil. The irony was that while professing to be fighting a War on Terror, the Reagan administration and its successors allied with Islamic fundamentalists—like Syria's Muslim Brotherhood and the Afghan mujahidin—that adopted terrorist tactics against secular nationalists and socialist regimes. The public relations value of the War on Terror was accentuated through the clever propaganda trick of portraying all Arabs in dispute with Israel as terrorists, meaning that brute force directed against them was said to be legitimate.[74]

Reagan specifically called Assad "the bad boy of the Middle East."[75] The Omnibus Diplomatic Security and Antiterrorism Act of 1986 and Omnibus Reconciliation Act of 1986 banned U.S. military equipment sales to Syria and denied foreign tax credits on income or war profits from Syria, with both laws citing ostensible Syrian government support for terrorism.[76] Assad was accused of masterminding terrorist attacks with Libyan leader Muammar Gaddafi, the Palestinian Liberation Organization (PLO), and Ayatollah Khomeini, though there was no credible proof that he nor the others were actually behind such attacks. In February 1984, when he ordered the use of American air and naval forces against anti-government positions in Lebanon, Reagan blamed Syria for the fighting that engulfed West Beirut and said Syria "facilitates and supplies instruments for terrorist attacks on the people of Lebanon."[77] The Lebanon government, however, said that Syrian troops were in Lebanon at its request.[78] In 1986, Syria was blamed for an attempted hijacking of an El Al flight to Tel Aviv whose culprit, Nezar Hindawi, is believed to have worked as a double agent for Israel (Syria was thus set up in a false flag operation).[79] Two years later, Assad was blamed with Gaddafi for the Lockerbie airplane crash, which evidence indicates, was set up by a rogue cabal of CIA agents led by Theodore Shackley in order to prevent the disclosure of criminal activities that they were behind.[80]

Syria may have itself been a victim of CIA terrorism in the 1980s—as it was in the 2010s. In March and April of 1985, a string of still largely unexplained car bombs rocked Damascus and at least five towns throughout Syria, leaving over 200 civilians dead in the most significant wave of attacks since the earlier 1979-82 war with the Muslim Brotherhood. Patrick Seale speculates of the bombings: "It may not have been unconnected that in late 1985 the NSC's Colonel Oliver North and Amiram Nir, [then Israeli Prime

Minister Shimon] Peres's counter-terrorism expert, set up a dirty tricks outfit to strike back at the alleged sponsors of Middle East terrorism."[81]

A Long Regime-Change Operation

In 1992, Charles Schumer (D-NY), a staunch supporter of the twenty-first century Syrian regime-change operation who then chaired the House Judiciary Committee's Subcommittee on Crime and Criminal Justice, oversaw the writing of a sensationalistic report, based largely on anonymous sources and hearsay. The report alleged that senior officials in Assad's government made between $350 million and $1 billion annually from the drug trade out of Lebanon and coordinated drug trafficking and terror tactics with the left-wing Sendero Luminoso in Peru. Rifaat Assad had long been accused in Western media of spearheading a large-scale drug trafficking operation, though Michael Hurley, who oversaw Lebanese operations for the Drug Enforcement Administration (DEA) from 1984 to 1990, said he "never saw hard evidence against Rifaat, only allegations." The Schumer report concluded by stating that "the Syrian government's continued support of terrorist groups based in Lebanon, its recent acquisition of several dud use technologies with the active support and encouragement of the Bush administration [which temporarily warmed over relations with Syria because of its support for the first Persian Gulf War], and its persistent involvement with known drug traffickers, make it clear that Hafez Assad's Syria has the capacity to become as great a threat to American interests in the Middle East as Saddam Hussein's Iraq ever was."[82]

Possessing particles of truth, Schumer's report gained traction after its claims were endlessly repeated in popular media. It shows the long roots of the demonization campaign targeting Assad, and how some of the same public officials involved in orchestrating the twenty-first century regime-change operation had been helping to lay the groundwork for it years earlier. Schumer's committee did not say precisely which American interests were threatened by Assad, however it is clear that they centered on control of West Asia's oil supply.[83] Though Hafez al-Assad may not have been a perfect leader, historians have compared him to Charles De Gaulle for presiding over his country's revitalization after a period of instability and weakness triggered by outside intervention. During his time in power, Hafez worked tirelessly to enhance the quality of life for average Syrians and to improve Syria's economy while effectively balancing the interests of the country's divergent political factions and religious groups. U.S. regime-change blueprints from the 1980s show how the U.S. was intent on exploiting religious and sectarian divisions in Syria and using the Turks to weaken and help oust Assad.

The U.S. military directly attacked Syrian forces in Lebanon during that decade, and the Reagan administration launched a large-scale propaganda/disinformation campaign branding Assad as a sponsor of terrorism, which was highly significant in creating a negative public image of the Assads. Many of those on the left who were traditionally weary of U.S. foreign intervention bought into the demonized image of Assad from that time and, in turn, became among the staunchest cheerleaders for U.S. covert intervention in Syria.

It must be said that, as Noam Chomsky has pointed out many times, the very fact that the U.S. was attempting to destabilize a country like Syria and to overthrow its government, including by exasperating sectarian divisions and supporting armed extremist groups, inevitably encouraged the government to be more repressive and less democratic. And indeed, despite all of the U.S.'s claims to the contrary, its very goal in dealing with both of the Assads was to provoke repression, which would trigger popular uprisings against the government that had long been yearned for, as well as justify military intervention in support of the uprisings, and cause death and destruction. As we discuss further in the next chapter, the U.S. would seize upon the rise of popular protest in West Asia during the period known as the "Arab Spring" to bring down the government of Bashar al-Assad. Specifically, the U.S. would support violent protests in Syria in which police were targeted and killed—protests that the U.S. government and the compliant press would call "peaceful"—to ultimately provoke the repression it needed (though Assad was initially quite restrained in response to this violence) to justify public support for regime change.[84]

CHAPTER 3

The Arab Spring
and U.S. Interference in Syria

"Things fall apart; the centre cannot hold;
Mere anarchy is loosed upon the world,
The blood-dimmed tide is loosed, and everywhere
The ceremony of innocence is drowned . . ."
–William Butler Yeats, "The Second Coming."

"The British and American intelligence along with the Israeli
Mossad worked to create the Islamic State of Iraq and Syria
(ISIS). A terrorist organization that is able to attract all extrem-
ists of the world to one place, using a strategy called 'The
Hornet's Nest.' It is created to protect the Zionist Entity of Israel
by creating it with religious and Islamic slogans. The only solu-
tion to protect the Jewish State is to create ISIS near its borders."
–Edward Snowden (former NSA employee).

Roger Harris, a bird biologist who makes his living leading tours
around the world, worked with the U.S. State Department for
about twenty years helping with tours for individuals that were
selected as "emerging leaders." In the early 2000s, the two State
Department employees Roger worked with told him that, by far,
the favorite country of those they took on tour was Syria. This was
because, at that time, it was a uniquely placid, friendly country
with amazing historical sites and antiquities.

In 2010, just before Syria's troubles began, over ten million people
visited Syria.[1] *CNN* noted that "[b]efore the civil war, tourism report-

edly accounted for 14% of Syria's GDP. With a history stretching back to antiquity, tourists were drawn to ancient sites like Palmyra, a Greco-Roman city largely destroyed by ISIS and desert landscapes dotted with Crusader-era castles like Krak des Chevaliers. Damascus is one of the world's oldest continuously inhabited cities, while the verdant Mediterranean coastline, once famed for its sun-drenched beach resorts, teems with turquoise waters and sandy bays." This tourist paradise, along with Syria's economy and social fabric, as well as many of its historic sites and antiquities, all came crashing down beginning in 2011. However, this was not due to "civil war" as *CNN* indicated, but rather, due to a brutal regime-change operation which was brought to Syria from the outside.

As already mentioned, we know from General Wesley Clark that as far back as November of 2001, the U.S. had its sights on attacking and transforming seven countries, "beginning with Iraq, then Syria, Lebanon, Libya, Somalia, Sudan and finishing off with Iran." What became clear with time was that the attack upon one country, such as Iraq, created the conditions for the attack upon the next countries, such as Syria. After the U.S. invasion of Iraq in 2003, 1.5 million Iraqis fled the violence into Syria,[2] which, at that time, had a population of seventeen million people. Not surprisingly, most of the Iraqi men who fled into Syria remained unemployed,[3] inevitably leading to the destabilization of Syrian society, which could not easily absorb all of these refugees. And, as the American Friends Service Committee, a project of the Quakers, noted at the time,[4] because Syria was seen as a "rogue nation," Syria received very little help to manage this incredible influx of refugees, which softened it up for the violent regime-change operation to come.

The other way in which the U.S. war on Iraq contributed to the regime change in Syria was the resulting emergence of the terrorist group Islamic State (EI or État islamique), which would migrate from Iraq into Syria and become the Islamic State of Syria (ISIS). As Swiss intelligence expert Jacques Baud explains,[5] the U.S. overthrow of Saddam Hussein and the resulting rise to power of the Iraqi Shia majority inspired the creation of Sunni terrorist groups in Iraq. The latter began to attract foreign fighters from around the world to challenge both the new Shia government and U.S. occupation of Iraq, and which would help form the Islamic State beginning in April 2004. While the U.S. opposed and fought the Islamic State in Iraq, it ended up backing ISIS in Syria in order to undermine the government of Bashar al-Assad.

While the emergence of EI in Iraq may have been an inadvertent result of U.S. policy there, this was not true in Syria. Baud writes that the U.S. "created, armed and supported the armed Islamist opposition in Syria, which later became part of the EI."[6] ISIS in Syria was seen by U.S. foreign policy-makers as "a useful ally in the fight against the 'regime' of Bashar al-Assad. In Syria, the Western interest was to have a sufficiently powerful, violent and radical rebel force to provoke a brutal response from the government and thus justify its overthrow or force it to negotiate."[7] Baud debunks the myth that the war in Syria began because Assad attacked a peaceful organic protest movement in part by citing Roland Dumas, the then foreign minister of France, who said that the U.S., along with Great Britain, had been "preparing . . . an insurgency aimed at bringing to power a dissident faction of the Syrian army" back in 2010 before the troubles in Syria had begun.[8] According to Baud, "[i]n the West, there is talk of a popular insurrection. This is not true. In Syria, discontent was not enough to trigger an insurrection. This is why, unlike other Arab countries [e.g., Tunisia, Egypt], the Syrian revolution was piloted from outside the country from the start."[9] The Assad government in turn, according to Baud, did not attack "the *entire* opposition militarily, but only the armed opposition."[10]

Ahmed Bensaada's book *L'Arabesque Américaine* argues that the U.S. helped manufacture the entire "Arab Spring" for self-serving purposes. He notes that none of the protests that erupted were spontaneous—all required careful and lengthy (5+ years) planning, by the State Department, CIA through foundations, George Soros, and the pro-Israel lobby. Focused exclusively on removing reviled despots without replacing the autocratic power structure that kept them in power, the "Arab Spring protests" made no reference whatsoever to powerful anti-U.S. sentiment over Palestine and Iraq. In addition, all the uprisings were led and dominated by middle class, well educated youth who mysteriously vanished after 2011.

In the section on Syria, Bensaada focuses on a handful of Syrian opposition activists who received free U.S. training in cyberactivism and nonviolent resistance beginning in 2006. One activist, Ausama Monajed, is featured in the 2011 film *How to Start a Revolution* about a 2006 visit with Gene Sharp, a CIA-backed intellectual who had been a conscientious objector to the Korean War who wrote a blueprint for overthrowing dictatorial regimes. Monajed and others worked through a State Department program funded by the Middle East Partnership Initiative (MEPI), which operated in countries such as Libya and Syria where USAID was banned. In February 2011, MEPI-funded groups posted a call on Twitter and Facebook for a Day of Rage. Nothing happened. When Sharpian techniques failed to produce a sizable nonviolent uprising, as in Libya, they and their allies (Saudi Arabia, Turkey, Qatar, and Jordan) were all set up to introduce Islamic mercenaries, many directly from Libya, to declare war on the Assad government.[11]

Leaked emails from the leading private intelligence firm Stratfor, which included notes from a meeting with Pentagon officials, confirmed that the war in Syria was waged from the outset as part of a subversive operation by NATO members that aimed to force a "collapse of the [Syrian] state from within."[12] Mohammed al-Jolani, who helped lead the overthrow of Assad and declared himself President of Syria, emerged quite tellingly from the U.S. Camp Bucca prison in Iraq to carry out his counter-regime work in Syria.[13] There is some mystery surrounding al-Jolani's transformation from jihadi militant fighting against the U.S. occupation in Iraq to Western tool for regime change in Syria; some believe that he was groomed in the U.S. prison by the CIA to play out this latter role.

After strolling out of Camp Bucca, al-Jolani became the leader of the strongest military force trying to oust Assad—the al-Nusra Front of Al Qaeda. Political analyst A.B. Abrams quotes al-Jolani stating that the peaceful protests, though unable to unseat Assad, "paved the way for us to enter this blessed land [Syria]."[14] A 2012 declassified report by the Defense Intelligence Agency (DIA) reported that the Syrian opposition was dominated by Al Qaeda elements who "wanted to set up an Islamic Caliphate in Damascus"—exactly what al-Jolani and his rebranded Al Qaeda group, HTS, are attempting to do now in Syria.[15]

Myth Versus Reality

The "Arab Spring" uprising in Syria officially began in the southwestern city of Daraa 90 kilometers from Damascus where Syria's soldiers allegedly brutalized a group of youth who sprayed anti-Assad graffiti on the walls.[16] Left out in Western media reports was the fact that Daraa was a center of Islamic resistance to Baath Party rule dating to the 1970s and 1980s.[17] The head of the Muslim Brotherhood in Syria, Muhammed Riyadh Al-Shaqfa, admitted that the Brotherhood "punched above its weight" during the uprising, indicating its sectarian, Islamist nature.

Shaqfa's remarks undercut National Security Council adviser Samantha Power's claim that the protesters were a "ragtag band of farmers and doctors and carpenters" who could be compared to the "revolutionaries who won America's war for independence."[18] Power's assessment was further undermined by Peter Ford, Britain's Ambassador to Syria at the time of the "Arab Spring," who said that the "besuited mild-mannered opposition [to Assad] were never going to play any role other than providing a cover for the hard men of the Islamist groups." The latter's goal according to Ford was nothing less than the "Talibanization of Syria" and destruction of the "civilized, multiethnic, multicultural Syria" that had flourished under Assad.[19]

The London *Daily Mail* showed pictures of guns, AK-47 rifles, and hand grenades that Syrian security forces recovered after storming the Omari mosque, where arms had been shipped to the "Arab Spring" insurgents from Saudi Arabia. Other reports highlighted the presence of snipers at the anti-Assad rallies and the torching of Baath Party headquarters and courthouses.[20] While Sunni businessmen may have felt that a corrupt Alawite class had come to dominate business enterprise under Assad, signs at the demonstrations called for the killing of Alawites and deportation of Christians into Lebanon. Muslim Brotherhood televangelist Adnan al-Arur was among those inciting violence by calling for protesters to "feed Alawite government loyalists to the dogs."[21]

In the first protests, seven police officers were killed and Baath Party headquarters, Daraa's main courthouse, the governor's office, and the Syria Telephone company offices were set ablaze. Sixty security forces were massacred two weeks later. The plan of the mob was to provoke a police response that would make it seem like the security forces were reacting harshly, which would discredit the Syrian government.[22] One Ahrar al-Sham fighter admitted that the jihadist group began forming brigades well before the protests started and recruited foreign fighters.[23] Majd al-Zaim, a Syrian, stated that what had happened in Syria during the Arab Spring was "not a revolution or civil war [as has been depicted in the Western media]. The terrorists are sent by your government [the U.S.]. They are Al Qaeda, Jabhat al-Nusra, Wahhabi, Salafist, Talibans and the extremist jihadists are sent by the West, Saudis, Qataris, Turkey . . .. Your Obama and whoever is behind him or above him are supporting Al Qaeda and leading a proxy war on my country."[24]

Father Frans van der Lugt, a Jesuit priest who lived in Homs and was tragically murdered by Jabhat al-Nusra in June 2014, told Australian professor Tim Anderson in January 2012 that most citizens in Syria "do not support the [armed] opposition—you cannot say that this is a popular uprising . . .From the beginning the protest movements have not merely been peaceful. I have seen from the beginning armed protesters in those demonstrations walking around; they were the first to fire on the police. Very often the violence of the security forces comes in response to the brutal violence of the armed insurgents . . . Most Christian leaders stand behind Bashar because they are convinced that they would be worse with any alternative."[25]

Even U.S. intelligence acknowledged that Assad remained popular in the face of the "Arab Spring" uprising, noting that Syrians were "pragmatists" who "do not want a Muslim Brotherhood government."[26] Roula Roukbi, a hotel manager in Damascus, told journalist Charles Glass that "a lot of people here, nationalists of the old generation, are with the regime because they think it's against imperialism and the Zionist project." Another physician told Glass that many people were against Assad because of what had happened in the last ten years and wanted change in Syria "but not like this [reference to violent uprisings and prospect of rule by jihadists]."[27]

On March 29, 2011, six million Syrians out of a population of 22.5 million attended pro-Assad rallies. *TIME* magazine quoted a member of the CIA-backed Free Syrian Army (FSA), who acknowledged that around 70 percent of Syrians supported Assad.[28] A Qatari poll put the total of Assad supporters at 55 percent.[29] Their ranks included minority groups who had done well under the Assads, Alawites, other Shiite groups, most of Syria's Christians, and parts of the Sunni merchant class.[30]

President Obama called for Assad to "step aside" in August 2011—he said for the "good of the Syrian people."[31] At that time, the U.S. ambassador, Robert Ford, was traveling around Syria telling demonstrators and rebel fighters that the U.S. was on their side, inciting them with promises of support.[32] In May 2011, Assad had offered to pardon all political crimes and initiate a national dialogue with opposition elements who rejected this offer of amnesty and dialogue. Assad further said he would allow for competitive presidential elections and registration of six new political parties.[33]

The private intelligence firm Stratfor determined that while some protesters had been killed, there was "little evidence of massive brutality" on the Syrian government's part "compared to other state crackdowns in the region."[34] Nir Rosen reported for *Al Jazeera* in 2011 that opposition activists were misrepresenting dead rebel fighters as civilians killed by security forces, which other sources corroborated.[35]

Foreign support for the rebel fighters came from Saudi Arabia, Turkey, and Qatar, which each hated Assad for different reasons (Turkey, for example, disdained Assad's long support for the Kurdistan Workers Party, PKK).[36] The U.S., Turkey, and Jordan had all deployed Special Forces to Syrian territory to support the covert military operation—which in a way recycled Kermit Roosevelt's 1957 plan to topple a secular nationalist government by enlisting Sunni Islamists to create an internal uprising.[37]

USAID and NED Play a Key Role

Benjamin Arthur Thomason's 2024 Ph.D. thesis at Bowling Green University details how the National Endowment for Democracy (NED), a CIA offshoot specializing in propaganda, financed opposition media and activists and helped mobilize them in the buildup to the anti-Assad uprising. Thomason cites an April 2009 Wikileaks cable by U.S. chargé d'affaires Maura Connelly describing a $1.25 million grant for the NED-financed International Republican Institute (IRI) to create and disseminate public opinion research and CDs containing footage by anti-Assad journalists and a report documenting human rights abuses. Connelly discusses a grant of over $2 million for the Aspen Strategic Initiative Institute in Berlin to organize conferences for Syrian opposition figures to meet international NGOs, media, and human rights activists.

Connelly also lists $6.3 million for the Democracy Council of California to discreetly collaborate with the Syrian opposition to produce a website and "various broadcast concepts," and $611,000 for the Czech NGO People in Need to train Syrian activists on "using the model of Eastern European democratization." The same cable describes $584, 904 for Etana Press, the publishing arm of the Syrian opposition research, activism and lobbying group Etana. A February 2010 cable reveals that the Middle East Partnership Initiative, a regional partner of USAID, was supporting Barada TV, a London-based Syrian opposition satellite TV network that vilified Assad and lionized the anti-government activists.[38] NED also financed *Enab Baludi*, an anti-Assad, anti-Iran, anti-Russian newspaper established in a Damascus suburb co-founded by a woman whose husband was allegedly tortured to death by the Syrian intelligence service.[39] A top ranking U.S. diplomat in Damascus had warned in an April 2009 cable that Syrian authorities "would undoubtedly view any U.S. funds going to illegal political groups as tantamount to supporting regime change."[40] Which of course it was.

The U.S. money for Syrian opposition figures had begun flowing under President George W. Bush after he effectively froze political ties with Damascus in 2005, and then continued under Obama. Recipients of grants included Freedom House for workshops for Syrian activists on "strategic non-violence and civic mobilization"; the American Bar Association, which held a conference in Damascus and then continued outreach for legal education programs in Syria; and American University, for research on Syrian tribal and civil society.[41] The $6.3 million Democracy Council of California loan was known to have resulted in the channeling of funds to the innocuous-sounding Movement For Justice and Development in Syria, a London-based Islamist group founded by former disaffected members of the Muslim Brotherhood, ostensibly to provide money to the families of opposition figures jailed by the Syrian government.[42] The founder of Barada TV, Malik al-Abdeh, was significantly a member of the Movement for Justice and Development.

Precedents of Serbia and Libya

The NED's regime-change strategies had been perfected in the post-Cold-War era in Serbia, where NED mobilized student activists with the group Optor as part of a successful operation to remove socialist leader Slobodan Milošević. Optor leaders were paid by the International Republican Institute (IRI) to attend a seminar on nonviolent resistance at the Hilton hotel in Budapest where they received training in such matters as how to organize a strike, how to communicate with symbols, how to overcome fear, and how to undermine the authority of a dictatorial regime. A principal lecturer at the IRI-financed seminar was retired U.S. Army Col. Robert Helvey, a Vietnam veteran who promoted non-violent resistance methods around the world. Helvey introduced Optor activists to the writing of Gene Sharp, "the Clausewitz of the nonviolence movement," whose lectures were later attended by anti-Assad dissidents.[43]

Besides Serbia, the regime-change operation in Syria also bore a lot of similarities to a parallel regime-change operation in Libya between March and October 2011. Russia had followed the operations in Libya very closely, and what it saw led it to intervene in Syria to try to prevent the same thing from happening there. Sold as a liberation operation in support of an indigenous "Arab Spring" revolution against Muammar Gaddafi's supposedly brutal dictatorship, the Operation Odyssey Dawn was in reality designed to establish Western control over Libya's oil resources and remove a defiant anti-imperialist leader who had resisted the U.S. Africa Command (AFRICOM). Journalist Patrick Cockburn reported that rebel militiamen had only a limited role in the overthrow of Gaddafi, "who was mostly brought down by NATO air strikes."[44] According to Cockburn, "[w]ithout NATO, the rebels would not have lasted more than a few weeks."[45]

The NATO campaign against Libya was ironically carried out just as Gaddafi was attempting to create good relations with the West, by, for example, compensating the victims of the Lockerbie Scotland plane downing even though Gaddafi continued to deny that Libya was responsible, and by forgoing any aspirations to obtain nuclear weapons.[46] At the urging of his son Saif—whom the U.S. has recently blocked from coming to power by repeatedly delaying elections—Gaddafi was working to create a constitutional form of government for Libya.[47] In short, it is when Libya was reforming in ways the West claimed it wanted that it decided to destroy Gaddafi and the nation of Libya along with him.

Internal emails between Secretary of State Hillary Clinton—one of the key figures behind the invasion and destruction of Libya—and various White House officials demonstrated that the Libya intervention, just as the Syria one which began around the same time, was knowingly based on lies.[48] In the case of Libya, there were three essential lies peddled by Clinton, et al., and amplified by the mainstream press and even human rights groups like Amnesty International. These lies were a) that Benghazi was being imminently attacked and subjected to genocide by the Gaddafi government, when in fact the emails show that Clinton and her colleagues knew that any possible threat to Benghazi had passed before the bombs started falling; b) that Gaddafi was handing out Viagra to his troops to carry out mass rapes—a lie which was thoroughly debunked, but not in time to prevent the NATO onslaught; and c) the claim that Gaddafi was using "Black mercenaries" to attack his own people, when in fact these were simply guest workers from sub-Saharan Africa who were not engaged in any fighting.[49] This third lie actually incited a very real genocide against Black Africans living in Libya.[50] The results of the NATO intervention were disastrous, as even Obama would lament later when he stated that the aftermath of the intervention represented the "worst mistake" of his presidency.[51] The term "mistake" is a misnomer here as the destruction of Libya was entirely predictable and indeed intended.

A 2022 article in *Al Jazeera* describes the darkness into which Libya, the most prosperous country in Africa before the NATO intervention, fell after NATO's regime-change campaign.[52] The article noted that since the fall of Gaddafi, "human rights abuses" abound, with people "regularly subjected to acts of slavery, rape and torture." Gaddafi himself was brutally killed and Libya was divided between rival governments—one in the east, backed by military commander Khalifa Haftar, a CIA favorite, and a UN-recognized administration in the capital of Tripoli. Each side was supported by different militias and foreign powers. A UN expert panel report to the Security Council detailed brutal torture inflicted on young women and girls in two different towns, including Bani Walid—a town of Black Libyans attacked by the NATO-backed jihadists in the course of the regime-change operation:

> The experts said four migrants suffered human rights abuses in secret detention facilities controlled by human traffickers in the areas of Tazirbu in the Libyan desert and Bani Walid near the northwest coast. They said victims were enslaved, severely beaten, deliberately starved and denied medical care.
>
> "Two former female detainees, who were 14 and 15-year-old girls at the time, further testified to the panel that multiple perpetrators repeatedly raped them, subjected them to sexual slavery and other forms of sexual violence during the period of over 18 months in a secret detention facility in Bani Walid," the report said.
>
> The panel said it also found that guards responsible for protecting the most vulnerable migrants in the government-run Shara al-Zawiya detention centre "took a direct part in or turned a blind eye to consistent acts of rape, sexual exploitation and threats of rape against women and girls" detained there between January and June 2021.[53]

In short, as all of these regime-change operations invariably do, they made Libya much worse off than before and actually turned it into a human rights nightmare. Mission accomplished! And so, if the NATO campaign in Libya was not in fact about protecting human rights as claimed, and was actually carried out just as Gaddafi was trying to cozy up to the West by making various reforms, including democratic reforms, what was it truly about? Maximilian Forte makes the strong case that this regime change was primarily about removing an African/Arabic leader who was a staunch supporter of Third World liberation organizations such as the Palestine Liberation Organization (PLO) and who was successfully building Pan-African unity that included plans for a gold-based African currency to compete with the U.S. dollar.[54]

From Gaddafi to Assad

Quite similar concerns motivated the U.S.-led attempt to unseat Bashar al-Assad. As with Muammar Gaddafi, the West made its moves against Assad even as he was attempting to curry favor with the West by making wide-reaching liberal economic reforms. As Dr. Khaled Al Wazani relates, "[u]pon assuming his presidential office in 2000, Assad introduced market liberalization that was designed to bolster the private sector and attract foreign investments. Key measures included: bank privatization, the licensing of private universities and other private schools, and establishment of an economic 'free zone.'"[55] Assad also cooperated with the Bush admnistration in the despicable extraordinary rendition program.[56] Despite these initiatives, Assad remained recalcitrant in matters unacceptable to the U.S. and its Western allies. For example, he permitted two communist parties to flourish in Syria along with communist and socialist-led trade unions. Indeed, as one of the authors of this book witnessed, the left-wing unions of Syria were critical in the revitalization of the Communist World Federation of Trade Unions (WFTU)—the oldest trade union confederation in the world, which had originally found its seat in Moscow after World War II, but which had experienced a decline after the collapse of the USSR.

But the biggest "crime" of Assad was his continued support for the Palestinian cause and for the resistance forces fighting against Israel. Frederic C. Hof, who was intimately involved in discussions with Assad, has detailed that progress was being made in negotiating with Assad in 2010 for a rapprochement with the West, but that, as 2011 approached, it was clear that he would not "deliver on Israel's price for peace: Syria's full strategic realignment away from Iran, Hezbollah in Lebanon, and Hamas in the Gaza Strip; and the liquidation of all security threats to Israel arising from Syria and Syrian relationships, including its relationship with Lebanon."[57]

When negotiations fell apart over these issues in 2011, the dogs of war were unleashed upon Syria. And when Assad was ultimately overthrown by the re-named Al Qaeda affiliate, HTS, that organization made it immediately clear that it wanted friendly relations with Israel. It made this statement, even as Israel was militarily assaulting Syria and destroying all of Syria's defenses. As *NPR* would report in a December 27, 2024 report entitled "New leaders in Damascus call for cordial Syria ties with a resistant Israel,"

> In a wide-ranging interview with NPR, [HTS] Governor Maher Marwan, 42, said that Syria's new government did not want to seek conflict with Israel, which has been striking strategic military installations in Syria since the regime of former President Bashar al-Assad fell earlier this month.

> "We have no fear towards Israel and our problem is not with Israel," Marwan said. "We don't want to meddle in anything that will threaten Israel's security or any other country's security."

Incredibly, the new HTS government would even release a new map of Syria shortly after taking power which did not include the Golan Heights[58]—a portion of territory illegally seized by Israel in 1967 but still recognized as part of Syria under international law. Of course, while it may initially sound strange that a radical Islamist group would want to be friends with Israel, this should not be surprising given the fact that, as revealed by *Foreign Policy* back in 2018, Israel armed and funded no less than twelve rebel groups in Syria in their war against Assad.[59]

The same article explained that this was in addition to the support being provided these groups during "the 7-year-old civil war . . . [by] Qatar, Saudi Arabia, Turkey and the United States." In truth, what was sold to the U.S. public as a "civil war" in Syria was in fact a world war against that country, with passports collected from over 100 different countries amongst the various militant groups fighting Assad. And the results of this world war were truly disastrous for the people of Syria.

CHAPTER 4

Voices from Syria[1]

> "Alawites to the grave; Christians to Beirut."
> –War slogan of the anti-Assad militants during the Syrian conflict.

As this chapter was being written, Syria was experiencing the worst day of violence since HTS (formerly the Al-Nusra Front of Al Qaeda) took power from President Bashar al-Assad. Reports from Syria published on social media, accompanied by gruesome videos mostly filmed by the killers themselves, indicate that hundreds, if not thousands, of Syrians (mostly Alawites, but also Christians) were killed in sectarian violence carried out by forces aligned with HTS on Friday, March 7, 2025—the day in which it may be said that a genocide began in earnest in Syria. According to witnesses, "most of the perpetrators of the massacres of civilians were foreign militants, Uyghurs, Chechens and Uzbeks affiliated with HTS, and only a small percentage were Syrians. Following the downfall of Assad, the HTS-led government absorbed foreign jihadists into its military and appointed some to senior roles."[2]

In the early morning hours of Monday, March 9, 2025, an Alawite friend of mine in Damascus, after not having responded to a text the night before, reached out to me with this message: "Dear Dan. I'm sorry. Was broken. When called a friend's phone in Latakia. To be answered by a jihadist. Telling me that he killed her. Offering me the same fate of my friend. I am sorry I didn't reply to your call. I think I had a panic attack. Breathing seems very hard now."

My friend asked me if I thought the jihadist might have been lying and whether her friend might still be alive. I responded that I prayed she was alive. Before noon, my friend wrote me again. She enclosed a photo of her friend in Latakia dead on the floor of her home next to another dead woman. They were clearly shot at close range. My friend's accompanying message read, "She's gone Dan. That's her in the pink pajamas. I just had some hope. Her name was Nagham. I hope she will be in a better place than Syria."

Another Alawite, who I had never met before, sent me a direct message on Twitter. The message is very moving, and so I share it here unedited:

Greetings,

I am an Alawite girl from the Syrian coast, a 26-year-old pharmacist. I am writing this letter in secrecy to protect my life and the lives of my family.

I was deeply pleased to learn that you have been appointed as an advisor to the Alawite Association in the United States, hoping that you might help put an end to the systematic genocide aimed at the ethnic cleansing of the Alawites.

Mr. Kovalik,

I have witnessed firsthand what has happened. Jihadi gangs, along with Hay'at Tahrir al-Sham, stormed the coastal region, massacring elderly people, children, women, and unarmed young men. They burned homes, livelihoods, and everything that sustained our existence.

I now live with my family in a remote village—six days without electricity or water. My friends in other villages are hiding in the forests with their families, despite the cold weather and the lack of food and milk for their children.

All of this has happened in just a few days...

And beyond these recent events, over the past three months, 9,000 young men who were in the Syrian army were arrested after surrendering their weapons under guarantees of safety. We have no information about them or their fate. My own 23-year-old brother is among them—I have not heard anything about him for three months.

After that, thousands of other young Alawite men were also detained. We have been dismissed from our jobs, while kidnappings, killings, and forced displacement continue.

I am hoping for help to stop this.

I am hoping to see my kidnapped brother again or at least to learn something about his fate.

I am hoping to return to my job and pursue the dreams that are being mercilessly destroyed.

I apologize for the length of my letter,

but our hearts are weary, and we place great hope in you.

Thank you.

The same young woman sent me a number of grisly videos which the killers themselves had taken and posted on social media to brag of their murders:

There are many more, but my heart can't take it anymore.

Please, help us. They want to exterminate the Alawites, that's what they're saying.

We are now fleeing in the forests.

Please, I'm sending this to you. If they find out, they will kill me and my family.

Please, we want peace.

I want to see my kidnapped brother.

I want to live in safety with my friends.

We are not remnants *of the regime.*

It turned out the forests were not safe as the HTS forces, in an effort to kill those fleeing there, began to burn down entire woods in order to cut off escape. Again, numerous photos and videos of the forests burning corroborated this. However, at the time of this writing, my new pen pal is still alive.

While there was scant reporting on the mass slaughter in the mainstream Western press, the *Greek City Times*, in an article entitled, "SYRIA: Turkey-backed jihadists massacre Greek Orthodox Christians and Alawites in latest bout of violence," reported the following:

> The Syrian Network for Human Rights (SNHR) said on Friday that more than 225 people have been killed since Thursday. However, this is believed to be a gross underreporting, with activists on the ground, such as Coast Youth Forum, believing the death toll could be as high as 1,800, mostly Alawites, but also Christians.
>
> Syria's new regime, led by so-called transitional president Ahmad al-Sharaa, has for months been massacring the Alawite minority, as well as Christians, under the guise of eliminating remnants of the former Assad dictatorship. . . .
>
> The latest massacres mark a sharp escalation though, with disturbing videos seen by Greek City Times showing the execution of civilians, women, children and the elderly. . . .
>
> One video shows the Turkish-backed jihadists desecrating a Christian icon in Tartous. The militant says, 'Our guardian is Allah, and you have no guardian,' accusing Christians of idol worship.[3]

The number of those murdered in what is clearly a genocidal campaign appears to be much higher than the official figures. As Greek European Union Minister Nikolas Farantouris reported after visiting Syria during the worst weekend of violence:

> As a member of the Security and Defense Committee, the Constitutional Affairs Committee and the Budgets Committee of the European Parliament, I paid a two-day visit to Damascus on 8-9 March at the invitation of the Patriarch.

On Sunday (of Orthodoxy), I attended the service in the Patriarchal Church together with [Greek Orthodox] Patriarch John X of Antioch and we had a long private meeting on the developments. I then met with representatives of national and religious communities, while I also visited the Ministry of Foreign Affairs of the new regime and spoke with the heads of International and European Affairs.

Reliable data indicate 7,000 Christians and Alawites slaughtered and unprecedented atrocities against civilians. Christian and other communities with a millennial presence in this region are at risk of extinction.

The new Islamic regime is leading Syria into an Islamic state and is claiming that it cannot control the paramilitaries, and the gangs associated with them who attack innocent civilians.[4]

A week later, on March 15, 2025, the Telegram channel *Syrian Christians* posted an interview that the famous Syrian actor Bashar Ismail gave to *Sky News* in which he estimated that 22,000 individuals (Alawites and Christians) had been killed since the genocide began in earnest on March 7.[5] As *Syrian Christians* noted, if this figure is correct, this number would have exceeded the entire number of civilians killed in Syria between the years 2018-2024, more than the *annual* number of civilians killed in 2011, 2016, and 2017, and roughly equal to the annual number of civilians killed in Syria in 2012 and 2015![6]

In addition to those killed, it is estimated that around 200,000 civilians were displaced in this violence.[7] The three main Patriarchs of the Syrian Christian Churches (Syriac Orthodox, Greek Orthodox, and Melkite Catholic) released a joint statement on March 8, 2025, stating, in pertinent part:

> In recent days, Syria has witnessed a dangerous escalation of violence, brutality and killings in attacks on innocent civilians, including women and children. Homes have been violated, their sanctity disregarded, and properties looted—scenes that starkly reflect the immense suffering by the Syrian people.

The Christian Churches while strongly condemning any act that threatens civil peace, denounce and condemn the massacres targeting innocent civilians, and call for an immediate end to these horrific acts, which stand in stark opposition to all human and moral values.

Quite surprisingly, the U.S. Department of State put out a statement on May 9, 2025, which accurately described and then condemned the violence. It stated, "The U.S. Department of State condemns the killings in Syria and says the U.S. stands with Syria's minorities, the Christians, Druzes, Alawites and Kurds, calling on Syrian Transitional Government to punish their killers."[8] Despite this condemnation, however, the U.S. has continued to collaborate with the HTS leaders of Syria. "The U.S. military, which continues to occupy one-third of Syria, has indeed been working behind the scenes to negotiate a deal between the HTS and various militia forces in order to unify the country under HTS rule.[9] This, despite the fact that HTS, and al-Jolani himself, continue to remain on the official U.S. terrorist list.[10]

For its part, the European Union (EU) released a scurrilous message that was indicative of most of the Western coverage of events and which only encouraged the violence. Thus, the EU stated: "The European Union strongly condemns the recent attacks, reportedly by pro-Assad elements, on interim government forces in the coastal areas of Syrian and all violence against civilians."[11] Not surprisingly, then, even after his weekend killing spree, Syria's HTS leader, al-Jolani, was invited to Brussels for an EU donor event.[12] To its credit, the *European Conservative* roundly condemned this invite, stating:

The European Commission, led by Ursula von der Leyen, has invited the interim Syrian government to Brussels for a donor conference. This decision—designed to promote investment in the country to secure strategic resources—comes just days after the massacre of thousands of civilians from ethnic and religious minorities at the hands of the army and militias affiliated with the Islamist terror group Hayat Tahrir Al-Sham (HTS).

Despite the severity of these events, the European Union continues to provide financial and political support to the new Syrian administration without questioning its ties to these extremist groups.[13]

The Associated Press (AP), quite representative of the Western coverage of these massacres of civilians, was late in reporting on them, and, when it did, attempted to write them off as "clashes between Syrian security forces and loyalists of ousted President Bashar Assad and revenge killings" against Alawites because Bashar Al-Assad was an Alawite.[14] But as always, the devil is in the detail, and the detail given by the *AP* itself belies the claims of "clashes" between armed groups. Thus, as the *AP* explained in its deceptively titled article, "2 days of clashes and revenge killings in Syria leave more than 1,000 people dead,"

> The Revenge killings that started Friday by Sunni Muslim gunmen loyal to the government against members of Assad's minority Alawite sect are a major blow to Hayat Tahrir al-Sham, the faction that led the overthrow of the former government. Alawites made up a large part of Assad's support base for decades.

> Residents of Alawite villages and towns spoke to The Associated Press about killings during which gunmen shot Alawites, the majority of them men, in the streets or at the gates of their homes. Many homes of Alawites were looted and then set on fire in different areas, two residents of Syria's coastal region told the AP from their hideouts.

Curiously, there is no evidence of "clashes" here; just wanton murder and mayhem. In addition, it must be noted that many women have been killed in these massacres as proven by the numerous photos of the female victims on social media. But, apparently, these deaths are not convenient to *AP's* narrative. Meanwhile, the *AP* description of the violence in one coastal town continues to paint the picture of unarmed civilians being gunned down. Thus, the *AP* writes,

Residents speak of atrocities in one town

Residents of Baniyas, one of the towns worst hit by the violence, said bodies were strewn on the streets or left unburied in homes and on the roofs of buildings, and nobody was able to collect them. One resident said that the gunmen prevented residents for hours from removing the bodies of five of their neighbors killed Friday at close range.

Ali Sheha, a 57-year-old resident of Baniyas who fled with his family and neighbors hours after the violence broke out Friday, said that at least 20 of his neighbors and colleagues in one neighborhood of Baniyas where Alawites lived, were killed, some of them in their shops, or in their homes.

Again, where are the alleged "clashes"? The violence perpetrated by the HTS militias has been so grisly and shocking, indeed, that some of their own members have been moved to denounce it. As DD Geopolitics on Twitter, with an accompanying video of such a member, explains: "Muhammad Abu Obaidah, a fighter from HTS, speaks out with tears in his eyes, condemning the brutal massacres committed in Baniyas and Jabalain. 'Did our religion command us to do this? Were the Prophet's teachings like this? Forcing people from their homes and executing them in cold blood?' HTS' own members are breaking ranks—the truth can no longer be hidden. Even their fighters can't stomach these crimes."[15]

And quite notably, while the HTS has had the wherewithal to carry out mass atrocities against Syrian civilians, it has had no stomach for challenging Israel's takeover of huge swaths of Syria. Thus, completely unmolested, at the time we are writing this book, Israel has set up seven military outposts in Syria since the HTS-takeover.[16] But of course, this was quite according to plan. Sadly, the horrible atrocities we are witnessing today were quite predictable from the conduct of Al-Nusra and allied terrorist groups during the Syrian conflict, and they have been enabled by the compliant Western press, such as the *AP*, which has sanitized, promoted, and even lionized these terrorists.

* * *

In 2021, I twice visited both Lebanon and Syria. What I learned there was quite at variance with what we were being told in the mainstream press. One of the first people I met in Damascus, Syria, was Yara Saleh, a lovely and affable woman who was serving as a reporter and anchor for the Syrian News Channel, an official state news agency.

Yara, while working for this channel back in 2012, was kidnapped by the Free Syria Army (FSA) just outside Damascus, and held for six days until rescued in a daring mission by the Syrian Arab Armed Forces (SAA). Yara's kidnapping and rescue became the subject of a movie which the delegation I was with were invited to watch for its premier. I contacted Yara afterwards to hear her story in her words.

Yara still seemed shaken by her abduction years before. She was thin, almost to the point of emaciation, ate nothing, but chain smoked as she told her story. As Yara explained, she was traveling with a driver (Hussam Imad), a camera man (Abdullah Tabreh) and an assistant (Hatem Abu Yehya) to do a report on the clashes between the SAA and forces which she described as "armed terrorist groups." She specifically wanted to report on the impact of the burgeoning war and terrorist threats upon the civilian population.

However, while traveling on the road to their destination (a Damascus suburb known as al-Tell), they were stopped by armed men. These armed men detained them, took their possessions, including their phones and money, and beat all of them, including Yara. Yara, a quite small woman, explains that the beatings upon her were quite hurtful. Yara said they decided to kidnap them after discovering that they were with the Syrian News Channel.

They were driven into town and to a location with hundreds of other armed militants. While en route, one of the armed captors held Yara's head down between her legs.

Yara related that the militants seemed to be led or guided by a sheikh of some sort who appeared to be of foreign origin and did

Yara Saleh, a reporter and anchor for the Syrian News Agency had been kidnapped by the Free Syria Army in 2012. She talks about how the "rebels" targeted people for their religious background. (Kovalik, 2021)

not understand Syrian traditions. I would later hear such stories again in other areas of the country, like Douma and Jabar. In these areas, armed terrorists took over the cities via huge tunnels connecting them to Jordan where they entered, and they began to kidnap people, beat them and enslave or even kill them if they were of religious faiths different from the fanatical doctrine of Wahabism advocated by the terrorists.

One of the first questions Yara and her colleagues were asked was about their religious background. All of them were of "mixed" traditions in Yara's words, and Yara stood out because she wore makeup and did not wear any head covering. I just found out recently that Yara is an Alawite. Yara, like many of her fellow Syrians, sees herself as a Syrian first and that is more important to her identity than being an Alawite. Before the sectarian violence brought to Syria from the outside, Syrians did not wear their religions on their sleeve and didn't go around asking others what their religion is; that would be considered rude.

The sheikh told them that they all were to be executed because they worked with the Syrian government and because of their mixed religious affiliations. In response to the sheikh's words, two of Yara's colleagues, Hussam and Hatem, were taken away to a nearby location. Yara then heard the sound of gun fire. She believed that both of her associates were killed at that time. However, Hussam was shortly brought back, and he told Yara, with tears in his eyes, that he witnessed Hatem murdered in a spray of bullets.

Notably, Yara explained that the fighters who held them openly told them that they were taking orders from someone in Turkey and that they had been told to move them to Turkey. The fighters explained that the plan was to negotiate their freedom with the Syrian Arab Army, and that if the SAA did not give in to their demands, they would kill them. However, when Yara asked one of the fighters if they would be released if the SAA gave them what they wanted, he answered in the negative, saying that they would continue to hold them for leverage to gain more concessions.

In addition, according to Yara, a significant number of the fighters were not Syrian. They were not certain where they all were from, but they could tell by their accents that some were from Saudi Arabia and Libya.

Yara related that they were subjected to awful physical and psychological torture during their six days of captivity. She explained that they were incessantly beaten, especially in the first two days, and that she was made to wear a hijab and abaya though that is not her practice. The fighters referred to their captives as "infidels." They forced her cameraman, a Christian, to pray as Muslims do. They were moved around quite a lot during their captivity and kept underground where there were rats and no sunshine. What little food they were given was poor.

Yara stated that she was threatened with sexual violence by the fighters. She believes that if she were not rescued as quickly as she was and if the fighters had not been distracted with clashes during their captivity that these threats would have been carried out.

Eventually, the Syrian Arab Army entered and surrounded the area in order to try to rescue them. The fighters holding them attempted to escape, using them as human shields. However, they were able to escape and run to the safety of the SAA. Yara said she was elated when the Syrian Army showed up and was moved to tears when she reached them and saw the flag of Syria they were flying.

After this experience, Yara was more convinced than ever that the militants fighting the government stood outside of civilization and the law and that darkness would descend upon Syria if they came to power. I still stay in touch with Yara, and while she is devastated by the fall of the Assad government and is worried about where the country is headed, she believes in Syria and the Syrian people and believes the country will rise again. She is truly one of the bravest people I have ever met.

Also in 2021, I visited a primary school in the Ikrimah neighborhood of Homs which witnessed one of the worst atrocities of the war in Syria. In October 2014, anti-government terrorists attacked this school with two car bombs. The first car bomb killed numerous children in the school. The second bomb was timed to then kill parents who rushed to the school to check on their children after news of the first explosion was reported on the radio. In total, 45 people were killed, including 37 children, and over 110 were injured, the majority of them children.

On October 2, 2014, the Permanent Mission of the Syrian Arab Republic sent identical letters to the UN Security Council and UN Secretary-General denouncing this crime, the foreign support for the terrorists who committed it and the world's silence in the face of such acts of terror in Syria. In a pertinent part, these letters read:

> The available information indicates that the two terrorist bombings were planned and executed by the terrorist groups which the Western States and their regional proxies enthusiastically refer to as the "moderate armed opposition."

Photo of the First Lady's visit to a primary school in the Ikrimah neighborhood of Homs that witnessed one of the worst atrocities of the war on Syria in 2014, which left 45 people dead including 37 children. It was committed by the so-called "moderate armed opposition" supported by the United States and other Western countries. (Kovalik, 2021)

The killing of innocent children and other civilians can have no justification. Yet the international community, as represented by the United Nations, has not condemned the crimes of the armed terrorist groups. Nor has it spoken out against the recent terrorist attacks on schools. The latest incident was but one example; others include the targeting of the Badruldin al-Husayni Faculty of Legal Sciences, the Darulsalam School and the Manar School. Failure to condemn those acts has merely emboldened the terrorist groups to carry out further atrocities. . . .

The murder of schoolchildren in Homs encapsulates the ideology and modus operandi of the terrorist groups, who have directed their hatred and lawlessness at Syria's children, and not for the first time. On another occasion, terrorist groups struck against children under the age of three, when fictitious health-care agencies belonging to the armed terrorist groups conspired with the Turkish authorities to cause a humanitarian disaster that claimed the lives of 15 innocent Syrian children, who had been given expired and poisoned vaccinations for measles. Dozens of other innocent children suffered asphyxiation.[17]

As for the assertion that the terrorists involved in the attack were amongst the "moderate rebels" being supported by foreign powers, including the U.S., this turned out to be true. Thus, as the principal of the school that I met explained to me, this attack was carried out by the FSA which, President Barack Obama openly stated, was the main group the U.S. was supporting in Syria at this time. The school principal expressed deep gratitude to President Assad who supported the swift rebuilding of the school, and she proudly gave me a tour of the restored facilities. She expressed particular thanks to and warmth for the First Lady, Asma Fawaz al-Assad, who visited the school shortly after the tragedy to give condolences to the families of the deceased and wounded. She proudly showed me photos of the First Lady from her visit to the school.

Also in Homs, I visited the Saint Mary Church of the Holy Belt, a Syriac Orthodox cathedral which claims to house a portion of a belt worn by the Virgin Mary. The current church was built in 1852, but the original church, which can be visited underneath and is essentially a cave, was built in 59 AD, making this one of the oldest Christian churches in the world. In 2012, the FSA attacked this Church, destroying ancient relics and burning the portions of the church that would catch fire. As the pastor of the church told me, before the FSA arrived, members of the church, escorted by the Syrian Arab Army, had moved the belt of Mary to another city and hid it there.

One of Many Relics Damaged by the Free Syria Army
attack on the Saint Mary Church of the Holy Belt in 2012.
It was the Hezbollah and the Syrian Arab Army that defended
the Church and drove the FSA away. (Kovalik, 2021)

Pastor of the Saint Mary Church of the Holy Belt describes
FSA attack. (Kovalik, 2021)

In truth, I was surprised to learn that it was Hezbollah, along with the SAA, which helped to defend the church and to drive the FSA away. The church, which was heavily damaged during the attack, was fully restored by 2014. The pastor seemed quite grateful to the Syrian government for its efforts in helping save the church and the belt of Mary which, by the time I had visited, was housed there again.

While those who opposed the Assad government have tried to blame Assad for somehow provoking the attacks upon Christians which began quite early in the war, the Telegram group *Syrian Christians* tells a very different story. As they explained recently, in a post captioned,

"Who is inciting against Christians in the Valley of the Christians,"

> Since the fall of the Baathist regime, the valley [in the western part of Homs Governate] has become a hotspot for escalating crimes and violence, marked by a distressing surge in murders and kidnappings orchestrated by jihadists. This once-peaceful region now grapples with fear and uncertainty. . . .
>
> A little background—Al Hosn, a Sunni town nestled near the Valley of the Christians is the site of the magnificent Krak des Chevaliers castle. Historically, Al Hosn was home to a small but vibrant Christian community, however the onset of the Syrian civil war in 2011 marked a dark chapter in its history. In January 2012, jihadist groups established a presence in the area, causing tensions.
>
> The first act of violence occurred in February 2012 when three unsuspecting policemen were ambushed and brutally murdered, a heinous attack attributed to the Al Qaeda-affiliated Nusra Front. This marked the beginning of a campaign of terror that targeted Christians, Alawites and even Sunnis in the region, causing widespread displacement from Al Hosn as first the Christians fled and then thousands of Sunnis who sought refuge in the Valley who were hosted in hotels free of charge and with food and amenities donated by the Valley of the Christians. The only Sunnis who stayed in Al Hosn are the jihadists & salafists who wanted to fight.

In December 2012, Al Hosn emerged as a jihadist emirate, establishing a new governance structure under the control of the Lebanese jihadist organization Jund Ash Sham, joined by international jihadists from several countries. This marked a significant shift in the region, as the group sought to enforce its ideological principles which are close to ISIS. The group utilizes ISIS flags as well.[18]

As *Syrian Christians* further explains, Christians ultimately took up arms to defend themselves against terrorist attacks during the Syrian war. And, on March 17, 2025, *Syrian Christians* reported that "Christian fighters who defended their town against jihadist terrorists during the war are now being taken and tortured in Jolani's prisons."[19]

Just as Christians took up arms to defend themselves, so did Alawites. Indeed, I am very close to some Alawite fighters who fought alongside the SAA against the terrorists. These individuals, it must be said, were not fans of Bashar al-Assad and were critical of many of his policies. However, as they explained to me, they knew full well that they were fighting against much darker forces than Assad. And now that Assad has fallen, these friends and their families live in terror in places like Homs and Latakia. They will not go outside to their work, to attend school or to worship. At most, they leave their homes to buy food, and sometime not even then. The darker forces they were fighting against have now taken over Syria, and all they wish to do now is leave the country. At least for the moment, however, they are trapped.

CHAPTER 5

Charlie Wilson's War Redux?
Operation Timber Sycamore
and Other Covert Operations in Syria

In August 2017, *The New York Times* reported on the Trump administration's shutting down what it termed "one of the costliest covert action programs in the history of the CIA"—the $1 billion dollar per year Operation Timber Sycamore, a four-year operation initiated by President Barack Obama to arm and train Syrian rebels trying to overthrow the Assad government. Until that time, Operation Timber Sycamore, which received comparisons to Charlie Wilson's War[1]—the CIA's training of mujahidin soldiers to expel the Soviet Union from Afghanistan—was largely unknown to the American public. *The Times* claimed that Timber Sycamore had had periods of success such as in 2015 when "rebels using tank-destroying missiles, supplied by the C.I.A. and also Saudi Arabia, routed government forces in northern Syria." However, it was acknowledged that "some of the C.I.A.-supplied weapons had ended up in the hands of a rebel group tied to Al Qaeda," which the *Times* said "sapped political support for the program."[2]

Prior to commissioning Operation Timber Sycamore, Obama ordered a study of the history of the CIA's covert arming of rebel groups, which determined that there were only one or two instances of "successful proxy wars." Despite the failure of the CIA's secret wars from Albania in the late 1940s through Angola in the 1970s, and 1980s, Obama assigned the CIA to train militants under Timber Sycamore in Turkey and Jordan.[3] A 2013 poll found that 64 percent of Americans were against arming the Syrian rebels.[4] Some of the weaponry—which included millions of rounds of ammunition—was routed through NGOs or humanitarian relief organizations.[5] A lot landed at the U.S. Incirlik Air Force base in Turkey, a main command center for U.S.-NATO covert operations in Syria. Seventeen countries were involved in Timber Sycamore. Weapons were bought in the Balkans and elsewhere around Eastern Europe, including Bulgaria, and flown in through CIA subsidiary aircraft and Silk Way Airlines, an Azerbaijan public company of cargo planes, under the oversight of the Israeli government.[6]

Because of the importance of Bulgaria as an arms supplier, the Obama administration forged closer relations with Bulgarian leader Boyko Borisov who was a mafia lord.[7] Arms were procured through the CIA's bolstering its connection to Eastern Europe's criminal underground.[8] A Bulgarian weapons supplier that provided arms to the CIA-linked mercenary firm Purple Shovel was run by a Bulgarian mob boss nicknamed "The Baron." Firms and executives who supplied arms were linked to fraud, foreign bribery, and every other corrupt activity imaginable.[9] Syrian rebels additionally looted government properties and extorted people to obtain cash to purchase the CIA-supplied weapons.[10]

U.S. arms manufacturers that shipped weapons included Orbital ATK (bought in 2018 by Northrop Grumman) and Chemring Military Products, which also supplied the Afghan National Police.[11] An article in *The Canberra Times* specified that two thousand tons of Eastern European weapons had been delivered to Aqaba alone by April 2016.[12] Qatar and the UAE assisted in covert arms supplies along with Saudi Arabia, which contributed both weapons and large sums of money—around $700 million per year (40 percent of the Syrian state's pre-war defense budget).[13]

As part of what CIA operative Doug Laux called the "multi-tiered plan to engineer Assad's ouster," CIA paramilitary operatives trained rebels in basic infantry skills and to use Kalashnikovs, mortars, antitank guided missiles and other weapons. They provided them also with $200 in cash.[14] Prior to his death in September 2012, U.S. ambassador to Libya Christopher Stevens oversaw a covert arms supply pipeline from Libya. Ships from there delivered Tube-launched optically tracked, wire-guided (TOW) surface-to-air missiles, and other high-tech weaponry to the port of Iskenderun in southern Turkey.[15] Secretary of State Hillary Clinton (2009-2014) was a strong booster of Timber Sycamore who stated that "the hard men with the guns are going to be the more likely actors in any political transition."[16] In an attempt to soften their images, the CIA provided these hard men with media training, encouraging them to promote their "achievements" on social media.[17] These "achievements" included the killing of 11,000 civilians in government-controlled West Aleppo in the first four years of the war using some of the weapons provided under Timber Sycamore, including "hell cannon" mortar fire and explosives.[18]

To limit appearances of its wide-scale intervention in Syria, Turkey outsourced military training operations to a private military company called SADAT International Defense Consultancy.[19] The same approach was adopted by the Obama and Trump administrations, which bolstered Timber Sycamore by contracting private mercenary companies—many owned by former intelligence or U.S. Special Forces operatives—to carry out military training, weapons supply, intelligence analysis and other covert military operations in Syria. One of the companies that received a $10 million Pentagon contract for intelligence analysis in 2016, Six3 Intelligence Solutions, was subsequently acquired by CACI International, which was ordered by a U.S. Federal Judge to pay $42 million in damages because of the role of its employees in torturing captives at Abu Ghraib prison in Iraq following the Bush administration's invasion of Iraq.[20]

The New York Times reported about Jordanian intelligence officers pilfering stockpiles of weapons the CIA had shipped to the Syrian rebels, selling them on the black market. A Jordanian

Police Captain, Anwar Abu Zaid, shot and killed three American soldiers who had been training Syrian rebels as part of the CIA program.[21] Another *New York Times* article quoted from Hassan Abour, commander of Soquor al Sham, an Islamist group known to carry out suicide bombings receiving weapons under Timber Sycamore, who said that there were "fake Free Syrian Army (FSA) brigades claiming to be revolutionaries," who, when they got weapons sold them on the black market.[22] A lot of Timber Sycamore weaponry was obtained by ISIS fighters in Iraq. Some of it was old Soviet weaponry whose sale pushed the Warsaw Pact countries to purchase newer hardware produced in the U.S. and Western Europe.[23]

Obama administration officials confirmed that senior White House officials were regularly briefed on arms shipments carried out under Timber Sycamore.[24] The briefings included reports that the CIA-trained rebels had summarily executed prisoners and committed other violations of the rules of armed conflict. John O. Brennan, Obama's last CIA director who was close to Saudi spy chief Prince Mohammed bin Nayef from his time as the CIA's Riyadh Station Chief in the 1990s, remained a vigorous defender of Timber Sycamore despite alleged divisions inside the spy agency about Timber Sycamore's effectiveness.[25] One top official justified the program on the grounds that the Gulf Arab States, Turkey, and Saudi Arabia, "were going to do it one way or another. They weren't asking for a 'Mother, may I?' from us. But if we could help them in certain ways, they'd appreciate that."[26]

These kinds of spurious arguments received almost no push-back in Congress. Senator Ron Wyden (D-OR), a member of the Senate intelligence committee who is considered on the dovish end of the political spectrum, raised questions about why the U.S. needed Saudi money for Timber Sycamore and demanded greater transparency but never questioned the underlying program.[27] According to CIA-linked researcher Charles Lister, there were at least fifty vetted rebel groups fighting in Syria that received weapons or training through Timber Sycamore. All of them, he said, worked with the Al Qaeda linked al-Nusra Front, because they were considered to be very good on the battlefield.[28]

David Ignatius wrote in *The Washington Post* that a knowledgeable official estimated that CIA-backed fighters trained under Timber Sycamore may have killed or wounded 100,000 Syrian soldiers and their allies between 2013 and 2017.[29] The Syrian rebels, however, lacked wide support among a population that perceived them to be "guns for hire." Peter Ford, the former UK Ambassador to Syria, told Robin Wright of *The New Yorker*, "American mercenaries, that's what I'd call them. They're trained by Americans. They're paid by Americans. They're supposed to fight for American goals—which are out of synch with local priorities."[30]

The British government acknowledged that between 2013 and 2017 it spent over $277 million to support the anti-Assad opposition, supplying it with satellite phones and other communications equipment. Intelligence was provided to the FSA through Turkey via a British military and intelligence base in Cyprus, and over 1,000 British Special Forces and private mercenaries helped provide military training alongside the CIA and to direct air strikes in Syria.[31] One British trainer characteristically complained to *Harper's Magazine* correspondent Charles Glass that Timber Sycamore was benefiting religious fanatics. The groups that received weapons included one led by Mohammed al-Jolani, which in August 2013 partook in a killing spree against Alawites in Latakia, Assad's hometown.[32]

A Green Beret associated with the training program in Turkey admitted that around 95 percent of rebels receiving arms and training under Timber Sycamore were "either working with terrorist organizations or were sympathetic to them." He added that "a good majority of them admitted that they had no issues with ISIS and that their issue was with the Kurds and the Syrian regime."[33] Some of the terrorists armed under Timber Sycamore carried out suicide bombings and tortured and beheaded captives. Others raped girls because their fathers refused to give them money or waterboarded and whipped people who refused to support them.[34]

A leading recipient of CIA support, the FSA, was "little more than a cover for the Al Qaeda affiliated al-Nusra," according to the above quoted Green Beret.[35] Journalist Patrick Cockburn reported that the FSA's military council meetings were attended by U.S., UK, Jordanian, and Qatari intelligence officers, lending the impression of an organization "wholly controlled by Arab and Western intelligence agencies."[36] One FSA offshoot, the 10th brigade, carried out attacks on Alawites on Syria's Mediterranean Coast.[37] Another CIA-backed offshoot, the Suleiman Shah Brigade, which had close ties to Turkish intelligence, had human rights sanctions placed on it by the U.S. State Department for committing pillage, rape, kidnapping, and torture.[38]

The FSA's ranks were bolstered by jihadists that came to fight with them from Chechnya, Afghanistan, Algeria, and China (Uyghur Muslims).[39] Syria's UN Ambassador at one point informed the UN that jihadists were pouring into Syria from 101 of the UN's 193 member states.[40] The FSA became notorious after releasing a video of a child beheading an unarmed prisoner at the behest of the FSA's Khalid ibn Al Waleed brigade, which was known to have beheaded at least eighty other prisoners.[41] U.S. officials themselves called FSA fighters and the Turkish militias that fought with them "thugs and bandits and pirates that should be wiped off the face of the earth," this after they began attacking Kurds.[42]

Although earlier designating them as a terrorist group, President Obama announced the day after the release of the beheading video, closely following France and Britain, that the FSA would be recognized, as "the legitimate representative of Syria by the U.S." — allowing for the more open provision of weapons.[43] Mere weeks later, FSA affiliates lived up to the earlier terrorist designation by bombing Aleppo University, causing 87 deaths and 200 casualties.[44]

Nour al-Din al Zenki, a Salafist fighting unit founded by Sheikh Tawfiq Shahabuddin, was singled out by Amnesty International for carrying out a wave of kidnappings and torturing activists and journalists in Aleppo. The neoconservative Institute for the Study of War listed al-Zenki as a "moderate rebel force," though a video captured them sawing off the head of a Palestinian captive who had been fighting for Assad's forces and dangling it before a cell phone camera.[45] Another "moderate rebel" group financed under Timber Sycamore, Ahrar al-Sham, was headed by Abu Khalid al Suri, who had fought alongside Osama bin Laden in Afghanistan during CIA-backed operations against the Soviet Union in the 1980s and was named by a Spanish court as a key figure in orchestrating Al Qaeda's Madrid train bombing in 2004.[46]

Incredibly, as reported by the *LA Times* in 2016, rebel groups supported by the CIA were fighting groups being armed by the Pentagon in a separate program from Timber Sycamore.[47] The U.S. military also battled FSA rebels who had been armed by the CIA and were now backed by Turkey.[48] None of the groups were moderate. Joe Biden told students at the Harvard Kennedy School in October 2014 "our biggest problem was our allies. The Turks… the Saudis, the Emirates, etc., what were they doing? They were so determined to take down Assad and essentially have a proxy Sunni-Shia war, what did they do? They poured hundreds of millions of dollars and thousands of tons of weapons into anyone who would fight against Assad. Except that the people who were being supplied were al-Nusra and al-Qaeda and the extremist elements of jihadis coming from other parts of the world."[49]

Though the Obama administration claimed that it was redirecting all operations against Al Qaeda after Biden's comments, journalist Rania Abouzeid talked to espionage sources among the U.S.-backed Nazan movement who complained to her that "the CIA seemed uninterested in such intelligence as the GPS-coordinates of ISIS leaders in Latakia."[50] Residents of Palmyra also told Charles Glass that they had seen American warplanes flying in support of ISIS, and a U.S. Special Forces soldier deployed to Syria in 2018 wrote about participating in firefights against Syrian army forces and Wagner group Russian mercenaries, but never against ISIS.[51]

By the end of Obama's term, a U.S.-led coalition had carried out more than 2,500 hundred air strikes as part of the regime-change operations.[52] The U.S. military claimed that the U.S. bombing operations were the most precise in history, though *Airwars* counted between 2,700 and 4,300 confirmed or reported civilian deaths from coalition airstrikes in 2017 alone.[53] A local source told journalist Shane Bauer that in Raqqa, the first thing that coalition jets targeted were ambulances, fire trucks, first responders, public services institutions, water pumps, and electricity stations. Phosphorus was likely used despite its being banned under international law.[54] In December 2020, Anand Gopal published an article in *The New Yorker* which discussed the methodical devastation resulting from the Trump administration's dropping of 10,000 bombs on Raqqa in 2017. Gopal wrote about witnessing charred schools, collapsed apartment buildings, and gaping craters and said that nearly 80 percent of Raqqa was totally destroyed.[55]

Columbia University Professor Jeffrey Sachs explained how "in Syria, instead of allowing for a political solution to emerge, the U.S. opposed the peace process multiple times. In 2012, the UN had negotiated a peace agreement in Syria that was blocked by the Americans, who demanded that Assad must go on the first day of the peace agreement. The U.S. wanted regime change, not peace."[56] At the end of the Obama Administration, Timber Sycamore was privatized and came to be coordinated by Kohlberg, Kravis, Roberts (KKR), a hundred-billion-dollar Wall Street private equity firm which appointed General David Petraeus, the original coordinator of Timber Sycamore, as partner and Chairman of the KKR Global Institute, a private intelligence agency.[57] KKR's involvement exemplifies the long nexus between Wall Street and the CIA and Wall Street's support for covert operations and imperialistic intervention in the Middle East designed to bring profits to corporate investors, weapons contractors, big oil companies, and Wall Street banks.

Cornerstones of the Covert Regime-Change Operation: NED and USAID

Founded in the 1980s as a CIA offshoot, the National Endowment for Democracy (NED) contributed significantly to the regime-change operation in Syria by funding anti-Assad opposition groups and media and trying to coordinate their dissident activities. A previous chapter detailed the importance of NED funding in supporting the "Arab Spring" uprising. According to publicly available records, between 2016 and 2021, the NED spent $5,155,623 on sixty-seven Syria-focused program grants, which were primarily geared towards bolstering the anti-Assad opposition movement and supporting pro-regime change media and right-wing parties that adopted a neoliberal economic program. Some of the funding went directly to Islamist groups and media that had affiliation with Syria's Muslim Brotherhood.[58]

Exemplifying the NED's hawkish stance on Syria, NED Director Carl Gershman gave a speech at New York University in 2012 criticizing the Obama administration for showing a weak response to the Syrian crisis. Gershman called for a mix of sanctions and military operations to facilitate Bashar al-Assad's downfall. John McCain, who was on the Board of the NED-affiliated International Republican Institute (IRI) and sat on the Senate Armed Services Committee, was one of the most influential figures in Washington promoting the arming of rebels and using the U.S. military to overthrow Assad. McCain secretly traveled to Syria in May 2013, becoming the highest-ranking American to enter Syria during the war. There he met with Salim Idris, chief of the FSA's Supreme Military Council and other FSA leaders from across Syria. His trip caused a minor scandal when a Lebanese newspaper reported that one of the rebels in a photo op with McCain, Mohammad Nour of the Northern Storm Brigade, had overseen the kidnapping of eleven Lebanese Shiite pilgrims in Syria. In 2017, McCain made another secret trip to Syria, this time to visit U.S. troops and Kurdish allies occupying the northeast.[59]

USAID bolstered Timber Sycamore and the larger regime-change operation in Syria by financing the White Helmets (discussed in Chapter 9) in collaboration with a Qatari development agency along with other anti-Assad groups. Under the Obama administration, USAID financed training for Syrian cyber activists, training them in computer encryption, circumvention of government firewalls and secure use of mobile phones.[60] A scandal erupted after it was uncovered that over $9 million in USAID-supplied food kits were being directed to Hayat Tahrir al-Sham (HTS), Al-Jolani's organization that was long characterized by the State Department as a terrorist organization. The USAID kits were given to HTS commanders by Mahmoud al-Hafyan, whose NGO received $122 million from USAID between 2015 and 2018. Al-Hafyan was later indicted for defrauding the U.S. government by a U.S. District Court in Washington, D.C.[61]

According to researcher Benjamin Arthur Thomason, USAID started funding Syrian civil society groups via the contractor Development Alternatives Incorporated (DAI) in July 2012 through USAID-DAI's Tunisia Transition Initiative. USAID gave $54.7 million to Syria Civil Defense from 2013 to October 2020.[62] Hungarian billionaire and color revolution guru George Soros assisted USAID by officially providing $1 million in humanitarian assistance through the International Rescue Committee (IRC), which since the Cold War had operated as a CIA front.[63] By 2022, the U.S. government, largely through USAID, had spent a total of $14.1 billion since 2011 on humanitarian assistance for Syria and Syrian refugees in neighboring countries, and $1.3 billion on "stabilization assistance" involving municipal services, education, economic development, and capacity-building programs that were targeted towards areas controlled by rebel forces fighting against Assad.[64] Charles Glass wrote in *Harper's Magazine* about a USAID transition-and-response team, going by the name START, which was set up to assist local administration in parts of Syria that the Assad regime had evacuated.[65] Under another initiative, communications equipment was smuggled into the country and instructors sent in to train activists with the aim of flooding social media with pro-opposition messages.[66]

USAID has a long history going back to the Vietnam War of channeling development and humanitarian assistance for political ends and serving as a front for covert operations. In South Vietnam, USAID provided significant support to the Strategic Hamlet program in which local peasants were forcibly relocated away from guerrilla insurgents into isolated villages where they were to be won over by aid inducements.[67] This pattern was continued in Syria with the targeting of development assistance to rebel held areas. Some USAID monies in Syria were further invested in media and propaganda efforts that were central to the regime-change operation. USAID worked in collaboration with human rights NGOs like the George Soros-funded Human Rights Watch, whose director Kenneth Roth sent out hundreds of tweets accusing Assad of ghastly crimes that were impossible for him to have carried out.[68] In June 2011, Human Rights Watch published a report that was picked up widely in the media entitled "We've Never Seen Such Horror: Crimes Against Humanity in the Syrian Security Forces," which claimed that Syrian security forces had committed egregious human rights crimes in crushing the "Arab Spring" protests in Daraa. Bowling Green University professor Oliver Boyd Barrett found that the report "lacked a credible methodology, made unverifiable claims and showed insufficient quality control."[69]

In other words, the report was part of the informational/propaganda war that Peter Ford stated publicly was crucial to the U.S.-UK regime-change operation in Syria.[70] Ford explained that this latter campaign was so effective that it amounted to "asymmetrical warfare," which the Syrian government gave up on trying to even counter. Ford laments the results of the regime-change operations as a defeat for the entire region. He said, "[o]ver the long term the loss of the last Arab state which unequivocally supported the Palestinian resistance may sound the death knell for Palestine. The beacon is gone. The beating heart of Arabism is dead."

Special Forces Run Amok

This chapter on U.S. covert military operations would not be complete without discussing the egregious war crimes committed by U.S. Special Forces in yet another secret war. In early December, *The New York Times* reported on the existence of a clandestine army unit in Syria which, from 2014 to 2019, had launched tens of thousands of bombs and missiles and repeatedly killed civilians, including farmers trying to harvest, children in the street, and villagers sheltering in buildings. The secret unit—which worked in collaboration with the CIA though officially did not exist—was called Talon Anvil, and it embraced a loose interpretation of the military's rules of engagement. A former Air Force intelligence officer told *The Times* that the Special Forces were "ruthlessly efficient and good at their jobs . . . . But they also made a lot of bad strikes."[71] One of these involved dropping a 500-pound bomb on a building in the farming town of Karama that was sheltering fifty people; another killed three men working in an olive grove near the city of Manbij; and yet another struck boats carrying civilians on the Euphrates River.[72]

From 2016 to 2017, Talon Anvil was overseen by four-star Army General Stephen Townsend, who, as commander in Syria, authorized low-level commanders to order air strikes. Under pressure to obtain results, these commanders, according to Air Force intelligence officers, would push analysts to say they saw evidence, such as weapons that could legally justify a strike, even when none existed. Larry Lewis, a former Pentagon and State Department advisor who was one of the authors of a 2018 Defense Department report on civilian harm, reported that Townsend was dismissive of reports from news media and human rights organizations describing the mounting human toll of U.S. Special Forces operations in Syria.[73] Townsend also covered up for the U.S. bombing of the Tabqa dam on the Euphrates River in March 2017 despite it being on a "no target" list. Rather than being hounded by anti-war protesters and fired, Townsend was promoted in July

2019 to become the head of the U.S. military's Africa Command, or AFRICOM, headquartered in Stuttgart, Germany. In that capacity, he sponsored yet more killing in U.S.-run dirty wars.[74]

CHAPTER 6

Strange Bedfellows:
The Multi-National Alliance
Against Syria

As we have mentioned, the war against Syria was truly a world war, and there have been many players who had a hand in Syria's ultimate destruction. The following are a list of the key countries which, in league with the U.S., contributed to the overthrow of the Assad government and to the destruction of Syria. While all of these countries had their own reasons for seeking the overthrow of Assad, there was a great level of coordination between them in this effort.

Turkey

One of the prime movers in the regime-change operation in Syria was Turkey, a member of NATO. Christopher Davidson, in his book, *Shadow Wars*, explains that the bulk of the supplies and funds for the Islamic State in Syria "have been flowing in through Turkey."[1] This fact has been acknowledged by numerous sources, including former NATO Supreme Allied Commander Wesley Clark who told *CNN* that the Islamic State is "serving the interests of Turkey and Saudi Arabia . . . . All along there's always been the idea that Turkey was supporting them in some way."[2]

In addition, Joe Biden, in his address as Vice-President to Harvard, explained that "Turkey was known to have allowed most of the Islamic State's foreign fighters to cross into Syria," while a detailed report published by Columbia University's Institute for Human Rights reached the same conclusion.[3] Such a role in facilitating the moving of jihadist fighters was not new for Turkey, as Turkey, with the "tacit approval" of President Bill Clinton, had airlifted such fighters from Bosnia to Turkey in the 1990s to fight the Kurdish Workers Party.[4]

It is important to point out that, while Turkey's role in the war on Syria has been one of the world's worst-kept secrets, it has been quite dangerous for journalists to report on it.[5] One tragic example of this is Serena Shim, an American journalist, who was murdered after reporting on seeing Islamic State troops being transported by truck from Turkey to the Syrian border town of Kobane.[6] An excellent report by the Washington-based Foundation for Defense of Democracies (FDD) details Turkey's critical assistance to terrorists in Syria and the reasons behind it.[7] As the FDD explains, Turkey and its President, Recip Tayyip Erdoğan,, had been close allies of the Assad government in Damascus. But this changed with the advent of the "Arab Spring." According to the FDD:

> Immediately following the outbreak of Syria's Civil War [sic.] in 2011, Erdogan abandoned Assad after assessing that the existing Syrian regime was on the verge of collapse amid the wave of successful Arab Spring uprisings in Egypt, Tunisia, and Libya. As the situation in Syria deteriorated, Turkey saw an opportunity to help install a Sunni Islamist regime—one that would be loyal to Ankara and might even be influenced by the same Muslim Brotherhood doctrine. The Turkish regime found a natural kinship with the largely Sunni Syrian opposition, which resented how Assad and other members of the country's Alawite minority dominated the government. In August 2011, Turkey facilitated the establishment of the Syrian National Council (SNC) in Istanbul, which purported to bring together several factions of the Syrian opposition but was clearly dominated by the Syrian Muslim Brotherhood.[8]

The FDD went on to note that "[s]tarting in early 2012, the head of Turkey's intelligence organization (MIT) directed efforts to bolster elements of the Syrian opposition by providing weapons, money, and logistical support. This support continued even as extremist groups became discernible by mid-2012, notably Ahrar al-Sham and Al-Qaeda's Syrian affiliate, Jabhat al-Nusra (JN). These rebel groups, many of which were designated by the U.S. and UN as terrorist organizations, came to depend on Ankara's provision of military and communications equipment, as well as the ability to cross into Turkey."

Then, in 2017, according to the FDD, Turkey moved in and began to occupy a large portion of Syria in the northern province of Idlib, playing host to the terrorist groups that operated out of there, including HTS (formerly the al-Nusra Front of Al Qaeda) which would eventually overrun Syria from there and unseat the Assad government. Up until the time HTS overthrew Assad, Turkey aided HTS by "maintaining troops in HTS-controlled Idlib province to shield HTS from Syrian government attacks and channeling humanitarian aid and trade into northern Syria, which helped HTS gain legitimacy among the population." And, with Assad gone, Turkey moved swiftly to recognize the new HTS government, support it with diplomatic cover, and promise it economic and military support.

It can be truthfully said that HTS could not have been successful in overthrowing Assad without the support of and sheltering by Turkey. Meanwhile, even with HTS in power, Turkey continues to back other terrorist groups in Syria, which act independently of HTS, and which are carrying out sectarian violence against Alawites and Christians, particularly in the coast region of Syria.[9]

Saudi Arabia

Another big player in Syria has been Saudi Arabia, a long-time ally of the U.S. and Britain in combating secular, progressive governments and movements in West Asia. During the U.S. war against the secular, socialist government of Afghanistan beginning in 1979, Saudi Arabia was an important partner in this fight. In 1980, U.S. National Security Council Advisor Zbigniew Brzezinski, the intellectual author of this war, cut a deal with Saudi Arabia by which the U.S. would match, dollar for dollar, Saudi money going to the Afghan resistance, which included the Saudi-born Osama bin Laden and the Mujahidin.[10]

Saudi Arabia around this time became the U.S.'s key ally against the Islamic Republic of Iran, which was created after the revolution unseating the Western-backed Shah. Home to the most important Muslim holy site in the world (Mecca), Saudi Arabia was viewed as "a perfect counterweight to the Islamic Republic of Iran and its efforts to become a leader of the Muslim world," to quote Stephen Gowans.[11]

Patrick Cockburn explains in his book, *The Rise of the Islamic State*, that the alliance between the U.S. and Saudia Arabia (and the Pakistani Army as well) "has proved to be extraordinarily durable. It has been one of the main supporters of American predominance in the region, but also provided a seed for jihadist movements, one of which Osama bin Laden's al-Qaeda was originally one strain."[12] And this is why the U.S. government and press invariably give Saudi Arabia a pass on its crimes, which appear to include involvement in planning the 9/11 attacks. As Cockburn notes, "[t]he 9/11 Commission report identified Saudi Arabia as the main source of al-Qaeda but no action was taken on the basis of it."[13] Subsequently, the U.S. went on to remove the secular nationalist governments of Iraq, Libya, and then Syria despite their opposition to Al Qaeda. Through it all, Saudi Arabia has remained a key ally of the U.S. even as officials such as Secretary of State Hillary Clinton feigned concern about that fact that Saudi Arabia was maintaining its support for Al Qaeda years after 9/11—a support that would actually prove useful.[14]

In the Syrian theater, for example, Saudi Arabia would play an important role for the U.S. in funding and arming Al Qaeda against the Assad government and its Iranian and Hezbollah

STRANGE BEDFELLOWS   103

allies. This support initially took place, as discussed elsewhere in this book, in the context of the "Arab Spring" which began in 2011. It is important to point out that Saudi Arabia received a pass again from the West even here. Thus, while the West used the "Arab Spring" to attack governments such as those in Libya and Syria, the Western governments and media looked the other way as Saudi Arabia cracked down on its own "Arab Spring" protests, including by beheading the popular Sunni cleric who led the demonstrations, and as Saudi Arabia invaded Bahrain to help violently put down the "Arab Spring" protests there.[15]

Meanwhile, Saudi Arabia was "[p]erhaps the biggest funder of al-Nusra" front of Al Qaeda, and the U.S. was quite happy for Saudi Arabia to play this role given the U.S.'s own limitations in doing it directly itself.[16] And, as Saudi Arabia directly supported Al Qaeda, the U.S., and specifically the CIA, trained and equipped "rebel groups which fought under Nusra command but maintained a separate identity," to quote Gowans. He wrote that "CIA-trained and equipped groups coordinated with Nusra on the battlefield and shared arms. They were so thoroughly intertwined with the al-Qaeda franchise that they could act as arms conduits to al-Nusra, as well as operate as Nusra Front auxiliaries."[17]

Qatar and *Al Jazeera*

One player which does not get enough blame is the Gulf state of Qatar. In addition to directly supporting Al Qaeda, Qatar played one of the most critical roles in the propaganda war against Syria through its wholly-owned news outlet, *Al Jazeera*. In terms of supporting Al Qaeda, Qatar played the role as bag man for the West, funneling the money to the al-Nusra Front to get them started and keep them sustained. This fact is not in dispute. As Davidson explains in *Shadow Wars*, "[i]n 2012, the *Wall Street Journal* reported that Lebanese officials had been tipped off that a prominent Qatari who was the cousin of the foreign minister was in Beirut to pass money to *Al-Nusra* and had already visited the Sunni-majority [Lebanon-Syria] border town of Arsal so as to distribute the funds."[18]

As Davidson related, while this Qatari was initially arrested on terrorism charges, he was quickly released. And, the town of Arsal would soon become the site of Islamic State checkpoints. Davidson opines that "it seems likely that Qatar or elements within it have . . . been actively encouraged to take on this high-risk proxy role."[19] Qatar's proxy role also included buying and transferring weapons to the Al-Nusra Front of Al Qaeda.[20] However, an arguably bigger contribution that Qatar made was as purveyor of propaganda through *Al-Jazeera*. *Al Jazeera* was founded in 1996 in Doha, but gained its international notoriety, and indeed street cred around the world, in the early 2000s with its excellent coverage of the false pretexts of the U.S. war on Iraq and the brutality of this war once it started. Peace activists of a certain age remember *Al Jazeera* quite fondly as one of the few voices of reason and truth in those days. And, to this day, *Al Jazeera* continues to receive deserved respect for its extensive and accurate coverage of the Palestinian struggle and Israel's genocidal war on Gaza.

All of this indeed led Noam Chomsky, one of the leading media critics in the world for half a century, to sing the praises of *Al Jazeera* in 2006, stating: "[i]n the Arab and Muslim worlds, there is a long history of attempts to advance democracy and human rights, often blocked by Western imperial intervention. In recent years, probably the most democratizing force has been *Al-Jazeera*, . . . the primary reasons why it is so despised by the Arab tyrannies and Washington."[21] Given this credibility, particularly amongst the left and peace movements in the West, the coverage of *Al-Jazeera* related to Syria has been critical, and it indeed has been critically bad, playing a key role in turning most of the left in the West against the Syrian government of Bashar al-Assad and putting the peace movement to sleep.[22]

The malign influence of *Al-Jazeera*, even to this day, cannot be understated. As A.B. Abrams explains in his aptly-titled, *World War in Syria*, "[t]he Qatari monarchy and its highly influential

Al Jazeera satellite television channel . . . played the leading role in backing calls for protest against the Syrian government and shortly afterwards in backing the emerging Islamist insurgency."[23] And, it did so, Abrams explains, for two reasons: a) because the U.S., as documents released by *WikiLeaks* prove, was able to influence *Al Jazeera's* news coverage through its top news director who was connected with the Pentagon; and (b) because of the Qatari monarchy's own ideological "support for jihadist uprisings against secular governments," and for Al Qaeda in particular—a commitment which continues to this very day.[24]

Abrams cites a paper by the Carnegie Endowment for International Peace which highlighted *Al Jazeera* as a soft-power tool used quite successfully by Qatar—a close ally of the Muslim Brotherhood—in mobilizing Arab support for regime-change operations not just in Syria, but also in Libya and Egypt.[25] And, as Abrams explains, *Al Jazeera's* support for regime change was not just a matter of editorial slant. Rather, *Al Jazeera* went so far as "coaching eyewitnesses to give false testimony and fabricate information" in support of these operations.[26] Its coverage did wonders, with "[m]edia channels in other Western-aligned Arab states, from Saudi Arabia to Jordan, quickly follow[ing] *Al Jazeera's* example with highly positive portrayals of the insurgency and multiple hit pieces targeting the Syrian state, the presidency, its military and the Ba'ath Party."[27]

After helping with the overthrow of Bashar al-Assad and the rise of HTS (formerly Al Qaeda), *Al Jazeera* continues to play a treacherous role in promoting the new HTS government in Syria and in sanitizing its crimes, not surprisingly given Qatar's close links with Al Qaeda. The media organization, Red Stream, which publicizes itself as the producer of "revolutionary educational documentaries," recently put out a long stream on X (formerly Twitter) detailing this continued propaganda role of *Al Jazeera* (AJ). Red Stream explains that, "*Al Jazeera's* latest coverage of Syria has ignited a backlash. Armed groups linked to Hayat Tahrir al-Sham (HTS) carried out brutal massacres on the Syrian coast.

AJ amplified Qatari propaganda-framing the killings as 'military operations' against 'remnants of the Assad regime.'"[28]

But it gets much worse than this, as Red Stream further relates: "[o]n an episode of AJ's The Opposite Direction, the host, Faisal Al-Qasim, gave airtime to calls for the genocide of Alawites. The so-called 'survey' he cited framed mass slaughter as a democratic choice, putting extermination up for a public vote."[29] Red Stream additionally noted that *Al Jazeera* "consistently echoes Israeli justifications for attacks on Syria. It brands Israeli airstrikes on Syrian defense infrastructure as hits on 'military depots of the former Syrian army'—a blatant distortion. The 'former Syrian army' no longer exists. These are strikes on Syria's land, people, and sovereignty."[30]

And, while it may sound strange that an Arab, Muslim country that supports Al Qaeda and the Muslim Brotherhood is running cover for Israel, it is nonetheless par for the course, especially amongst the Gulf states such as Qatar. Indeed, even as we write this chapter, Qatar, along with the UAE, is quietly involved in joint military exercises with Israel in Greece, even as Israel was engaged in a massive bombing campaign of Gaza and Syria and Iran as well.[31] In addition, a scandal broke out in Israel after it was reported that that Qatar has been funneling hundreds of thousands of dollars to aides working for Benjamin Netanyahu, including to Netanyahu's former spokesman Eli Feldstein who reportedly "worked for Qatar via an international firm contracted by Doha to feed top Israeli journalists pro-Qatar stories."[32]

Qatar and Israel may seem like strange bedfellows, but what about Al Qaeda and Israel? A number of commentators have noted that Al Qaeda, despite claiming to be a radical Islamist group sympathetic with the plight of the Palestinians, never attacks Israel, but rather, seems more preoccupied with attacking and killing other Arabs and Muslims.[33] As the comedian and news commentator Jimmy Dore queried after making this observation, "it's interesting, isn't it, that Al Qaeda and ISIS never attack Israel? I wonder why that is . . . . It's almost as if the United States created Al Qaeda and it's almost as if the Israelis created ISIS . . . . It's crazy how that works . . . . Israel is sharing parts of Syria with the Al Qaeda."[34]

And this brings us to Israel itself.

Israel

Israel, for its own reasons of state, has decided to make the same devil's bargain with Al Qaeda and other terrorist groups that the Arab Gulf States have made with Israel, even as Israel decries the evils of terrorism and vows to fight against it. And Israel has supported these groups even as it has publicly and vehemently denied that it was. In the rare moments of candor, Israeli officials have admitted to its devil's bargain in Syria. Moshe Ya'alon, Israeli Defense Minister from 2013-2016, for example, stated that, "in Syria, if it is a choice between Iran [an ally of Assad] and the Islamic State, I choose the Islamic State . . . . Our greatest enemy is the Iranian regime that has declared war on us."[35]

But it was only after the fact that Israel admitted to actually supporting groups like the Islamic State in Syria to combat Iran and Hezbollah there, but above all to overthrow Assad. In January of 2019, *The Times of Israel* published an article entitled, "IDF chief finally acknowledges that Israel supplied weapons to Syrian rebels." The article read :

> Outgoing IDF Chief of Staff Gadi Eisenkot this weekend acknowledged for the first time that Israel had indeed provided weaponry to Syrian rebel groups in the Golan Heights during the country's seven-year civil war.

> Until Sunday, Israel would say officially only that it had given humanitarian aid to Syrian opposition groups across the border, while denying or refusing to comment on reports that it had supplied them with arms as well. . . .

> Israel's supply of weapons to these opposition groups has been reported for years—both by the Syrian army, looking to discredit the rebels as stooges of the Zionists, and by the opposition groups,

Israel bombed a home across the street from this sheep field after the Hayat Tahrir al-Sham (HTS) led by Western-cleansed Al Qaeda terrorist Mohammed Al-Jolani came to power. They claim that members of Hezbollah were living there. (Kovalik 2025).

interested in expanding their cooperation with Israel in the fight against Syrian dictator Bashar Assad—but was never confirmed by Israeli officials.[36]

The last line in this passage is notable, in that it shows that, as was often the case, the claims of the Syrian government which were written off as conspiracy theories and propaganda were actually true, and that it was the Western countries opposing Assad, like Israel, who were lying the whole time about their involvement amongst other things. At the same time, the press was always happy to print the lies of Israel as fact. At least, to the credit of *The Times of Israel*, it did not mince words about the lack of veracity of its own government on this matter, saying quite bluntly, "the acknowledgment of Israel's support for rebel groups in Syria was highly irregular as, for years Israeli officials repeatedly declared that the country was not getting involved in Syria's internal fighting—*now evidently a lie . . . .*"[37] (emphasis added).

In terms of the specifics of Israel's support for the opposition fighters, *The Times of Israel* article explains that, from 2013 to 2019, Israel provided twelve different armed groups weaponry and supplies—including "assault rifles, machine guns, mortar launchers, and vehicles"—and also paid these groups' fighters $75 a month in salary.[38] Israel only ended this assistance when Syria appeared to be winning the war and when, in any case, the uneasy truce was about to be agreed to in 2020. And, Israel only admitted to its support of the rebels once this support was over.

However, this direct aid to the armed groups was the tip of the iceberg of Israel's efforts to unseat Assad and destroy Syria as a functioning nation. Thus, Israel also admitted to another thing it had been less than candid about—the fact that it was directly involved in military operations in Syria in support of the terrorist groups and operated as these groups' air force for years, and to this very day. Thus, *The Times of Israel* explains that "Eisenkot acknowledged that the IDF carried out hundreds of raids in Syria—in some interviews, the number given is 200, in others it's 400—and dropped 2,000 bombs" in 2018 alone.[39]

While *The Times of Israel* attempted to excuse Israel's bombing of Syria by claiming that Israel's bombs were dropped on "Iranian targets" in Syria—and that is certainly true in some cases—it states in the same article that Israel was also periodically bombing the Damascus airport, the main, international airport of Syria. As a result, Syria, which had received billions of dollars from tourism before the war, was effectively cut off from the world for years because it was impossible to fly there. In other words, Israel played a key role in bringing Syria's economy to its knees by bombing its civilian airport—a war crime.

Other non-Iranian targets of Israel's Air Force included various Syrian military sites and assets, such as the Syrian Scientific Studies and Research Center; military bases, such as the Jamarya Military Facility near Damascus; Syrian anti-aircraft units; arms depots and arms shipments coming in from Russia—all reportedly bombed in coordination with the terrorist groups fighting Assad.[40]

Israel also bombed the Syrian Military Intelligence Building
as the HTS was coming to power. (Kovalik 2025)

A.B. Abrams explains in his *World War in Syria*, that "[b]y erod-
ing the Syrian Army's fighting capacity from the air, the Israeli
Air Force was providing direct air support to insurgent forces.
It usually did so flying F-16 fighters, notably the same aircraft
Pakistan had flown in Afghanistan in the 1980s for much of the
same purpose [i.e., in support of the mujahidin fighting against
Afghanistan's secular, socialist state and the USSR], drawing
another parallel between the two conflicts and the roles played
by American client states bordering the target areas."[41]

It may sound strange to think of Israel as acting as an "American
client state" in Syria, but in many ways, this is an accurate charac-
terization. In 2022, *CovertAction Magazine* (*CAM*), citing a *Wall
Street Journal* article, explained that, in addition to targeting the

south of Syria which borders the Israeli-occupied Golan Heights, Israel targeted its bombing in the east of Syria which the U.S. occupies.[42] And, as *CAM* explained, "Israel secretly coordinates with the U.S, on many of the airstrikes it carries out in eastern Syria near the Al-Tanf military base, a U.S. outpost near the Syria-Jordan border. Since 2017, the Israeli Air Force has cleared all planned flights with the U.S. Central Command, which conducts an assessment. The command also reports details of planned flights to the U.S. Defense Secretary and others, who can also choose to conduct assessments."[43]

And, why was Israel targeting this area at all? In order to help protect the U.S. military base there from drone attacks, *CAM* explained. The U.S.'s Al-Tanf base "houses prisoners of war and has been used as a base to train jihadists and other fighters seeking the overthrow of Assad. It is also located strategically near oil fields; U.S. troops have generally been positioned in Syria to 'keep Syria's oil,' as Donald Trump acknowledged when he was president."[44] And so, Israel has coordinated military action with the U.S. to protect this key asset there and help the U.S. maintain its illegal occupation of Syria.

As of the time of this writing, the U.S. continues to occupy about a third of Syria's territory in the east, despite Trump's claims in both his first and second terms of office that he would end this occupation. Presenting itself as protectors of Syria's beleaguered minority groups including the Druze, Israel has moved IDF troops deeper into the Quneitra and Daraa Governates in extending its occupation of the Golan Heights.[45] The IDF troops were reportedly bulldozing trees, demolishing buildings and homes, detaining civilians, and trying to depopulate Syrian villages, destroying electricity and water networks as they attempt to forcibly evict residents to make way for Israeli settlers.[46] An Israeli "loot unit" reportedly stole cash, gold bullion, and jewellery from Syrian homes from which residents had to flee.[47]

In late April 2025, IDF Chief of Staff Eyal Zamir approved orders to continue Israeli military operations in Southwest Syria, with top Israeli officials specifying Israel's intentions of remaining in Syria indefinitely.[48] Though in March it started to condemn Israel's advances as "hostile expansionism" after previously being silent[49] the new HTS/Al Qaeda government has so far done absolutely nothing to try to end Israel's occupations or land grabs, showing that Al Qaeda was in league with Israel, and the U.S., the whole time.

Jimmy Dore put it best when he said,

> Right now, in fact Israel is sharing parts of Syria with the Al Qaeda, right? . . . You got Turkey. You got the United States and you got Israel.

> They have, just like Gaddafi predicted 15 years ago, that Israel wanted to split up Syria into five different parts. They have it split up into four different parts right now. And so he was prescient. He knew.

> And that's why they had to kill him. And that's why they killed Gaddafi. And the propaganda in the United States was that he was the madman and he was the terrorist.[50]

Indeed!

CHAPTER 7

Shades of the Gulf of Tonkin: Chemical Weapons False Flag

> "The first casualty of war is truth."
> – U.S. Senator Hiram Warren Johnson (R-CA), 1918.

On August 20, 2012, President Barack Obama told a group of reporters that the use of chemical weapons by Bashar al-Assad's regime in Syria would cross his "red line." A year later, the Obama administration accused the Syrian government of carrying out a chemical attack in Eastern Ghouta near Damascus, resulting in the death of 1400 people, including 426 children.[1] The timing of the allegations was convenient because it coincided with the official launching of Operation Timber Sycamore, a covert twelve-billion-dollar weapon supply program to arm and train "moderate rebels" based in Jordan and Turkey. Obama in turn used the pretext of Assad's alleged chemical weapons attacks to promote air strikes on Syria, ordering the Pentagon to draw up targets for bombing while going on television to state: "We are prepared to strike whenever we choose. What message will we send if a dictator can gas hundreds of children to death in plain sight and pay no price?"[2]

Obama ultimately backed off on bombing when he realized he lacked the votes in Congress. The British House of Commons refused to support the strikes and France backed down as well. Assad's government was forced to join the International

Organisation for the Prohibition of Chemical Weapons (OPCW), and a U.S.-Russian agreement to dismantle Syria's chemical weapons capability was signed in Geneva on September 14, 2013. In August 2016, a UN and OPCW commission again alleged that Assad had deployed chemical weapons against his own people, dropping chlorine in two locations in northwest Idlib Province. Then on April 4, 2017, the OPCW accused Assad of deploying chemical weapons in Khan Sheykhoun in Idlib province that killed eighty-nine people, prompting the Trump administration to order fifty-nine tomahawk cruise missile strikes on the Syrian military's al-Shayrat airbase on the night of April 6-7, 2017, ostensibly with the goal of destroying Syrian chemical weapon stocks. Within hours of the supposed sarin gas attack, Trump had issued a statement describing Assad's "heinous actions" as being a consequence of the Obama administration's "weakness and irresolution" in addressing what he said was Syria's past use of chemical weapons.[3]

Not uncharacteristically, Trump's statements were pure hyperbole as rigorous scientific study of the attacks determined that they could have only come from rebel-held territory—if they were carried out at all.[4] A senior intelligence official told journalist Seymour Hersh that Trump's decision to bomb made no sense as "we KNOW that there was no chemical attack . . . the Russians are furious. Claiming we have the real intel and know the truth."[5] These remarks suggest that the allegations of chemical weapons attacks were crucial to the propaganda offensive directed against Assad and to an escalation of the U.S.-Western regime-change operation in Syria. They fit with a long pattern of U.S. deception and false-flag operations and atrocity fabrication whose function was to manipulate public opinion.[6] A senior intelligence official told Hersh that Barack Obama's altering of intelligence and distortions regarding the Syrian chemical weapons attacks "reminded him of the 1964 Gulf of Tonkin incident when the Johnson administration reversed the sequence of National Security intercepts to justify one of the early bombings of North Vietnam [and sending of U.S. ground troops.]"[7]

Speaking of the Vietnam War, it must be noted that from 1962 to 1971, the U.S. Air Force sprayed nearly 19 million gallons of chemical herbicides, of which at least 11 million gallons was Agent Orange in a military project called Operation Ranch Hand. The result was the destruction of millions of acres of South Vietnam's forests and creation of "villages of the damned" where large numbers of children were born with debilitating handicaps and deformities.[8] In September 1970 near Savane, Laos, U.S. Air Force Skyraiders dropped cluster bombs filled with the deadly sarin nerve gas Assad was accused of deploying.[9] Even if all the accusations against Assad were true, they pale in comparison to U.S. chemical weapons use over the years in Indochina and Korea and Iraq as well. As this chapter details, there is scant proof, however, that Assad ever deployed chemical weapons. Moreover, U.S. intelligence agencies themselves could never confirm this.[10] The evidence indicates rather that the chemical weapons attacks were part of false flag operations in which rebel forces backed by Turkey and the U.S. carried out crimes that were blamed on Assad or staged in order to justify an escalation of the war against him.

Khan al-Assal Attack in March 2013—and Other Attacks on Syrian Soldiers

The Obama administration and its media echo chamber first accused Bashar al-Assad of carrying out a chemical weapons attack in Khan al-Assal near Aleppo in April 2014. Doctors and hospital staff who treated victims said that the chemical weapons attack was actually carried out by al-Nusra Front, according to an investigation carried out by former UN prosecutor Carla Del Ponte. Swiss doctor Franco Cavalli found the same thing as Del Ponte, as did Gunther Meyer, head of the Center for Research in the Arab World of the Johannes Gutenberg University of Mainz, who stated that "the jihadists were responsible for the first deployment of chemical weapons in Khan-Al-Assal where 29 people died."[11]

Significantly, some of the dead in the Khan-al-Assal attack were Syrian soldiers. The London-based Syrian Observatory for Human Rights, an organization aligned with the Muslim Brotherhood and a frequent source of Western media, claimed that their death resulted from the Syrian army accidentally hitting themselves—which seems implausible. A UN investigation later determined that Syrian soldiers were killed in three of five alleged chemical weapons attacks carried out in 2013, which indicates that the real perpetrator of the attacks were the rebels who were fighting the Syrian army.[12]

Rebel capacity for manufacturing chemical weapons was detailed in a *Russia Today* report on a school used as a bomb factory, where quantities of Detia Gas-Ex-B, an agricultural pesticide that can be used to create phosphine gas, were discovered. Phosphine gas was previously used as a chemical weapon by the Islamic state. Russian forces also published video footage of a chemical weapon production facility they purported to have found in the suburbs of Aleppo.[13] This was all ignored by the Western media and political establishment, which continues to advance the illusion that Assad waged chemical warfare on his own people.

Cherry Picking Intelligence—the August 2013 Eastern Ghouta Attack

In April 2014, famed journalist Seymour Hersh published an article in *The London Review of Books* debunking official claims about the alleged chemical weapons attack in Eastern Ghouta. Hersh claimed that President Obama "ignored the data regarding al-Nusra and their ability to use Sarin and continued to claim only the Assad government had chemical weapons," adding that "the cherry picking of intelligence was similar to the process used to justify the Iraq War."[14]

Hersh's article included an interview with a senior U.S. intelligence officer who told him that U.S. military leaders had raised attention to the fact that Turkish Prime Minister Recep Erdoğan, who was supporting the al-Nusra Front, was advised that they could "get Assad's nuts in a vice by dabbling with a sarin attack inside Syria," hence "forcing Obama to make good on his red line threat."[15] A U.S. intelligence consultant told Hersh that a highly classified briefing prepared for Martin Dempsey of the Joint Chiefs of Staff and Defense Secretary Chuck Hagel described the "acute anxiety" of the Erdoğan administration about the rebels' dwindling prospects, which led the Turkish leadership to feel like it "needed to do something that would precipitate a U.S. military response."[16]

Another former intelligence official told Hersh: "we now know it was a covert action planned by Erdoğan's people to push Obama over the red line. They had to escalate to a gas attack in or near Damascus when the UN inspectors—who arrived in Damascus on August 18 to investigate the earlier use of gas—were there. The deal was to do something spectacular. Our senior military officers have been told by the DIA [Defense Intelligence Agency] and other intelligence assets that the sarin was supplied through Turkey—that it could only have gotten there with Turkish support. The Turks also provided the training and [were involved in] producing the sarin and handling it."[17] Left out of this analysis was the likely role of the CIA and that of Saudi Arabia, whose intelligence chief, Prince Bandar bin Sultan, was believed by residents of East Ghouta and rebel fighters interviewed by journalists Dale Gavlak and Yahya Ababneh to have supplied the rebels with sarin allegedly used in the attack.[18]

Hersh wrote that the Joint Chiefs of Staff knew that the Obama administration's public claims that only the Syrian army had access to sarin were wrong. The American and British intelligence communities had been aware since the spring of 2013 that some rebel units in Syria were developing chemical weapons.[19] On June 20, 2013, analysts for the DIA issued a highly classified five-page "talking points" briefing for the DIA's Deputy Director David Shedd, which stated that al-Nusra maintained a sarin production cell: its program, the paper said, was "the most advanced Sarin plot since al-Qaida's pre-9/11 effort."[20]

The previous May, more than ten members of the al-Nusra Front were arrested in southeastern Turkey with what local police told the press were two kilograms of sarin. In a 130-page indictment the group was accused of attempting to purchase fuses, piping for the construction of mortars, and chemical precursors for sarin. Five of those arrested were freed after a brief detention. The others, including the ringleader, Haytham Qassab, for whom the prosecutor requested a prison sentence of twenty-five years, were released pending trial (which appears never to have occurred).[21]

An investigation carried out by Turkish parliamentarians that made use of documents from the investigation of a sarin trader and drew upon phone recordings showed how ISIS received all necessary materials to produce deadly sarin gas via Turkey. The Deputy who headed the investigation, Eren Erdem, was charged with treason by Erdoğan. Erdem told the media that Westerners were "hypocrites about the situation" while noting that he had an investigative file with all the details about how sarin was procured in Turkey and delivered to the terrorists.[22]

When British intelligence obtained a sample of sarin gas used in the August 21 attack on Eastern Ghouta, analysis demonstrated that the gas used hadn't matched the batches known to exist in the Syrian army's chemical weapons arsenal. Actual exposure to sarin appeared to have been minimal or non-existent for thirty-one of the thirty-six people sampled (88 percent) in East Ghouta in a UN probe. The latter indicates that no sarin gas attack may have actually taken place.[23] A Syrian study examining detailed video evidence found that bodies had been manipulated for the images and that many children allegedly poisoned by sarin in East Ghouta appeared ill or drugged. Most of the children strangely were unaccompanied by any parent when they were outside at 2 a.m. when the attack allegedly occurred.

Two weeks earlier, it was discovered that there had been a large-scale abduction of children in Ballouta in Northern Latakia by armed gangs. Several sources link kids who had been abducted and then killed to the photos of children supposedly killed by the chemical gas attack in East Ghouta. Though the official death toll was over 1,000, videos showed less then 500 bodies, many of them still alive, and only eight burials. The rebels claimed they had to bury the bodies quickly because the bodies might have decomposed due to the heat, though this is unconvincing.[24]

Additional anomalies included the fact that symptoms that would indicate a sarin gas attack such as universal vomiting were not seen. First responders who handled the alleged victims without protective clothing didn't exhibit any symptoms, and the number of survivors outnumbered the dead by an 11-1 ratio, which should have been the opposite. No actual video footage of search and rescue operations or victims being treated in hospitals were ever found and the final death count was never corroborated by local authorities. Some of the children seen on video later appeared in other videos of alleged gas attacks in other places.[25]

Mohammed al-Aghawani, administrator of the Tuberculosis Hospital which treated hundreds of alleged "chemical victims," told journalist Eva Bartlett: "There was no chemical attack. I wasn't at the hospital that night, but my staff told me what happened. Around 2 a.m., there was suddenly noise, shouting, cars arriving at the hospital, bringing civilians. Some people, armed men, said there was a chemical attack. Some of them had foreign accents. They took people's clothes off and started pouring water on them. They kept bringing people in till around 7 a.m. Around 1,000 people, mostly children, alive, from nearby villages like Ein Terma, Hezze, Zamalka. Many people later said their children never came back."[26]

Journalist Aaron Maté reported that U.S. intelligence never itself confirmed Assad's use of chemical weapons. James Clapper, Director of the Office of National Intelligence, explicitly refused to release an intelligence product accusing Assad's military of guilt. At the president's daily briefing, Clapper told Obama that the evidence implicating Assad's forces in the sarin attack in Ghouta was not a "slam dunk." This was a deliberate reference to the term used by George W. Bush's CIA Director, George Tenet, in vouching for the falsified intelligence that Iraq possessed weapons of mass destruction, the pretext for the Bush administration's decision to invade.[27] Clapper later claimed in his 2018 memoir that the intelligence community "obtained evidence" of the Assad government's guilt in Ghouta. Yet Clapper also hinted that this evidence was far from convincing. The intelligence community's classified assessment on Ghouta, Clapper recalled, "gave alternate explanations" to an Assad regime chemical attack "and highlighted the things we didn't know." The former intelligence chief also disclosed that Obama's National Security Adviser, Tom Donilon, was another skeptic. Donilon, Clapper wrote, "seemed to keep raising the evidentiary bar we needed to meet before he believed our reports."[28]

Secretary of State John Kerry's claim that the Obama administration had irrefutable physical evidence that Assad had carried out chemical weapons attacks in Eastern Ghouta was disproven in a scientific study carried out by Theodore Postol, an MIT scientist and former top policy adviser to the chief of naval operations, and Richard Lloyd, a ballistics engineer with forty patents who worked at one point for Raytheon. The study determined that the deadly rockets allegedly carrying sarin gas could not have been fired from Syrian government-controlled areas as far as ten kilometers away—as Team Obama alleged. The shape of the rockets resulted in extreme aerodynamic drag, limiting their range to about 2 to 2.5 kilometers, which was within the range of rebel-controlled territory in relation to the scene of the attacks.[29] Postol and Lloyd further analyzed the impact debris from the single rocket for which data was available and showed that those who argued that the Syrian government had fired the rockets had incorrectly determined the direction of arrival as being from the northwest, when the actual direction was from the north. While not claiming to know exactly who was behind the alleged chemical attack, Postol and Lloyd wrote in *The London Review of Books* that "the mainstream American media have done a disservice to the public by allowing politically motivated individuals, governments, and non-government organisations to misrepresent facts that clearly point to serious breaches of the truth by the White House."[30]

Another Covert Action at Khan Sheykhoun

Following the alleged April 4, 2017, chemical attack in Khan Sheykhoun, an al-Nusra Front-controlled town in the Idlib province, President Trump tweeted: "you kill innocent children, innocent babies, little babies—with a chemical gas that is so lethal that crosses many, many lines beyond a red line, many, many lines. And I will tell you that attack on children yesterday had a big impact on me. That was a horrible, horrible thing and it doesn't get any worse than that." Sixty-six percent of the public supported the fifty-nine tomahawk cruise missile strikes that Trump ordered in response, which killed at least seven Syrian soldiers and nine civilians, including four children.[31] House Minority leader Nancy Pelosi (D-CA) characterized the strike as a "proportional response to the regime's use of chemical weapons," while Senate Minority leader Chuck Schumer (D–NY) said, "Making sure Assad knows that when he commits such despicable atrocities he will pay a price is the right thing to do."[32]

Three years later, Theodore Postol published an article with Goong Chen, a mathematician from Texas A&M University, and five other scientists, "Computational Forensics for the Alleged Syrian Sarin Chemical Attack on April 4, 2017: What Actually Happened?" The article used forensic computer simulations and three-dimensional image analysis to model the crater that was identified as the source of sarin allegedly released at Khan Shaykhoun.

Postol and his co-authors determined that the crater and related fragments were almost certainly caused by a vehicle-launched improvised rocket-propelled artillery round with a high-explosive warhead—which the rebels could have possessed—and not an aerial bomb from a Syrian airplane. No fragments characteristic of an aerial bomb such as tail fins were observed and the size of the crater was too small to be caused by a bomb. This finding—which was confirmed by a senior intelligence official with experience assessing bomb damage and by the Pentagon's flight track map—called into question the scenario of attack described by the U.S. intelligence community, and the OPCW Joint Investigative Mechanism (JIM).

According to Postol's team, there was extensive tampering with the crater and debris, which led to misreporting in the media. A dead goat was found at the scene displaying symptoms of sarin inhalation; however, tracks were found indicating that the goat had been dragged to the scene along with a rope around its neck. Dead birds were also found that appeared to have been very recently released from a cage. Postol and his team determined that there was no physical evidence of any sarin-containing vessel at the scene. A pipe was inaccurately identified by the OPCW as a container filled with sarin; in truth it was the casing of the rocket motor that propelled the warhead to the location of the explosion. Chemical weapons generally do not make large craters in the ground and since no workers sent to clean up the scene were exposed to sarin or died—when any contact with the asphalt around the crater would have been highly lethal in the wake of an attack—it is unlikely sarin was actually used, as in Eastern Ghouta.[33]

Seymour Hersh reported that the impression that sarin had been used at Khan Shaykhoun was created by a toxic cloud that resulted from the bombing of an agricultural supply depot near the crater possessing fertilizers, disinfectants, and other goods whose release caused neurotoxic effects similar to those of sarin.[34] Other investigators suggest the possibility that the Syrian opposition used smoke generators they had in their possession. Oddly, hospital records near the site of the attack showed a normal volume of patients, though fifty-seven patients were admitted to a nearby hospital before the attack, possibly to make it seem like there was an emergency that day. To add to the odd circumstances, rescue workers, as in Eastern Ghouta, doused children with water in near sub-zero temperatures, and then piled them onto trucks mixed with the alleged dead, and filmed themselves resuscitating children hours later, which makes it further look like the whole thing was staged.[35]

Postol, Chen et al.'s article "Computational Forensics for the Alleged Syrian Sarin Chemical Attack on April 4, 2017," was published in the *Global Journal of Forensic Science and Medicine* in November 2020, and was featured by Tulsi Gabbard on her website when she was running for president. However, the article was withdrawn from publication by the more prestigious journal *Science & Global Security* one year earlier after the article had initially been accepted and was circulated at the page-proof stage. Postol had served for more than thirty years on the editorial board of *Science & Global Security* and mentored the three main editors who ultimately blocked publication of his piece. The removal and censorship of Postol's piece exemplified a growing authoritarian environment in the U.S. synonymous with widening imperialistic interventions like in Syria that were accompanied by massive lies and deceit. Postol stated that he "reviewed the [White House's] document carefully [making the case for Syrian government culpability in chemical gas attacks], and I believe it can be shown, without doubt, that the document does not provide any evidence whatsoever that the U.S. government has concrete knowledge that the government of Syria was the source of the chemical attack in Khan Shaykhoun, Syria at roughly 6 a.m. to 7 a.m. on 4 April, 2017."[36]

In his book, *The Syria Scam: An Insider Look into Chemical Weapons, Geopolitics and the Fog of War* (Green Hill Publishing, 2025) OPCW whistleblower Ian Henderson points to the significance of the fact that no traces of tell-tale chemicals allegedly used by the Syrian army to carry out chemical weapons attacks were found in the bombed-out rubble of the Shayrat air base after Trump ordered air strikes on it. Henderson says the bombing attack would have been irresponsible if the motive of destroying Syrian chemical weapon stocks was sincere because it would have resulted in the release of toxic nerve agents and could in turn be classified as a chemical weapons attack. However, since no nerve agents were released or found in the soil or around the rubble, it affirmed the deceit of U.S. policy-makers once again.[37]

Douma and OPCW Coverup

On April 7, 2018, Assad was alleged to have carried out another chemical weapons attack in Douma. Trump tweeted: "many dead, including women and children in mindless CHEMICAL attack in Syria. Russia and Iran are responsible for backing animal Assad. Big price to pay."[38] Six days later, the Trump administration and its allies launched cruise missiles from the air and from nearby warships and submarines at targets said to be associated with what remained of the Syrian government's chemical weapons program. Those targets included a scientific research center in Damascus and a chemical weapons facility near Homs that had been used for the production of sarin. The alleged chemical gas attacks by Assad on April 7, according to Trump, represented "a significant escalation in a pattern of chemical weapons use by that very terrible regime." In an additional information sheet, the White House noted that "a significant body of information points to the regime using chlorine in its bombardment of Douma, while some additional information points to the regime also using the nerve agent sarin." In another characteristic tweet after the U.S. airstrikes, Trump declared, "Mission Accomplished!"[39]

Trump's narrative of events was put into question by Ian Henderson who leaked a suppressed engineering assessment that challenged the OPCW's official conclusions about Assad's culpability. The leaked report found that the gas cylinders at the scene in Douma were likely "manually placed," which suggested that the attack was staged—a view reinforced by a photo showing a man standing next to the crater who should have immediately died from exposure to the gas (he did not die).[40] Henderson also wrote about the repositioning of bodies and doctoring of photos posted by apparent intelligence agents on social media.[41] Subsequently, another member of the OPCW team—the second whistleblower—came forward and delivered testimony in front of a panel convened by The Courage Foundation, a journalist and whistleblower protection organization founded by Wikileaks. In a statement, the panel said: "We are unanimous in expressing our alarm over unacceptable practices in the investigation . . . . We became convinced by the testimony that key information about chemical analyses, toxicology consultations, ballistics studies, and witness testimonies was suppressed, ostensibly to favor a preordained conclusion."[42]

A Douma resident interviewed in Mark Taliano's documentary, *Crimes Against Syria*, had said that he never saw evidence of any chemical attacks; he thinks it was a play or show—a lie that never happened. How was it possible, he asked, that people were walking around the area openly—without getting sick or killed when these chemicals were supposed to be deadly? And why would Assad use these weapons on his own people when he had liberated most of the country without them?[43] Noted Middle East correspondent Robert Fisk visited Douma a few days after to interview local residents and doctors and similarly found no evidence the attacks had occurred. One doctor told Fisk that a bombing operation by the Syrian Air Force had kicked up some dust that caused some respiratory problems among residents. Then after, a member of the White Helmets came by and shouted "chemical attack" and started taking video footage, though this did not show any evidence that a chemical attack actually occurred.[44]

After reviewing the evidence put forward by the OPCW whistleblowers, Theodore Postol told journalist Aaron Maté: "the evidence is overwhelming that the gas attacks were staged." Postol continued: "If I were advising somebody, as I did when I was in the Pentagon, I advised the chief of naval operations, and part of my job was to take technically detailed analysis and translate it into information that could be readily understood by an intelligent non-expert, so if I were briefing the chief on this particular document, I would not caveat it quite the way that the [OPCW] professionals did, although they did a good job. I would simply say that the evidence is overwhelming that the gas attacks were staged, and then I would explain why this evidence is overwhelming."[45]

Corrupt U.S. politicians—including most members of the Democratic Party—predictably dismissed the OPCW's Douma controversy as "Kremlin disinformation," even when Trump's Defense Secretary James Mattis stated in February 2018 that the U.S. had "no evidence to confirm" reports from aid groups and others that the Syrian government has used the deadly chemical sarin on its citizens.[46] U.S. media predictably also fell into line, with the once antiwar *Guardian* declaring "that Syria's renewed use of chemical weapons against its own people...is shameless and barbaric."[47] *Newsweek* journalist Tareq Haddad resigned in protest after the magazine's editors refused to publish his report on the OPCW whistleblower leaks. When Haddad announced on Twitter his reasons for leaving, a *Newsweek* spokesperson smeared Haddad, telling *Fox News* that he had "pitched a conspiracy theory rather than an idea for objective reporting."[48]

The deceit of the media was further evident in a January 2025 *Washington Post* article that sought to discredit Tulsi Gabbard's skepticism of Syria chemical weapons allegations, published just days before her scheduled confirmation hearing as Director of National Intelligence. Authored by Isaac Stanley-Becker, the article made no mention of the OPCW whistleblowers and leaked documents that are on the public record and cited Bellingcat as a scientific authority when it is a regime-change propaganda agency that has received financing from the National Endowment for Democracy (NED), a CIA cutout.[49] Bellingcat's founder, Elliot Higgins, who tried to attack Theodore Postol, was a college dropout who had never set foot in the Middle East and had no scientific training nor any interest in learning about science. Before the Arab Spring, Higgins admitted that he "knew no more about weapons than the average Xbox owners; any knowledge he had came from Arnold Schwarzenegger and Rambo."[50]

Another Unjust War Rooted in Lies

The chemical gas hoax showed the importance of false flag deception operations to the U.S. regime-change operation in Syria. Documents leaked from Stratfor, a Pentagon-linked private intelligence agency, showed that air operations against Syria to tip the balance in favor of anti-government militant groups were under serious consideration from the war's earliest days, and that the Pentagon was intent on demonizing the Syrian state through "media attention on a massacre" by government forces, that "would be vital to facilitating an air attack."[51] The chemical weapons attacks were the perfect form of massacre whose staging was designed to mobilize public opinion in the same way as Saddam Hussein's alleged possession of Weapons of Mass Destruction (WMD) in Iraq.

A.B. Abrams and Tim Anderson's books show repeated false flag incidents where war crimes committed by The Free Syrian Army (FSA) and other U.S.-backed groups were blamed on Assad. In May 2012, for example, Western media outlets—drawing on official State Department and rebel-linked human rights NGOs—reported that the Syrian army had killed large numbers of civilians without provocation in the town of Houla, though an investigation by a German newspaper found that insurgent militias had been responsible.[52] A subsequent massacre of 245 people in Daraya reported as a war crime by Assad's forces in Western media was determined by Robert Fisk to have been carried out by the FSA. Abrams mentions another example of the massacre of 120-150 villagers in the town of Aqrab that *The New York Times* said was carried out by "members of Assad's sect [Alawites]." British journalist Alex Thompson, however, determined that the FSA was the perpetrator and held 500 villagers from the Alawite religious minority hostage for nine days before carrying out mass executions.[53]

Amazingly, besides all these cases and others, the U.S. government and its media echo chamber accused Assad of using a nerve gas agent in Homs that does not even exist![54] Further, Assad was accused of launching 13,000 barrel bombs that were said to be of the same ferocity as the atomic attacks on Hiroshima—an impossibility.[55] Despite the above reality, the media massaging was so powerful and consistent regarding the chemical weapons attacks and Syrian army brutality that most people could not see beyond it. The alternative media played a crucial role in limiting the growth of an antiwar movement by advancing the same disinformation as the mainstream media. The niche program *Democracy Now,* which has a following among left-wing political activists, for example, featured guests from opposition NGOs that blamed Assad for the Houla massacre and the chemical warfare attacks in Eastern Ghouta.[56] The alternative media also followed the mainstream in denouncing Syrian war critics as "defenders of Syria's bloodthirsty dictator and butcher," to quote Spencer Ackerman in the hip *Wired* magazine.[57]

When the truth came out with regards to the chemical weapons attack, it was only in obscure publications because of systemic media censorship. Most people, therefore, do not know what really happened to this day. In a website post urging Donald Trump to explain the purpose behind his military escalation following the April 2017 Khan Sheykhoun attack, Bernie Sanders (D-VT)—a hero to many on the left—wrote that "in a world of vicious dictators, Syria's Bashar Assad tops the list as a dictator who has killed hundreds of thousands of his own citizens to protect his own power and wealth. His regime's use of chemical weapons against the men, women and children of his country, in violation of all international conventions and moral standards, makes him a war criminal."[58]

These statements show Sanders' embrace of the demonized image of Assad and his lack of comprehension of the nature of the Syrian conflict. Sanders was either ill-informed or willfully blind to the evidence uncovered by independent investigators regarding chemical weapons attacks. Additionally, he showed a lack of common sense: Assad had no incentive to use chemical weapons when he was winning the war; the rebels and U.S., however, had all the incentive to stage a false flag attack that could be blamed on Assad. As an antiwar activist during the Vietnam era, Sanders should have recognized the propensity of the U.S. government to manipulate public opinion and stage false-flag incidents in order to secure public support for military aggression. The Syrian chemical weapons hoax bore comparisons to the Iraq WMD fraud; the fake Viagra and Gaddafi atrocity stories in Libya, the Lusitania incident in World War I, false flag bombing operations by Bosnian Muslims and the Kosovo Liberation Army (KLA) that were blamed on Serbs in the 1990s Balkans conflict, fake atrocity stories and provocations directed against North Korea during the Korean War and the Gulf of Tonkin incident in Vietnam. Fake atrocity stories were also spread to justify genocidal campaigns against Native Americans.[59] The pattern of deception is apparent to anyone who studies history. The Syrian conflict is no exception and one of the unjust wars waged by the U.S. this century.

CHAPTER 8

A War by Other Means: Sanctions and the U.S. Regime-Change Operation

Economic sanctions have been a key in the U.S. regime-change toolkit for operations around the world. The goal is usually to weaken the country's economy and facilitate popular disaffection and civil unrest against the targeted government, culminating in regime change.[1] In 2017, Congressman Dennis Kucinich called the U.S. sanctions imposed on Syria—which were among the harshest in the world—"a war by other means," noting that they had the effect of "compounding the deteriorating context in the country" by "strengthening economics of plunder and acting as a bonus for groups such as ISIS, among other Islamists. These groups successfully recruit from unemployed youth, many of whom are from destitute families where the main breadwinner has been killed or injured."[2]

Kucinich's remarks help explain the underlying motive behind the U.S. sanctions policy, which James Jeffrey, U.S. Special Representative to Syria from 2019 to 2020, bragged were helping to "crush Assad."[3] Jeffrey and his colleagues in the U.S. foreign policy establishment were unconcerned about the horrific human costs of the sanctions, which Jordanian political figures characterized as a "form of economic terrorism," and the UN's Special Rapporteur on sanctions, Alena Douhan, said "may have amounted to a crime against humanity, against all Syrian people."[4] *Reuters* reported that Syria's economy contracted by 84 percent between 2010 and 2023—due in part to dwindling oil sales and tourism revenues resulting from the war and sanctions and a $7.8 billion decline in Syrian exports.[5] Syria's manufacturing sector contracted in the same period by a staggering 70 percent.[6]

In 2023, more than 609,000 Syrian children under the age of five were reportedly stunted from chronic undernutrition; twelve million Syrians lacked enough food to meet daily dietary needs, and 90 percent of Syrians were estimated to be living in poverty.[7] Food shortages were caused in part by militias affiliated with both the U.S. and Turkey blocking the sale by Syrian peasants of wheat and barley east of the Euphrates. The same militias sold oil illegally in northern Iraq and set fires in an attempt to decimate Syria's yield of strategic crops. Many of the fires targeted olive trees that were used to produce olive oil—a source of livelihood for many Syrians. The economic sanctions further prevented needed medical supplies and equipment from getting into Syria and caused milk shortages resulting in the deaths of children and a cholera outbreak that was reported on by the World Health Organization (WHO).[8]

Syrian doctors told an international tribunal on U.S. imperialism, that had been assembled in 2023 to investigate the impact of U.S. sanctions on Syria, that jihadist rebels shelled Syrian hospitals and murdered doctors and destroyed pharmaceutical factories. The doctors compared the impact of the sanctions in Syria with Iraq in the 1990s, where sanctions that followed the bombing of Iraq's infrastructure in the first Persian Gulf War resulted in the deaths of half a million Iraqi children, according to Secretary of State Madeleine Albright.[9]

Dr. Hizla al-Assad said that the U.S. war and sanctions had threatened to return life in Syria back to the Stone Age. Electricity in the country was sporadic and basic social services—excellent before the war—were severely reduced. Living standards were miserable and social cohesion was coming undone. People had to endure long food lines, public transport was lacking, and students could not study because their schools had been destroyed. Goods could no longer get in because of restrictions on Syrian airplanes and imports and exports were way down.[10]

In addition, much of the country's oil had been stolen, taken to Iraq and Turkey. This theft was facilitated by Turkey's occupation of northwest Syria, and the U.S.'s occupation of the northeast, both of these being oil-rich areas.[11] The Syrian Ministry of Foreign Affairs provided evidence to the Secretary General of the UN in June 2022 that unlawful trafficking of Syrian oil caused direct and indirect losses of about $107.1 billion to Syria's oil and gas sectors between 2011 to June in 2022.[12] Robert Ford, the former UK Ambassador to Syria, noted that, "[i]t would be hard to over-state the importance to the Syrian state of its being deprived of a resource, oil and gas, which represented over 20% of its GDP and which was crucial to electricity supply." Ford added that the northern areas occupied by the U.S. and Turkey were the bread basket of Syria, a primary source of grain. "No state can survive indefinitely being shut off in this way from its own major sources of wealth," he said, as the U.S. and Turkey well knew.[13]

The U.S.-Turkish plan was clearly to intentionally impoverish a country that was part of an axis of resistance against Western imperialism. According to Hizla al-Assad, an earthquake in Syria in 2022 showed the inhumanity of the Americans who prevented the delivery of needed medical and humanitarian aid into the country. That inhumanity was also evident in the behavior of American occupying troops in the northwest, who kidnapped Syrian youths and dragged them unconscious for the crime of possessing a picture of Bashar al-Assad.

Imposing a Heavy Toll: Bush and Obama Sanctions

U.S. sanctions on Syria were first adopted in the twenty-first century by the Bush administration in response to Syria's alleged support for Iraqi insurgents that targeted the U.S. after its illegal invasion of Iraq in 2003 along with other alleged acts of inter-national terrorism.[14] Eliot Engel (D-NY), the head of the Senate Foreign Relations Committee who co-sponsored the congressional sanctions bill signed by President Bush, stated that "we will not tolerate Syrian support for terrorism . . . .We will not tolerate Syrian occupation of Lebanon . . . . I do not want to witness horrors worse than 9/11."[15] Under the sanctions, American exports to Syria were all but prohibited, except for food and basic medicines, and U.S. busi-nessmen were banned from operating or investing in Syria. Syrian aircraft were also prohibited from landing in the U.S. In 2006, after calling Syria "an unusual and extraordinary threat to the national security, foreign policy, and economy of the United States," the Bush administration banned transactions with the Commercial Bank of Syria and froze the assets of Syrians involved in supporting policies considered to be hostile to the U.S.[16] These measures "took their toll" on the Syrian economy, according to various reports, which detailed the expansion of power shortages and electricity failures in Syria; how U.S. energy companies with capacity to build big power plants like Conoco Phillips, were pulling out of the country; and how the Syrian airlines industry was adversely affected by the lack of access to airplane parts of U.S. origin.[17]

Despite the severity of the sanctions, the trade volume between Syria and the U.S, remained high and President Bashar al-Assad was still able to make improvements in the Syrian economy. An economic analysis put out by the Berlin-based Konrad-Adenauer-Stiftung foundation found that liberalizing initiatives combined with construction of industrial cities in Rif Dimashq (Adra), Homs (Hissiya), Aleppo (Sheikh Najjar) and Deir ez-Zur contributed to a whopping 20 percent annual rise in the Syrian Gross National Product (GNP) from 2000 to 2010, "surpassing all other rates recorded for other countries in the region."[18] However, this was about to change as President Obama would turn the screws on Syria to try in earnest to topple Assad.

The pretext for the Obama administration's sanctions was Assad's allegedly brutal crackdown of the "Arab Spring" protests that erupted in Daraa in March 2011. As we have previously discussed, the official narrative surrounding these protests was false. The State Department website stated that the U.S. pursuit of "calibrated sanctions" was designed to "deprive the regime of the resources it needs to continue violence against civilians and to pressure the Syrian regime to allow for a democratic transition as the Syrian people demand."[19] However, the goal of democratic transition was really a pipe dream in light of the fact that the Syrian uprising was led by Muslim fundamentalists who wanted to create a medieval-style theocracy—as Obama was well aware. As an additional pretext for the sanctions, the Obama administration repeated Reagan-era tropes about Assad's support for terrorist groups, and followed George W. Bush's playbook in accusing Assad of developing weapons of mass destruction.[20]

The harshest aspect of Obama's sanctions was a prohibition on the importation of Syrian oil and further restrictions on Syria's central bank that made it virtually impossible for the Syrian government to tap into international financial markets or receive foreign aid. The sanctions also resulted in the illegal freezing of all Syrian government assets subject to U.S. jurisdiction and prohibited U.S. persons from engaging in any transaction involving the Syrian government. Obama said that "'unprecedented sanctions' were imposed in order to deepen the financial isolation of the Assad regime and further disrupt its ability to finance a campaign of violence against the Syrian people."[21] Put another way, they were designed to facilitate regime change.

The "economic siege on Syria," as observers called it, was compounded by the Obama administration's pressuring the European Union (EU), Arab League, Turkey, Canada, and Australia to impose their own sanctions on Syria.[22] The Syrian Center for Policy Research estimated that 28.9 percent ($6.8 billion) of Syria's GDP loss in 2011-2012 was attributed to U.S. and other foreign sanctions and that 877,000 Syrians were pushed into poverty because of the sanctions.[23] A study by *The Lancet* determined that the cost of illegal sanctions imposed on Syria by 2014 totaled

$143.8 billion.[24] Alena Douhan, the UN's Special Rapporteur on sanctions, found that whereas Syria was one of the largest oil producers and exporters in the Eastern Mediterranean region between 2000 and 2010, after the imposition of sanctions it became a net importer of crude oil, with half of the domestic consumption coming from imported oil.[25]

Additional studies detailed how Obama's sanctions undermined food security as basic foods (milk, rice, and tomatoes) tripled in price over the first year. The sanctions further fueled an increase in domestic inflation and unemployment, contributed to a decrease in salary levels and collapse of small businesses, helped depreciate Syria's currency, depleted government financial reserves, and seriously restricted trade.[26] The impact was most sharply felt among the poorest sectors of the population, as is often the case.[27] Kids were direly affected by the closure of schools and lack of proper textbooks because of a shortage of paper in the country.[28]

Doctors Without Borders reported that before the sanctions and war, Syria had a well-functioning health system with trained health workers, medical expertise, and its own pharmaceutical industry. The sanctions drove international pharmaceutical companies out of the country and caused a shortage of medicines and drugs, hindering the treatment of illnesses.[29] British journalist Vanessa Beeley reported that the U.S./EU sanctions resulted in an inability to replace used-up medical equipment and hindered medical and scientific research. Sanctions additionally prevented the transfer of medical equipment from France among other countries that was vital to the functioning of various Syrian hospitals.[30] Canadian journalist Eva Bartlett reported that a cruel feature of the U.S. sanctions was to prohibit key materials needed in prosthetic limbs manufacturing, including resin, the primary material used in the manufacture of prosthetic limbs. This was designed to punish Syrian soldiers who had been wounded in the war and to prevent their rehabilitation.[31]

The immense damage done to the Syrian economy and health and education system was confirmed by a 2017 World Bank report, which noted that: a) on average about 538,000 jobs were destroyed annually during the first four years of the conflict; b) young people faced an unemployment rate of 78 percent; c) the specific targeting of health facilities disrupted the health system, with communicable diseases such as polio reemerging; and d) the education system was similarly disrupted by damage to facilities and the use of schools as military installations. Additionally, fuel shortages reduced the supply of electricity to major cities to around two hours per day, affecting a range of basic services."[32]

More Fraudulent Pretexts—the Caesar Sanctions

All of the above problems were worsened[33] by draconian sanctions imposed by the Trump administration that were legitimated by more false propaganda. The Caesar Syria Civilian Protection Act, sponsored by Eliot Engel (D-NY), then chairman of the Senate Foreign Relations Committee, and signed into law in December 2019 by President Trump, dramatically expanded the U.S.'s ability to sanction individuals, businesses, and governments for doing business with Assad's regime.[34] Among the effects of the Caesar Act was to strangle Syrian trade with Lebanon. The underlying political agenda was reflected in an exemption placed on the HTS-controlled Idlib Province occupied by U.S. and Kurdish troops, which received $50 million in humanitarian aid.[35] The Trump administration further granted a sanctions waiver to a Delaware-based oil company, Delta Crescent Energy LLC, with close ties to his administration, allowing it to develop oil fields captured by Kurdish U.S. proxies.[36]

Supported by the Syrian American Council, a neoconservative-backed lobby group,[37] the Caesar Syria Civilian Protection Act was named after a government defector, Caesar, who leaked thousands of photographs alleging torture of civilians by Assad's security forces. Nearly half the photos actually showed government soldiers who had been killed and victims of car bombs and other war-related violence, and many others showed soldiers who had died in combat—not government torture centers. Caesar's identity was initially unclear, though he later identified himself as First Lieutenant Farid al-Madhhan and said he had been the head of the Forensic Evidence Department of the Military Police in Damascus. When he appeared before Congress, Caesar wore a hood over his face to mask his identity and was brought there by his "case officer," implying that he was working for the CIA.[38] Caesar was also said to have ties to the Qatari monarchy, a sponsor of Al Qaeda which supported the anti-Assad insurgency.

Media Participates in Psywar Operation

The media bought into Caesar's story and failed to question the possibility that he was a CIA "asset." *The Guardian* was characteristic in claiming that Syrian government officials could soon face war crimes charges in light of the "huge cache of evidence smuggled out of the country" by Caesar who claimed that his job had been to take pictures of detainees that had been killed.[39] One of the reporters promoting Caesar's story, Michael R Gordon of the *Wall Street Journal* and *The New York Times*, also wrote a disinformation story blaming Assad for a chemical weapons attack in Khan Shaykhoun, and had been a key figure advancing disinformation about Iraq and WMDs in the period before the Bush administration's 2003 invasion, which Gordon championed.[40]

Media studies professor Greg Shupak found a general pattern in which the mainstream U.S. media grossly under-reported the effects of U.S. sanctions in contributing to the suffering of the Syrian population. Shupak surveyed the three most widely circulated U.S. newspapers—*The New York Times*, *USA Today*, and the *Wall Street Journal*—and found that they regularly failed to mention the sanctions as a source of Syria's economic collapse.[41] Instead, they lent the impression that Syria's problems were all the result of misrule by Bashar al-Assad. Long infiltrated by U.S. intelligence and State Department agents, these media outlets were at the forefront in a psychological warfare operation designed to manufacture public consent for the U.S. regime-change operation in Syria and cruel policies accompanying it, which were branded as "well intentioned."[42]

Key to Regime Change

The U.S. sanctions policy in Syria ultimately succeeded. By December 2024, a destitute population lacked the will to continue to fight for Bashar al-Assad and an independent Syria and succumbed to the foreign-backed jihadists who took over the country. Demoralized youth facing a bleak future had been made vulnerable to recruitment by Al Qaeda offshoots that paid a lot more than the government.[43] Syrian-American activist Johnny Achi told Eva Bartlett in 2020 that "these final sanctions [Caesar Act] have broken the back of Syrians, who after 10 years of war are exhausted, resources depleted, and simply put, were looking forward to the rebuilding process and economic recovery. And that is precisely what these sanctions are to stop. Any country, or entity that attempts to help Syria get back on its feet, will become a target of the brutal U.S. sanctions."[44]

This assessment was echoed by former UK Ambassador to Syria, Peter Ford, who explained that "the sad truth is that sanctions do work, if sustained long enough and if the target state has no effective work-arounds. For a long time, it seemed that Syria could survive, but sanctions work not just on essentials like electricity and food but also on morale, on the morale of the people and the military. Thanks to the simultaneously waged information warfare, the Syrian people blamed Assad for deprivations wholly attributable to Western sanctions. Even corruption, one of the major causes of discontent, was in large part due to the fact that sanctions always give rise to corruption as part of a war economy. Unpaid soldiers demand fees at road blocks, for example, which turns the people against them."[45] Ford added that since Syrian soldiers were left as destitute as the rest of the population, they became run down as time progressed and unable to defend the country.[46]

A parallel can be drawn with Nicaragua in the 1980s where the U.S. applied economic sanctions and a full trade embargo in an attempt to undermine popular support for the socialist Sandinista government, which had triumphed in a revolution and won free and fair elections—as Assad did in Syria. By 1990, the Nicaraguan population had suffered so greatly under the policy of collective punishment that they voted out the Sandinistas in order to end the economic siege and terrorist activity of CIA-backed counterrevolutionaries (Contras) who were the equivalent of Syria's foreign-backed jihadist terrorists.[47]

Like today, liberal proponents of "humanitarian intervention" supported U.S. economic warfare on Nicaragua in the 1980s as a supposedly humane alternative to military invasion. Stephen Solarz (D-NY) called it "an appropriate approach. . . . I don't see how you can support sanctions against Nicaragua and not against [apartheid] South Africa. In both instances, you have Governments deeply committed to policies we are opposed to. In South Africa, it is apartheid and in Nicaragua it is repression at home and revolution abroad."[48] Solarz' views were echoed in the 2010s by leading Democratic Party hawks like Caesar bill sponsor Eliot Engel who called the Caesar sanctions act "long overdue" and a "positive step" in pushing the current administration to address the "carnage in Syria" that he blamed all on Assad.[49]

Both Solarz and Engel—recipient of over $1.8 million in American-Israeli Public Affairs Committee (AIPAC) donations[50]— were oblivious to the fact that the sanctions themselves were a great source of human carnage. The sanctions were generally part of an imperialist foreign policy designed to oust governments that opposed U.S. hegemonic designs—whether in Central America and the Middle East—and will continue to be adopted unless a large anti-imperialist movement develops in the U.S.—and world-wide—that seeks to restore the country's republican roots and put an end to U.S. imperialism.

CHAPTER 9

The White Helmets: Al Qaeda's Partner in Crime

The White Helmets organization (officially, the "Syria Civil Defense") was the darling of the Western media and Western governments during the Syrian War. It was portrayed as a purely humanitarian aid group akin to the Red Cross and unaffiliated with any side in the conflict.[1] Indeed, the White Helmets itself claimed that it is "fiercely independent and has not accepted any funding from governments, corporations or anyone directly involved in the Syrian conflict."[2] However, somehow, they always happened to turn up in areas in which the Al-Nusra Front of Al Qaeda, now HTS, was advancing.[3]

Indeed, recent articles by even pro-White Helmet publications—such as *Al Jazeera*, a news outlet owned by Qatar, a country deeply involved in supporting anti-Assad forces during the war— demonstrate the link between the White Helmets and Al Qaeda/ HTS. For example, in a March 2, 2025 puff piece entitled, "Syria's White Helmets continue to help people in devastated Aleppo," *Al Jazeera* related that the White Helmets moved into a building in Aleppo "that used to be a regime military outpost housing soldiers, tanks and ammunition during the Syrian war . . . a little more than a month after an opposition offensive led by Hayat Tahrir al-Sham (HTS) took Aleppo on November 30 and went on to topple Bashar al-Assad eight days later."[4] Another pro-White Helmet article, this time in *The New Arab*, explained, "When

Hayat Tahrir al-Sham burst out of the Idlib province in late November, the White Helmets were as surprised as anyone. But they did not hesitate to follow . . . ."[5]

With the job of Assad's overthrow accomplished, the mainstream press could now admit what only a few were brave enough to point out during the war—that the White Helmets go wherever Al Qaeda goes. And, with HTS in power, the White Helmets, ever critical of the Assad government and now focused on revealing the alleged crimes of this government, is an uncritical apologist for the new regime, even to a ludicrous degree. Thus, in an interview with the *Voice of America*, White Helmet co-founder Abdulrahman Almawwas denied the sectarian nature of the new government and the fact that a designated terrorist group had come to power. In response to a question about concerns regarding "the rise of Islamist forces in the country," Almawwas responded:

> This was the [Assad] regime's narrative since 2011. It was trying to export this image about Syria: You have Bashar al-Assad, or you will have ISIS, you will have Islamic groups. ...
>
> If you look at Syria, you will find a lot of civil society organizations. You will find that a lot of Syrians are not to the right or to the left — they are in the middle, they are just normal people, like in any country. . . .
>
> We have Muslims, Christians, other groups, and we used to live together. And the only one who divided these groups was the regime. So we hope that the next government will be a serious transitional government . . . and it will lead us to a new Syria that all Syrians dream of.[6]

Of course, the very fact that Al Qaeda, albeit renamed, came to power belies the claims of Almawwas here. And the sectarian violence carried out by the new government—violence amounting to a genocide—soon after these remarks were made would show these claims to be preposterous. Not surprisingly, the White Helmets, preoccupied with uncovering the alleged past crimes of Assad, has had no comments, much less criticism, about this violence which, as already described in this book, has claimed thousands of civilian lives in Syria.

All of this raises the question of what the White Helmets is, where it came from, and who it serves. First of all, as everything about the war on Syria, the White Helmets was not an indigenous organization but instead was brought to Syria from the outside by the West. Thus, in addition to the aforesaid Abdulrahman Almawwas, the White Helmets was co-founded by "James Le Mesurier, a former British military intelligence officer and private security contractor for the United Arab Emirates" who "organized the initial civil defense teams from a Turkish base."[7] Le Mesurier had also been a member of the Oliver Group security firm which would go on to merge with the U.S.-based Blackwater,[8] the private military contractor infamous for committing atrocities against civilians in Iraq. Russia openly suspected that Le Mesurier had also been an agent for MI6—the British analogue of the CIA—which would not have been uncommon for Brits with Le Mesurier's background.[9]

Le Mesurier founded the parent company of the White Helmets, Mayday Rescue Foundation, in Dubai in 2013, but later moved it to the Netherlands.[10] And the White Helmets received massive funding from the collective West. By 2021, they had received approximately €100 million from the UK, Germany, Holland, and Denmark, $54.7 million from USAID, and several million dollars more from Japan, Canada, and Qatar.[11] The White Helmets direct involvement in military operations was exemplified by their establishment of an early warning system for airstrikes that benefitted anti-Assad insurgents.[12]

While the Western press loudly declared that criticisms of the White Helmets as a fraud was nothing but Russian, Iranian, or other propaganda, Le Mesurier himself would later fully admit to its fraudulence and would commit suicide in Turkey three days later. In 2020, Le Mesurier confessed to taking tens of thousands of dollars for himself and other directors, including his wife, in undeclared bonuses after being caught by a Dutch accountant auditing the organization.[13] But this was just the tip of the iceberg, with the Dutch government ultimately cutting off funding to the White Helmets, an ostensibly humanitarian relief organization, after discovering that much of the money was going to weapons and that, what's more, the White Helmets was working with "unacceptable" groups—that is, terrorists—on the ground in Syria.[14]

Sadly, the Netherlands was the only Western government to acknowledge what the legacy press had been disparaging as mere propaganda for years—that the White Helmets was allied with designated terrorist organizations in Syria.[15] And even after Le Mesurier's suicide following his admission of corruption, the Western media attempted to portray him as a hero who was somehow a victim of false accusations of fraud and other misdeeds.[16]

One emblematic example of this campaign to salvage the reputation of Le Mesurier, and consequently of the White Helmets, was a piece entitled, "Why no-one could save the man who co-founded the White Helmets," in which the *BBC* insinuates—without any evidence and despite the fact that his own wife admits that he committed suicide out of despair[17]—that Le Mesurier may have been killed by the Russians.[18] In this piece, the *BBC* dismisses the "deep suspicion" that some had about Le Mesurier serving as a British intelligence agent even while with the White Helmets.

However, the *BBC* did acknowledge the following: "A former soldier, he had served as a military intelligence officer in Bosnia. After leaving the army, he worked as a private security contractor in the Middle East. It led some to question: why was a former British soldier running a humanitarian group in Syria? The fact the White Helmets are funded by states including the UK and the U.S. was, for some, further grounds for suspicion." Nothing to see here, though, was the takeaway that the *BBC* urged upon its audience. Strangely, this piece ends abruptly with the tantalizing lines:

> And then there were reports that in the days before his death, he had been accused of fraud and embezzlement.

In death, James Le Mesurier left behind a tangled knot of truth and lies. Untangling that knot would mean finding out who he really was and how he came to die. It's a story which goes to the heart of a very modern war.

However, the *BBC* had no intention of untangling the ostensible "knot of truth and lies" or to really tell the reader who Le Mesurier and the White Helmets really were. That is the job we undertake here. The main service the White Helmets did for its terrorist partners was to whitewash their crimes (which they continue to do to this day) and frame the Assad government for atrocities with the hope to provoke Western military intervention on the side of the jihadists. Indeed, well-respected journalist John Pilger referred to the White Helmets as a "'complete propaganda construct' of the Al Qaeda affiliated Al Nusra Front."[19]

While the White Helmets were founded in 2013, they were the main fount of information from rebel areas in Syria by 2014.[20] Indeed, the White Helmets ONLY operated in areas controlled by the al-Nusra Front of Al Qaeda, now rebranded HTS, and some of their members even appeared alongside the Al Qaeda fighters with guns and the Islamic flag in hand.[21] One of their top leaders, Farouq al Habib, was a leader of the Homs uprising against Assad.[22] Videos demonstrate that members of the White Helmets engaged in such nefarious acts as the beheading of a child and the making of devices to project "barrel bombs."[23] In places like Aleppo and Daraa, White Helmet members were "filmed attending executions . . . , parading several heads and dismembered bodies before dumping them in a garbage heap."[24]

Even *Newsweek*, while attempting to defend the White Helmets, acknowledged despicable acts by its members, such as overseeing a grisly execution of a man by the jihadists (the subject of a viral video), as well as helping the jihadists dispose of the bodies of people they had killed.[25] In other words, the White Helmets has been a full-service outlet for the jihadists. Even beyond that, it can honestly be said that the White Helmets WERE the jihadists.

And indeed, the jihadists themselves praised the White Helmets for being "comrades in arms against the Syrian government."[26]

As Dr. Tim Anderson explains, "videos and photographs appeared showing men in White Helmet uniforms not only mingled in alongside and helping the jihadist groups—including in the torture and murder of Syrian soldiers and civilians—but switching their medic uniforms for armed group logos and civilians. There are now compilations of many dozens of such photos."[27] As Anderson notes, "the head of Al Qaeda in western Syria, Abu Jaber al Sheik, praised TWH [the White Helmets] as 'hidden soldiers of the revolution.'"[28] And many Syrians who were impacted by the jihadist terror agreed. Dr. Anderson explains that after the eastern part of Aleppo was liberated by the SAA, former residents of the area called the White Helmets "'Nusra front [Al Queda] civil defense,' saying they worked together with the armed groups and rarely provided assistance to ordinary people."[29]

None of this should be too surprising, Dr. Anderson explains, because a number of the White Helmets' associates had strong attachments to the violent armed groups in Syria. For example, Khaleb Diab, before joining the White Helmets, had worked for "Qatar's Red Crescent, where he was accused of providing about $2.2 million to terrorist groups in Syria."[30] Farouq al Habib of the White Helmets was also a member of the anti-Assad armed group known as the "Homs Revolutionary Council."[31] In July of 2018, 422 White Helmets members were rescued from approaching SAA troops by British, Israeli, and Jordanian forces, with a British official saying this was necessary because they feared that the SAA would question them about chemical weapons attacks and that the White Helmet members might answer those questions.[32]

White Helmet members who were injured were treated in Israeli field hospitals on the border with the occupied Golan Heights.[33] Eventually, a number of these White Helmet members were brought to Jordan and then given refugee status in Canada, Germany, and other Western countries. Germany's offer of asylum to White Helmets members, including White Helmets' long-time director Raed Al-Saleh, became a matter of controversy, with Germany's Left Party raising alarm about the White Helmets' jihadist ties. As Heike Hansel, the deputy chairman of the Left Party, argued: "'It is completely contradictory that Interior Minister Horst Seehofer on the one hand wants to fight Islamist terror, but on the other hand wants to bring in these members of Islamist terrorist militias to Germany.'"[34]

This brings us to the biggest propaganda service the White Helmets provided for Al Qaeda and the West—the framing of the Assad government for chemical weapons attacks at critical moments in order to justify the bombing of Syria by the West. Thus, in 2017, the White Helmets claimed that the Syrian government carried out a chemical weapons attack in the Idlib Province, a claim quickly embraced by the anti-Assad alliance of the U.S., Britain, France, Turkey, Saudi Arabia, and Israel.[35] For their part, Russia and Syria, along with a number of independent journalists, claimed that it was the White Helmets itself which staged the chemical weapons attack to provoke a military attack against the Assad government in the absence of UN Security Council authorization.[36] Not surprisingly, this claim was quickly written off by the Western press corps as a mere conspiracy theory. However, this theory could not be so easily dismissed after the emergence of "a White Helmets film set in Syria showing an SAA chemical attack being staged, with actors appearing in multiple scenes playing roles of both victims and paramedics."[37]

Eventually, even some Western officials began to express doubt about the White Helmets' claims. Thus, by 2018, U.S. Defense Secretary James Mattis admitted that there had been no evidence of a Syrian attack. "We have other reports from the battlefield from people who claim it's been used [but] we do not have evidence of it," Mattis stated, meaning the White Helmets had essentially been taken at their word as a pretext for military action.[38] But such doubts came too late as the U.S., Britain, and France had already bombed Syria in response to the alleged chemical attack. Mission accomplished, then, for the White Helmets.

The White Helmets' chemical attack gambit worked so well in 2017 in Idlib that it decided to run it again in Douma on April 7, 2018—coincidentally, just before OPCW inspectors were due to arrive in Syria and as Assad was actually winning the war.[39] The governments and press of the West were happy to feign shock at this event even though they were given fair notice that it was coming and indeed who it was coming from. Thus, in mid-March of 2018, the Russian Military publicly warned "that the White Helmets and militants were planning to stage and film a chemical attack on civilians as a means of gaining Western military support."[40] And, once the alleged attack happened, Britain, France, and the U.S. tellingly vetoed a Russian resolution at the UN Security Council to investigate the event.[41] Moreover, in spite of the fact that Russia vetoed a Western-backed resolution to attack Syria in light of the alleged chemical attack, Britain, France, and the U.S. went ahead and bombed Syria anyway on April 14, 2018.[42]

The alleged Douma chemical attack became one of the most infamous episodes of the war in Syria. And, while many were fooled by the hoax, not all were. For example, Lord Alan West, former senior British government security advisor and former head of the British Navy, opined, "[t]he reports that came from there [Douma] were from the White Helmets who, let's face it, are not neutrals, you know, they are very much on the side of the disparate groups who are fighting Assad."[43]

Even as HTS was well on its way to overthrowing Assad and taking over Syria, the White Helmets continued to raise the specter of possible chemical attacks by the Assad government in order to gin up support from the international community for the regime change which would soon come. On December 3, 2024, the Director of the White Helmets, Raed Al-Saleh addressed the UN Security Council, and stated, in pertinent part:

> I am gravely concerned about the lives of every Syrian because of the real threat of chemical attacks. The Syrian regime has a long history of using chemical weapons for military gain, such as in Douma in the Damascus countryside in 2018. According to a report

Terrorist Tunnel under Douma, Syria, where the White Helmets staged
a false chemical weapons attack just before the Organization of the
Prevention of Chemical Weapons (OPCW) was to arrive. This became
a pretext for Britain, France and the U.S. to bomb Syria. (Kovalik, 2021)

of the Director-General of the Organization for the Prohibition
of Chemical Weapons, the regime has admitted to continuing
production and development of chemical weapons. This is a dangerous indicator of the safety of civilians and a clear violation of
UN Security Council Resolution 2118 and the Chemical Weapons
Convention. The failure of the international community to hold
the regime accountable for these violations puts civilians at risk
of chemical attacks at any moment.

In addition to raising the specter of chemical weapons attacks
which, by the way, never came even as the Assad government was
crumbling, Al-Saleh ended his remarks to go off script and make

a bizarre claim. According to one news outlet covering his presentation, he "denounced the Assad regime for turning Syria into a hub for terrorist militias . . .. 'Syria's civilization is 7,000 years old,' he said. 'But the Syrian regime has turned it into a passage for terror . . . .'"[44] That is, Al-Saleh claimed that it was Assad's fault that terrorists had infiltrated Syria in an attempt to overthrow him, destroying Syria in the process. Talk about blaming the victim. But this has been the typical discourse for the White Helmets over the years. As Christopher Davidson explains in his momentous book, *Shadow Wars: The Secret Struggle for the Middle East*:

> [A]lmost all of its press releases have sought to portray the Syrian regime, rather than any opposition group or even jihadist militias, as the main destabilizing force in the country. In October 2015, for example, its website's first headline claimed that the regime's infamous 'barrel bombs' have been the biggest killers of civilians, while earlier in the year the New York Times reported that the organization was campaigning because 'the West is so focused on the Islamic State that it is ignoring the far greater killing by Assad.' . . . The White Helmets have, thus far, never claimed that any of their personnel have been harmed by any of the US or rebel-led actions.[45]

This selective, pro-jihadist coverage, continues to this day even as the White Helmets, given free reign of the whole country by the HTS authorities, are stationed in places like Latakia and Tartus where Alawites and Christians are being killed in the thousands by HTS-linked forces. As of the date of this writing, it is estimated that perhaps 40,000 innocents have been killed in this slaughter in just two weeks.[46] While the White Helmets vaguely acknowledge the killings, it refuses to name who the killers are, and to criticize the HTS government that oversees the massacres.[47]

CHAPTER 10

The Liberal Intelligentsia Plays Its Role

> "There is work to be done to prevent this war of ours from passing
> into popular mythology as a holy crusade."
> –Randolph Bourne, "War and the Intellectuals," 1917.

Liberal intellectuals have always played a pivotal role in U.S. regime-change operations by providing moral and ideological justification for them and by casting them in moralistic terms. America's liberal intelligentsia routinely obfuscate the true purposes behind U.S. interventions around the world and provide a gatekeeping function by which they help to marginalize genuinely radical and dissenting voices. Additionally, they adopt the colonialist mindset of the masters in that they feel they can judge other peoples, other countries, other governments, other forms of democracy on the basis of their own hallowed (in their opinion) system.

A key historical precedent was established during World War I when the Wilson administration enlisted leading intellectuals to rally support for the war effort after setting up the Committee on Public Information (CPI), a large-scale propaganda agency that used techniques of modern advertising to persuade the public that it was in their interest to send U.S. troops into the Great War. Much of the CPI's propaganda involved the demonization of Germany, which was presented as a dark autocracy under Kaiser

Wilhelm II responsible for heinous human rights crimes, such as ripping open the stomachs of pregnant women and killing their unborn babies. Foreign correspondent Irwin Cobb, who covered the German invasion of Belgium, said that only about one-tenth of the atrocity stories reported in the U.S. media were true. To help whip up anti-German hatred, the CPI enlisted noted historians and intellectuals like Walter Lippman, a staunch champion of progressive reform, who presented U.S. intervention as a necessity to spread the noble ideals laid out in Woodrow Wilson's twelve-point platform for the League of Nations (national right to self-determination, free trade, etc.). Many later became disillusioned when the U.S. Senate never ratified U.S. membership in the League of Nations, and the 1934-1936 Nye Committee exposed the role of private bankers and munitions makers (AKA "merchants of death") in driving U.S. intervention in the war.[1]

Despite the public fallout that led to the growth of the America First Committee, the largest antiwar organization in U.S. history, the CPI set the groundwork for the next hundred years of government propaganda campaigns that have adopted the same approach of demonizing enemy leaders (and U.S. dissenters) and spreading exaggerated or false atrocity stories to help mobilize public support for regime change.[2] One fallacy that CPI intellectuals helped advance—like today's proponents of humanitarian intervention—was that military intervention could facilitate progressive change.[3] During the Cold War, the CIA adopted the infamous Operation Mockingbird by which it planted its "assets" in the media who promoted Cold War interventions. The CIA-financed Congress of Cultural Freedom further sponsored intellectual journals that advanced anticommunist themes and directed social criticism at U.S. adversaries.[4] Their contemporary heirs will occasionally admit that the U.S. has done some bad things as a result of military interventions in places like Vietnam and Iraq. Rarely, however, do they acknowledge that the U.S. is an empire with over 800 overseas military bases and that it routinely adopts humanitarian pretexts in order to rationalize intervention in countries like Syria for crass economic motives and based on self-serving geopolitical interest.

The propaganda campaign directed against Bashar al-Assad can be compared with that directed against the German Kaiser during World War I. Liberal intellectuals and mainstream media depicted Assad as a brutal tyrant who committed a litany of atrocities against his own people, many of which were unverifiable, such as chemical weapons attacks, which independent analysts attributed to rebel groups or may never have occurred at all. Like most propaganda, there was certain truth to claims of Assad's brutality, however, little nuance was adopted in trying to analyze why a majority of Syrians supported Assad after the so-called "Arab Spring" and how the Assads had sustained legitimacy in ruling Syria over decades. Rebel forces were typecast as democratic champions seeking to courageously overthrow the tyrant. Their links to Islamic fundamentalism and adoption of terrorist methods and large-scale atrocities was grossly underplayed or ignored.[5] So was the longstanding pattern of the U.S. allying with jihadists against Arab nationalists because of a drive to control Middle Eastern oil.[6]

The one-sided portrayal of the Syrian conflict was similar to Libya, where Muammar Gaddafi was demonized by Western intellectuals and media in a similar manner to Assad, while his major accomplishments were suppressed.[7] In both cases, even self-described left-wing magazines repeated the false U.S. State Department claim that the 2011 "Arab Spring" uprisings were "a mass peaceful movement composed primarily of working- and middle-class people," as journalist Anand Gopal stated of the situation in Syria in a December 2024 interview with *Jacobin Magazine*, the voice of the Democratic Socialists of America.[8] Denying the existence of ethnic cleansing and massacres by rebel forces in former government controlled territory, a charge he attributed to "Assad propagandists," Gopal—who had elsewhere reported critically on U.S. bombing operations—does not so much as mention U.S. intervention in Syria. Accusing Assad of leading one of the most "brutal regimes of the 21st century" and of "gassing his own people," Gopal told *Jacobin* that "in what are generally dark times around the world, the victory of the Syrian revolution [in December 2024] is something every leftist, and indeed every human being, should celebrate."[9]

The brave reporters who were not cheerleading Assad's downfall were labeled not only as "Assad propagandists" but also "conspiracy theorists," and said to be "part of a coordinated Russian campaign" to "distort the reality of the Syrian conflict" and "deter intervention by the international community," to quote the liberal-left *Guardian* in June 2022. The *Guardian* identified journalists Vanessa Beeley, Eva Bartlett, and Aaron Maté as primary culprits who supposedly misrepresented the White Helmets as Al Qaeda adjuncts, and denied or distorted facts about the Assad regime's alleged chemical weapons use. Author Mark Townsend suggested that these and other "Syrian conspiracy theorists" were helping to "normalize Syria's Assad regime" and "emboldening Russian President Vladimir Putin in Ukraine," with Syria functioning as a "testing ground for disinformation activity."[10]

Liberal Hawks and the Syrian Dilemma

The dominant liberal intellectual approach to Syria during the years of the U.S. regime-change operation was epitomized in a 2013 book published by *The Boston Review* called *The Syria Dilemma* edited by Nader Hashemi and Danny Postel, directors of the Center of Middle East Studies at the University of Denver.[11] Most of the contributors in this volume were known for their support for the Democratic Party and opposition to Donald Trump. Hashemi set the tone by attacking Western leftists who opposed U.S. military intervention in Syria for allegedly "enabling Assad's savage repression" and for "betraying the Syrian people's yearning for self-determination," which Hashemi felt was embodied by the rebel movement.[12]

A lead essay in the volume supportive of U.S. military intervention in Syria was written by Michael Ignatieff, the former head of

Canada's Liberal Party, who failed miserably in that position, and a professor at Harvard University's Carr Center for Human Rights who is a well-known proponent of the concept of "humanitarian intervention." In the 1990s, Ignatieff served as a cheerleader for the bombing of Bosnia-Herzegovina and Kosovo, believing that it was necessary to save the Bosnian Muslims and Kosovars from alleged Serb ethnic cleansing and genocide and for ushering in a multi-cultural society there.[13]

Ignatieff's essay, titled "Bosnia and Syria: Intervention Then and Now," suggests that the collapse of the legitimacy of the Assad government and prospects of state collapse in Syria, like the Balkans in the 1990s, resulted in a devolution into sectarian warfare and the population seeking outside protection.[14] Ignatieff praised Syrian opposition figures (whose names he does not cite) fighting "courageously to create a pluralist, multi-confessional democratic Syria upon the ruins of the Assad regime."[15] Subsequently, he acknowledges that the Al-Nusra brigade aimed to create an Islamic caliphate, but in the same sentence laments how Western governments have "found it easier to identify those they want to lose than those they want to win."[16]

Ignatieff seems to suggest here that the West should not let the presence of fundamentalists dissuade support for the pro-Western factions within the insurgency that want to create a liberal, multicultural society—at least in his mind. Ignatieff notes his amazement at "how much they [opposition leaders] sound like Yugoslavs, especially the Bosniaks of the early 1990s. They too sought to create a post ethnic politics after Tito's death. They too sought to preserve the complex, multi-confessional heritage of tolerance that many in the Syrian opposition are struggling to preserve."[17]

This assessment is highly problematic on numerous levels, including in its adoption of an idealized view of the opposition/ rebel movements in both Syria and Bosnia-Herzegovina that ignores the anti-liberalism and dominant strain of fundamentalist Islam in both of these movements. In 1970, the leader of the Bosnian

Muslims, Aliza Izetbegovic wrote a manifesto, which exalted Pakistan as a model Islamic state, considered Western feminists as a "depraved element of the female sex," and declared: "There can be no peace or coexistence between the Islamic faith and non-Islamic social and political institutions . . .. the state should be an expression of religion and should support its moral concepts."[18]

Ignatieff himself adopts a colonialist perspective in expressing belief in the U.S. as the savior of Bosnia-Herzegovina—like Syria. He praises Bosnian Sarajevans for getting Westerners to support military intervention by "marshalling outrage" over Serb atrocities like the Srebrenica massacre and market bombing in Sarajevo, though the latter was found to have been carried out by Muslim forces, to show the Serbs in a bad light.[19] Ignatieff's blinkered viewpoint extends to his triumphalist assessment of the Dayton peace agreement, brokered by Richard Holbrooke, which offered more territory to the Serbs than an earlier agreement the Clinton administration sabotaged.[20] Dayton's neocolonial character was further reflected in its mandating the occupation of Bosnia by 60,000 NATO troops, 20,000 of them American, and the drafting of a new constitution granting full executive powers in all matters to a Swedish official appointed by the UN Security Council who could overrule the prime ministers and appointed ministers.[21]

At the end of his essay, Ignatieff laments that "when western governments consider Syrian pleas for intervention, it is not Bosnia that comes to their minds but Iraq, Afghanistan and Libya."[22] Ignatieff is sad that "euphoric confidence in the superiority of the Western democratic model in the unipolar moment that followed the collapse of the Soviet empire had waned." On the bright side, however, he writes that "after much internal debate the Obama administration has concluded that Syria does matter" and that "lethal and non lethal aid" was "being funneled to Syrian fighters through Turkey and through Jordan, under the watchful eye of the CIA."[23] The only remaining question was as to whether external aid had "come too late to confer any leverage at all, as the rebels close in and the final battle for Damascus gets underway."[24]

These latter statements show Ignatieff's underestimation of Bashar al-Assad's political strength as the final battle for Damascus took place over a decade after his essay was published. Supportive of a covert operation that is comparable to Iran-Contra, Ignatieff is further naïve about the U.S.'s ability to "confer leverage over the rebels" and the fact that even if it did, it likely wouldn't help advance liberal democracy. Historically, the U.S. has empowered hardline anti-democratic elements in foreign countries valued for their willingness to sell of their country's natural resources to multi-national corporations and station foreign military bases on their soil—something to which Ignatieff feigns obliviousness.[25]

Ignatieff's line of argumentation is similar to many other contributors to *The Syrian Dilemma* volume. Notable is the lack of critical perspective on the geopolitical calculations driving U.S. intervention in Syria and the importance of oil—which Donald Trump came right out and said (In 2019, Trump said that "we left troops in Syria only for the oil").[26] The first essay in the volume by Shadi Hamid of the Brookings Institute rues the Iraq War because it dampened the interventionist impulse for places like Syria.[27] Liberal humanist Mary Kaldor wrote that "there should be intervention because of the regime's brutality towards its own people . . . what is needed is a humanitarian intervention to protect the Syrian people."[28]

A few of the essays in *The Syrian Dilemma* to be sure were not supportive of military intervention and pretty-well reasoned.[29] However, the overwhelming majority adopted hawkish positions and presented one-sided analysis of the Syrian conflict that thoroughly demonized Assad, presenting him in the vein of a modern day "Oriental despot" with caricatured features.[30] *Atlantic* editor Anne-Marie Slaughter's essay quotes from Pulitzer Prize-winning Samantha Power's 2002 book, *"A Problem From Hell": America in the Age of Genocide* to suggest that Western indifference with regards to Syria would enable Assad to commit genocide.[31] Slaughter[32] proposed that the Arab League and Turkey, backed by NATO members, should provide specialized anti-tank and anti-mortar weapons to Syrian towns willing to declare "no kill zones" and to defend themselves against Assad. Towards the end of the piece, Slaughter quoted a warning from CIA agent Robert Baer that the international community would not act unless the level of killing in Syria reached Rwanda type levels. "Surely," she writes, "mass murder in the tens of thousands [as was already occurring in Syria] is enough for action on both moral and strategic grounds."[33]

Slaughter may be oblivious to the fact that the U.S. did intervene in the Rwandan genocide, in support of the worst killers, the Tutsi-led Rwandan Patriotic Front (RPF), who functioned as a U.S. regional proxy force.[34] She fits the norm in presenting Assad as responsible for all the killing in Syria's "civil war," when many of the atrocities were committed by jihadist rebels along with Kurdish militias financed by the U.S., and when a significant proportion of people killed in the conflict—about a third (or, 200,000 out of 500 to 600,000)—were combatants fighting on the side of the Assad government.[35] The West, in Slaughter's assessment, could serve as Syria's savior, though in reality it helped trigger the deadly conflict and wanted to weaken and Balkanize Syria so it could better exploit its natural resources and allow its proxy, Israel, to take more of its territory.

Imperial Apologia of Fools

Slaughter's assessment was echoed in an April 2021 article in *The Nation* magazine—a traditionally liberal antiwar outlet—by Gilbert Achcar, a Professor of International Relations at the University of London. Entitled "How to Avoid the Anti-Imperialism of Fools," the article took aim at leftists who allegedly valorized Assad's brutal rule along with other of Washington's opponents like Vladimir Putin and Slobodan Milošević.[36] Like Michael Ignatieff, Achcar supported military intervention in Syria under the dubious doctrine of Responsibility to Protect

(R2P), which champions foreign military intervention if it will stop large-scale human rights abuses.[37]

A Lebanese socialist who wrote a book critical of Israeli policies towards the Palestinians with Noam Chomsky,[38] Achcar quoted favorably from a 2019 statement signed by several prominent figures on the American Left—including Judith Butler, Noam Chomsky, David Graeber, and David Harvey—demanding that the United States "continue military support for the Kurdish-led Syrian Democratic Force," in the face of Donald Trump's announced withdrawal. Supported by "progressive Democrats" like Bernie Sanders and Elizabeth Warren, this position was based on fear that if the U.S. withdrew, the Kurds would be slaughtered by Turkey, the Islamic State in the Levant (ISIS), or the "murderous Assad regime," as Achcar termed it.

The Kurds, however, were being used as a proxy force by the U.S. in a regime-change operation that would enable foreign exploitation of Syria's oil and military domination of the Middle East—and would inevitably be abandoned. After Assad's ouster, the U.S. set up two military bases in Kurdish-controlled areas and left 400 troops there.[39] Western empires had used the pretext of human rights many times before to justify colonization, and recruited disaffected minority groups, which was no different in this case. A twist this time was that many of the Turkish fighters brutalizing the Kurds had actually been trained by the CIA under the Operation Timber Sycamore,[40] which Achcar and others in his camp never drafted any letter to denounce.

In January 2025, Stansfield Smith published an article in *CovertAction Magazine* reviewing alternative media's coverage of the fall of Assad in December 2024. Smith was appalled to find that the majority of pieces celebrated another successful U.S. "regime change." *Portside*, which assembles daily news articles "of interest to people on the left," ran an article, "Liberation in Syria Is a Victory Worth Embracing" by Layla Maghribi, a former producer for *CNN International* whose father was active in the Libyan anti-Gaddafi movement, which criticized "some self-styled

Western 'anti-imperialists'" for their lack of enthusiasm for the "victory."[41] Smith lamented that "one finds no mention of the long U.S. blockade imposed on Syrians" in the piece.

Counterpunch, an ostensibly left website, was especially outspoken in its hostility towards those exposing U.S. coup operations in Syria, calling them "campists" and "tankies."[42] On December 10, *Counterpunch* published "Understanding the Rebellion in Syria" by Swiss-Syrian socialist Joseph Daher, which made the outlandish assertion that "some on the Left have claimed without foundation that their rebellion was orchestrated by the U.S. and Israel . . . .. Neither the U.S. nor Israel had a hand in these events. In fact, the opposite is the case."[43] Daher went on to write off as "campists" and "tankies" those of us who recognize the obvious, "that this military offensive is led by 'Al Qaeda and other terrorists' and that it is a western-imperialist plot against the Syrian regime intended to weaken the so-called "Axis of Resistance" led by Iran and Hezbollah....the campists claim that the fall of Assad weakens it and therefore undermines the struggle for the liberation of Palestine."[44]

On December 11, *Counterpunch* turned to academic Stephen Zunes for an "exclusive interview" presenting him as a "foreign policy expert" for the left.[45] Zunes, back in 2011, praised the U.S.-NATO destruction of Gaddafi's Libya in *Truthout.*[46] In this interview, he impugned Assad for his "savage repression" and "endemic corruption" and blamed him for Syria's growing poverty without mentioning the draconian U.S. sanctions policy or ravaging effects of a war that had been triggered by outsiders. Zunes went on to characterize the anti-Assad rebels as a "popular resistance movement," obscuring its domination by jihadist elements, and said that the rebellion "would have happened regardless of U.S. policy," which obscures the crucial nature of U.S. support. Zunes showed his true colors further when he defended President Barack Obama who inaugurated the largest covert operations in Syria since the U.S. support for the Afghan mujahidin in the 1980s, and illegally bombed Syria based on fraudulent pretexts, a phony charge of chemical weapons attacks.[47] According to Zunes, "many of these Western 'anti-imperialists' are themselves stuck in an imperialist mindset which denies agency to people of color in the Global South (or Slavs in Eastern Europe) who are struggling for their freedom against tyranny." However, the struggle against tyranny in this case was financed heavily by outside powers, including the U.S., and was led not by "freedom fighters" but jihadist terrorists who came from eighty-four different countries.

Truthout mimicked *Counterpunch* in running its own pro-U.S. regime-change article, "As Assad Regime Falls, Syrians Celebrate—and Brace for an Uncertain Future" by Shireen Akram-Boshar, a socialist writer and Middle East/North Africa solidarity activist. The article repeats the same apologetics for U.S. imperial rule: "Contrary to common misconceptions, the U.S. and Israel did not aspire to remove Assad after 2013."[48] The flagship "lefty" program *Democracy Now* hosted by Amy Goodman and Juan Gonzalez similarly ignored the U.S. involvement in the operations against Assad and triumph of Al Qaeda. It interviewed an *AP* reporter, Sarah El Deeb, who pointed to cheering crowds and expressed enthusiasm about the new post-Assad Syria. El Deeb further echoed the mainstream media in spotlighting the Assad's brutality, while ignoring the record of ethnic cleansing, suicide bombing, and massacres carried out by the rebel forces backed by the U.S. who succeeded in deposing Assad and their involvement in organ harvesting.[49]

One of *Democracy Now*'s main go-to guests on Syria for much of the war, Shane Bauer, is a suspected intelligence agent who in a series of in-country dispatches for the leftist *Mother Jones Magazine*, blamed Assad and his Russian supporters for carrying out a litany of horrors, including mythic chemical gas attacks that allegedly "poisoned children." Having almost nothing to say about the atrocities of U.S. forces while quoting from Kurds who made it seem like Americans were acting as liberators in Syria, Bauer used the language of U.S. intelligence in branding principled critics of U.S. intervention like *Grayzone* founder Max Blumenthal,

Lebanese journalist Rania Khalek, and British journalist Vanessa Beeley as "online attack dogs of the Assad regime."[50] Additionally, like Mark Townsend at *The Guardian*, Bauer branded skeptics of the official narrative of the chemical weapons attacks, "conspiracy theorists," a term that was weaponized by the CIA beginning in the late 1960s to discredit critics of the Warren Commission and other CIA coverups.[51]

The weakness of the left's analysis on Syria is generally reflective of what appear to be two countervailing trends: a) its cooptation by corporate foundation money and/or intelligence agencies, and b) a strong anti-authoritarian and anarchistic strain in its thought remnant from the 1960s. This latter strain has resulted in its over-identification with protest/rebel movements and knee-jerk condemnation of authoritarian leaders; even when those leaders are attempting to retain their country's national sovereignty and adopt forward thinking economic policies.

Regarding the first point, the CIA and its related corporate foundations have long sought to infiltrate, coopt, and weaken the political left. A particular focus has been on journalists and intellectuals who have the capacity to mold public opinion and spark outrage that could lead to the growth of a formidable antiwar movement.[52] CIA operative Cord Meyer Jr. told Timothy Leary in the 1960s that "the CIA creates the radical journals and student organizations and runs them with deep-cover agents. Dissident organizations in academia are also controlled."[53] The Democratic Party itself has a long history going back to the late nineteenth century of creating astro-turf organizations and infiltrating left-wing groups to coopt them.[54] This strategy extends to alternative media outlets that echo Democratic Party talking points and support Democratic Party politicians from the left-end of the party's spectrum (like AOC, Bernie Sanders, etc.) who often support foreign military and regime-change operations under the guise of stopping human rights abuses.

Related to the second point, Kirkpatrick Sale, author of a landmark study of the Students for a Democratic Society (SDS), the dominant New Left organization of the 1960s, has emphasized that a rejection of authoritarian institutions and championing of participatory democracy and community empowerment was key to the New Left's political outlook.[55] Since Assad was an authoritarian leader, there was very little sympathy for him—much like with other targets of U.S. regime change (Gaddafi, Putin, Lukashenko, Kim Jong-un, etc.). There was also a tendency to cheer opposition movements that were seen to embody the New Left's liberatory spirit. While rejection of authoritarianism is admirable, a fatal flaw regarding Syria and some other countries is the development of an idealized viewpoint of opposition movements and failure to recognize their manipulation by predatory outside powers. Like everyone else across the political spectrum, leftists also often disregard how colonialism and neocolonialism stifled democratic development in countries like Syria, which require a strong state to avoid becoming Balkanized—the goal of U.S. foreign policy.

A key general weakness of the 1960s New Left movement was its turning away from the working class and embrace of identity politics.[56] A significant number of people who opposed the Vietnam War retreated from antiwar activism when the war was over. This stemmed in part from the 1960s era antiwar movement never having developed a political-economic analysis of U.S. imperialism that became broadly accepted. In the 1970s and 1980s, the concern for human rights abuses was effectively coopted by the State Department, which channeled liberal compassion towards victims—real or imagined—of governments targeted by the U.S. for regime change and in support of so-called "humanitarian intervention."[57] By the 1990s, many liberal intellectuals who had opposed the Vietnam War and were active in the New Left, supported the Clinton administration's bombing of Bosnia-Herzegovina and Kosovo on supposed humanitarian grounds.[58] They supported the latter 78-day bombing campaign despite the fact that it focused almost entirely on civilian and civilian infrastructure targets, as pointed out by then UN High Commissioner for Human Rights, Mary Robinson, who stated at that the time:

"[i]n the NATO bombing, . . . large numbers of civilians have incontestably been killed and civilian installations targeted on the grounds that they are or could be of military application."[59]

The same liberals who supported the bombing of Kosovo had by then abandoned past critiques of the CIA and other U.S. intelligence agencies. While opposing the Bush administration's war on Iraq, they became mesmerized by the rhetoric of Barack Obama and, unwilling to go against America's first Black president, supported disastrous military interventions in Afghanistan, Libya, Ukraine, Somalia, Uganda, Yemen, and Syria.[60] The opponents of these latter interventions started to come more and more from the right. With the Democratic Party becoming increasingly a party of war hawks, those who were leery of U.S. military intervention found themselves either in the political wilderness or wound up supporting Donald J. Trump, believing, naively, that he would end America's forever wars and reign in the "deep state."

The Rojava Fraud and U.S. Psywar

During the middle 2010s, a segment of the North American and European left expressed enthusiasm about the perceived development of a socialist egalitarian experiment in Rojava in Kurdish territory in Northern Syria. Leftists began making pilgrimages to Rojava and gushed over the adoption there of a "third way" between the tyranny of Assad and Islamic fundamentalists that had taken over the rebel movement.[61] Some leftists took up arms with Kurdish militias in Rojava to fight against ISIS, seeing themselves as akin to members of the Abraham Lincoln brigade that volunteered to fight fascism during the Spanish Civil War. Magazines featured glamorized portraits of female fighters and interviews with boyish North American anarchists who saw the Kurdish struggle in Syria as their generation's Spanish Civil War or somehow part of an anti-capitalist struggle.[62]

Kurdistan Workers Party (PKK) leader Abdullah Ocalan, who had been held for years in solitary confinement after his abduction by Turkey, was said to be inspired by the writings of Murray Bookchin, an anarchist thinker who emphasized the link between capitalism and environmental catastrophe and pushed for a reconfiguring of society through grassroots participation. The Rojavan revolution was also supposedly driven by women guerrilla fighters advancing a new feminist social order, with Rojava's constitution enshrining gender equality and religious freedom.[63]

According to a 2020 article on popularresistance.org, Rojava became "a place onto which European and American leftists could project anti-capitalist dreams and radical democratic illusions."[64] These leftists criticized "anti-imperialists" opposed to U.S. intervention in Syria for "avoiding the appearance of being on the same side as an imperialist in any context." David Graeber, a leader of the Occupy Wall Street movement and author of a book that looked to pre-modern societies as a preferable alternative to modern capitalist ones, wrote that "this attitude [of anti-imperialists] only makes sense if you've secretly decided that real revolutions are impossible. Because surely, if one actually felt that a genuine popular revolution was occurring, say in the city of Kobani [in Rojava], and that its success could be a beacon and example to the world, one would not also hold that it is better for all those revolutionaries to be massacred by genocidal fascists than for a bunch of rich white intellectuals to sully the purity of their reputations by suggesting that U.S. imperial forces already conducting airstrikes in the region might wish to direct their attention to the fascist tanks. Yet astoundingly, this was the position that a very large number of self-professed 'radicals' actually did take."[65]

While legitimately concerned about the plight of the Kurds and possibility of retribution being taken upon them, Graeber's position, like that of other leftist enthusiasts of the Rojava experiment, was problematic on numerous levels. First, the condescending attitude towards anti-imperialist intellectuals, whom Graeber assumes to be "rich" and "white," mimicked establishment efforts to denigrate them. Related to this, Graeber failed to recognize how Kurdish nationalist parties' decision to ally with U.S. imperialism represented a betrayal of the Kurdish people's struggle to obtain democratic and cultural rights and set the Kurdish people up for disaster.[66]

What was going on in Rojava was not generally as wonderful as Graeber and others made it seem. An analysis published on left.com accused Graeber and his comrades of relaying the propaganda of the Kurdish Democratic Union Party (PYD), an affiliate of the PKK which monopolized power in Kurdish-run territories in Iraq, Syria, and Turkey, and ruled in an authoritarian way, detaining and assassinating political opponents, firing on unarmed protesters, and conscripting child soldiers.[67] Amnesty International accused the YPG of committing "war crimes" by razing entire Arab villages as punishment for harboring ISIS fighters—a tactic once used by the Turkish government against the PKK.[68]

Additional reports highlighted ethnic cleansing operations of Arabs to make way for Kurdish arrivals from Turkey, reliance on black market petrol revenues, and a school curriculum that elevated Ocalan to almost god-like status. Women may have been somewhat freer in Kurdistan than in surrounding territories, but there were accusations of a rapist/sexist culture in the Kurdish Peshmerga.[69] Private property was further enshrined in the Rojava declaration, safeguarding the privileges of landowners who were encouraged to invest in agricultural projects sponsored by the Rojava authorities.[70] Alex Lantier wrote on the *World Socialist Website* that "Rojava was not a democratic haven but a garrison protected by U.S. troops. As has now been widely reported, it contained prison camps where over 11,000 people were imprisoned at the say-so of the imperialist powers, simply on suspicion of being Islamic State (IS) fighters."[71] These comments directly contradict Graeber's triumphalist account, which, among other things, avoided any discussion of class.

According to the left.com analyst, the 1871 Paris commune and Russian revolution were "a lot further down the road to real proletarian autonomy than what is being sold to us today in Rojava or anywhere else in Kurdistan."[72] Bill Rood, a 2022 candidate for Minnesota State Senate with the Legalize Cannabis Party, wrote that "Bookchin's ideas might be workable, even beneficial, in an environment where there is no regional hegemon attempting to lord it over all locales. That's not the situation in the Middle East, where Israel, European powers and Turkey have all long attempted to dominate. The only prospect Kurds, Assyrians, Arab Christians, Alawites and other minorities have of maintaining any amount of local control is by working together to keep the Syrian state strong. Assad is willing to give locales some autonomy, but he can't give Kurds more autonomy than other ethnic or religious minorities. That's not acceptable to PKK fanatics as long as they have the backing of the US and Israel."[73]

Leftist celebrants of the Rojava experiment ultimately helped weaken the potential growth of the antiwar movement in the U.S. regarding Syria and other ongoing military operations. Channeling political energy into support for something that existed only in their own fantasy, they failed to adequately assess how the U.S. was intent on using the Kurds as a battering ram against the Assad government and then discarding them, fitting the pattern of past CIA recruitment of ethnic minorities like the Hmong, Montagnards, Kachin, and Nicaragua's Mosquito Indians.[74] And as in the past, covert operations were financed through criminal activity, in this case, the selling of looted Syrian oil on the black market in Iraq.[75]

A.B. Abrams emphasizes in *World War in Syria: Global Conflict on Middle Eastern Battlefields* that Russian intervention in Syria "strengthened an already prevailing trend for the Western bloc to seek to work more directly with parties other than jihadist groups to achieve its ends in the country," including most notably "ethno-nationalist paramilitary groups from Syria's Kurdish minority, which sought autonomy from Damascus and had been active from the war's early stages defending Kurds from jihadist attacks."[76] The Obama administration came to see the Kurdish militias as the most "effective fighting force in Syria," and as such deployed Special Forces who helped to organize a unified Kurdish fighting force—the Syrian Democratic Forces (SDF)—that was openly hostile to Damascus. The Green Berets were led by General Christopher Donahue, a "star of the clandestine world of Special Forces," according to *The New York Times*, who had previously "hunted terrorist chiefs in the shadows of Iraq, Libya and Afghanistan" and went on to command murderous U.S.-Ukrainian operations in eastern Ukraine and Russia.[77]

Like their mainstream counterparts, leftist intellectuals were silent about the atrocities committed under Donahue's oversight—which ranged from kidnappings, ethnic cleansing, use of child soldiers and torture—as the U.S. used its growing support for the SDF to establish more of a foothold on Syrian soil.[78] The embedding of Special Forces within the SDF disguised what amounted to a U.S. invasion of Syria. The SDF even directly signed agreements with U.S. energy companies to allow for the exploitation of the Deir Ezzor oil fields.[79] Delusional belief in the creation of a utopian socialist experiment in the middle of a warzone led people who might have helped mobilize opposition to champion yet another "humanitarian intervention" whose real purpose was to destroy a nationalistic government that had resisted predatory outside powers.

The timing of the left's discovery of the Rojava experiment was all too convenient for U.S. psychological warfare operators who would use any trick to get segments of the U.S. left to support military intervention in Syria and even take up arms as over 100 mercenary volunteers for the SDF did.[80] If things in Rojava were so great, why hadn't leftists enthused about it and made pilgrimages earlier—before the period when the U.S. military began recruiting Kurdish militias to fight the Assad government and factions of ISIS it didn't support? Or after Assad's downfall in late 2024? As it stands, people like Graeber served as unwitting dupes for what has all the appearances of a U.S. intelligence/psywar operation. Special Forces deployed to Syria in support of the SDF significantly included psychological warfare teams.[81] Their targets included people in the West who knew so little about Syria they could believe almost anything they were told if the source had the appearance of being credible.

Tulsi Gabbard and Neo-McCarthyism

During the 2020 Democratic Party primary, Tulsi Gabbard was the lone antiwar candidate regarding Syria. She was mercilessly attacked by Hillary Clinton and Kamala Harris, who adopted the language of U.S intelligence in calling her an "Assad apologist" and Russian "favorite." Gabbard had criticized U.S. support for jihadists in Syria and how it compromised the waging of the War on Terror. Gabbard also met with Bashar al-Assad in an attempt to open channels for U.S. diplomacy with him and favored diplomacy with Vladimir Putin and the Russians. Gabbard was again attacked mercilessly when Donald Trump nominated her to be Director of National Intelligence. A group of National Security officials penned a letter directed to U.S. Senate Majority Leader Charles Schumer (D-NY) and Senate Majority Leader Elect John Thune (R-SD) claiming that she had "aligned herself with Russian and Syrian officials" and "sympathized with its dictatorial leaders" (Putin and al-Assad).[82]

Gabbard, however, had never lionized Assad but rather sought to better understand his perspective and find means of engaging in diplomacy with him so as to end the deadly conflict in Syria that the U.S. had helped trigger. Gabbard was accused in the letter of purveying "conspiracy theories" because she questioned the false claim that Assad had used chemical weapons against his own people. In seeking the truth, Gabbard met with MIT scientist Theodore Postol who carried out a detailed scientific study of the crime scene using sophisticated computer models that disputed official U.S. government claims.[83] Through these and other acts, Gabbard showed herself to be a responsible politician who wanted to find out the truth and advance diplomacy in the interests of world peace. She was attacked accordingly by the corrupt elements that were behind the U.S. regime change operation in Syria and other foreign policy interventions that have resulted in thousands upon thousands of deaths.

CHAPTER 11

Syria After the Western-backed Al Qaeda Triumph—As Witnessed by Dan Kovalik

> "American policy has very often been directed against
> movements that were essentially 'modernizing' . . .
> To defeat such progressive movements, Western powers have often
> supported the most feudal and obscurantist tendencies."
> –Jean Bricmont, *Humanitarian Imperialism*.

During her confirmation hearing for Director of National Intelligence on February 1, 2025, Tulsi Gabbard was grilled about having been a purveyor of "Putin's talking points" about the U.S. supporting Al Qaeda in Syria. Gabbard responded with a history lesson of sorts, noting that Russian involvement in Syria had been triggered by the CIA, which beginning under President Obama, carried out one of its most expensive regime-change programs termed "Operation Timber Sycamore"[1]—a $1 billion-a-year program which included the arming and funding of terrorist groups like Al Qaeda and ISIS to undermine the government of Bashar al-Assad.

Seymour Hersh wrote in *The New Yorker* magazine in 2007 that the U.S. began supporting such groups in Syria back in 2005 under President George W. Bush. Hersh's article was entitled, *The Redirection*—the title referring to Bush's having reversed course in having targeted Al Qaeda for destruction after 9/11 to supporting

Al Qaeda to undermine governments, such as the one in Syria, which challenged U.S. hegemony in Northern Africa and West Asia.[2]

The Western support for groups like Al Qaeda actually goes back nearly a century. Al Qaeda takes its inspiration from the Muslim Brotherhood which, as CIA officer Robert Baer has explained, has been the tool for the U.S. throughout its interventions in the Middle East going back to the 1950s.[3] As Stephen Gowans explains in his book, *Washington's Long War on Syria*, Baer insisted that it was more accurate to say that it was the Muslim Brotherhood who was behind the 9/11 attacks, and that it was "[t]he Brothers, cum Al Qaeda . . . [who] were the 'same crew' the United States used to do its 'dirty work in Yemen, Afghanistan, and plenty of other places,' countering secular leftist movements and governments."[4] In the 1980s holy war against the Soviet Union, one of the U.S.'s key allies in Afghanistan was Osama bin Laden who went on to create Al Qaeda. Bin Laden was inspired by the Muslim Brotherhood and appointed members of the Egyptian and Syrian Brotherhood to Al Qaeda's senior ranks.[5] And, it must be said that Britain has been backing the Muslim Brotherhood to undermine secular, nationalist states of the Middle East and Northern Africa—most famously against the secular government of Egyptian President Gamal Abdel Nasser—since the Brotherhood's very beginnings in Egypt in 1928.[6]

The U.S. and its Western partners have now reaped what they have sown for nearly 100 years with the Al Qaeda offshoot Hayat Tahrir al-Sham ("HTS") taking charge in Syria. Immediately after declaring himself president, Mohammed Al-Jolani scrapped the socially-progressive Constitution of 2012 and announced that there will be no elections forthcoming for at least four years and possibly five.[7] Replaying the Truman administration's behavior following the 1949 CIA backed coup, the Biden and Trump administrations raised no qualms about these and other antidemocratic measures because the HTS government served U.S. and Israeli geopolitical objectives, including by undermining the Palestinian cause.

According to the Arab Center, Washington D.C.,

> HTS's first big decision [after it took power] was to dissolve the Palestinian Liberation Army (PLA) and ask other factions to surrender their arms. Syria's new de facto president, Ahmed al-Sharaa, has since communicated that under his leadership, Syria will not serve as a base for launching attacks against neighbors and other nations and Syria will continue to adhere to its 1974 disengagement agreement with Israel.[8]

The Cradle reported in March 2025 how the HTS had frozen out the more radical Palestinian liberation groups, including Hamas, while cozying up to the Palestinian Authority (PA) which collaborates with Israel in maintaining its brutal occupation of the West Bank.[9]

The day after HTS forces entered Damascus, they launched a wave of closures targeting Palestinian faction offices. "Those belonging to Fatah al-Intifada, the Baath-aligned Al-Sa'iqa movement, and the PFLP-GC were shuttered, with their weapons, vehicles, and real estate seized. What followed was a systematic decapitation of the Palestinian factional structure in Syria."[10] Fatah al-Intifada's Secretary-General Abu Hazem Ziad al-Saghir was among those arrested and detained. The HTS essentially held al-Saghir hostage until Fatah al-Intifada paid $500,000 for his release, and al-Saghir was then deported to Lebanon. *The Cradle* went on to report that:

> The Palestinian Baathist faction, Al-Sa'iqa, fared no better. Its Secretary-General Muhammad Qais was interrogated and stripped of the group's assets. . . .

> HTS also clamped down hard on the PFLP-GC, whose Secretary-General, Talal Naji, was placed under house arrest and interrogated multiple times. All the group's offices, vehicles, and weapons were confiscated, their headquarters shuttered, and its members beaten and humiliated. Their radio station, Al-Quds Radio, was seized, and their Umayyah Hospital is reportedly next in line.[11]

As for the Nidal Front, a left-wing Palestinian liberation group, its Secretary-General, Khaled Abdul Majeed, was forced to resign by HTS, and all of his personal property, including his home, vehicles and $5,000 in cash, were seized.[12]

Very worrying, the HTS is now putting the fate of Syria's over half a million Palestinian refugees in grave doubt. "Of particular concern," *The Cradle* explains, "is a reported settlement proposal, conveyed through Turkish mediation. It allegedly offers Palestinians in Syria three options: Syrian naturalization, integration into a new PA-affiliated "community" under embassy supervision, or consular classification with annual residency renewals. The implicit fourth option is displacement, mirroring what happened to Palestinians in post-U.S. invasion Iraq."[13]

As of the time of this writing, the other great betrayal of the Palestinians that HTS may be offering to carry out for the West is aiding and abetting Israel's ethnic cleansing of Gaza, potentially doing something which even the vassal states of Egypt and Jordan refuse to do—allowing Israel to transfer hundreds of thousands of Palestinians out of Gaza and to Syria.[14] Certainly, both the U.S. and Israel are hopeful that the HTS will collaborate with this ethnic-cleansing project.[15]

The second goal which the new HTS regime is compliantly serving for the West is collaborating with Israel in its capturing of territory in both Syria and Lebanon in an apparent attempt to advance its Greater Israel project. Thus, the HTS has offered no resistance to Israel even as it was bombing Syria's military bases and destroying all of Syria's defenses just after the fall of Assad, and as Israel has been advancing deep into Syrian territory.[16]

In early May 2025 it was reported that "Israeli forces are about 24 kilometers away from Damascus and just ten kilometers away from Khan Eshieh Camp for Palestinian refugees."[17] HTS has also allowed Israel to build at least seven new military installations in Syria, including on Syria's Mt. Hermon (known in Arabic as Jabal al-Shaykh)—the highest point in all of Syria.[18] Lest one be led to believe that this seizure of land is merely temporary, the Syrian

The HTS government of Syria allowed Israel to build new military installations in Syria, including on Mount Hermon, Syria's highest mountain. Mount Hermon, as seen from South Lebanon. (Kovalik, 2025)

Interior Ministry has released a new map of Syria which no longer includes the Golan Heights, occupied by Israel since 1967, despite the fact that international law still recognizes this as Syrian territory.[19] This same new map also effectively cedes territory to Turkey in northern Syria known as Alexandretta.[20] Meanwhile, the U.S. continues to occupy about one-third of Syria, and this happens to be the most oil- and grain-rich area of the country.

As a friend in Damascus told us, the HTS is so deferential to Israel that it is now forbidding people from talking about the "Zionist entity" or "Occupied Palestine" publicly or in the media as was the custom for decades in Syria. Instead, people are required to refer to the "State of Israel." As the friend lamented, she is so ashamed that now Syrians must recognize the State of Israel if they speak publicly—something they used to be taught in schools never to do.

While the HTS regime can be said to be passively allowing Israel to take over huge swaths of Syria, it is quite actively assisting

Israel in its take-over of Lebanon.. Thus, HTS forces have been engaged in numerous incursions into northern Lebanon, clashing with armed Lebanese citizens defending their country and land, as Israel has provided air cover for these raids.[21] Meanwhile, these HTS attacks themselves have provided a safety valve for Israel in South Lebanon as it continues to occupy land and homes there. Now, should a full-scale war be visited upon Lebanon again, Lebanese forces, including and especially Hezbollah, will now be forced to defend the country from the north as well as the South, leaving Lebanon incredibly vulnerable.

In addition to all this, the HTS regime gave tacit sanction for Israel's bombing of Iran in June 2025, which resulted in the death of top Iranian military commanders and scientists along with an estimated 200 civilians in the first few days. *The New York Times* reported that while most Arab leaders denounced the Israeli strikes as "heinous attacks" and "violations of international law," Syria remained noticeably silent. According to the *Times*: "the decision by Syria's new government, led by President Ahmed al-Shara, to remain silent is a sign of just how much the geopolitical sands have shifted in the country since rebels toppled the Assad regime in December [ie. the U.S. regime change operation]."[22] What's more, Syria is actually allowing Israel to use its airspace to attack Iran, something unthinkable under the Assad government.[23]

The third goal of the West, which HTS quickly advanced, was destroying the left opposition within Syria as well as the progressive social policies of the Assad government. Thus, the new regime in Damascus outlawed opposition parties, such as the Baath Party (the former governing party) as well as both Communist Parties of Syria. For its part, the banned Syrian Communist Party (Bakdash) put out a statement denouncing the new regime, writing, in part:

> Since seizing power in our homeland Syria on December 8, 2024, as a result of a military attack fully supported by colonial powers that are members of the aggressive NATO, the dark clique has begun to

restrict the social rights of the people. Tens of thousands of workers in the state and public sector facilities have been laid off, with many of these facilities being liquidated, which has led to a worsening of the economic and social situation. In addition, discrimination between citizens on the basis of their beliefs and affiliations is escalating. Kidnappings and assassinations have taken place and are taking place, accompanied by theft, looting and extortion.[24]

As referenced at the end of this statement, the other task the new regime quickly turned its attention to was pursuing its long-standing goal of setting up a religious Caliphate in Syria. An integral part of this plan is to violently eliminate religious groups and sects that the HTS extremists see as infidels or apostates.

The U.S. Department of Defense Intelligence (DDI) had stated truthfully back in 2012 that the goal of creating a religious Caliphate was in fact the ultimate intention of Al Qaeda—the group which the DDI acknowledged was being backed by the collective West.[25] Now, the Office of the U.S. Director of National Intelligence (DNI)—that is, of Tulsi Gabbard—is acknowledging that what the DDI had said back then has become a reality with the triumph of HTS. As the DNI stated in a worldwide terror assessment released on March 18, 2025:

The fall of President Bashar al-Assad's regime at the hands of opposition forces led by Hay'at Tahrir al-Sham (HTS)—a group formerly associated with al-Qaʻida—has created conditions for extended instability in Syria and could contribute to a resurgence of ISIS and other Islamist terror groups. . . .

• The HTS-led interim government forces, along with elements of Hurras al-Din and other jihadist groups, engaged in violence and extrajudicial killings in northwestern Syria in early March 2025 primarily targeting religious minorities that resulted in the death of more than 1,000 people, including Alawi and Christian civilians.

• The leader of HTS claims to be willing to work with Syria's array of ethnosectarian groups to develop an inclusive governance model. Many of these groups remain skeptical of HTS's intentions, especially considering the leader's past al-Qaʿida association, suggesting protracted negotiations could devolve into violence.[26]

Mission accomplished, then. And, with the goal of overthrowing Assad accomplished, the U.S. had no more use for the White Helmets and their anti-Assad propaganda. And, so, in March of 2025, the Trump Administration cut off nearly all the funding amounting to $30 million—for this organization.[27]

While the DNI is essentially correct in its analysis of the situation in Syria, it is wrong about one important fact—the number of people killed by HTS since it took power in December of 2024. Between March 7, 2025—when the mass slaughter began in earnest—and March 30, 2025 alone, there are estimates of as many as 50,000 killed under the new HTS government.[28] No less a person than Israel's Defense Minister Israel Katz said in March that "Jolani (Sharaa) took off his galabiya (robe), put on a suit, and presented a moderate face—now he has removed the mask and revealed his true identity: a jihadist terrorist from the Al-Qaida school, committing atrocities against the civilian population."[29]

These atrocities have been specially directed against the Alawite community. Journalist Pamela Geller wrote:

> What is happening in the Syrian coast against the Alawite community amounts to genocide in all its forms: physical, biological, cultural, economic, and political.
>
> Hayat Tahrir al-Sham, led by al-Jolani, is carrying out systematic extermination practices including:
>
> – Mass executions and field killings with tens of thousands of victims, including women, children, and the elderly
> – Arbitrary detention of more than 30,000 Alawites subjected to torture in al-Jolani's prisons
> – Daily kidnappings, especially targeting women
> – Destruction of religious shrines and prohibition of religious practices
> – Economic marginalization, dismissal from jobs, assassination of academic elites, and shutting down service institutions.[30]

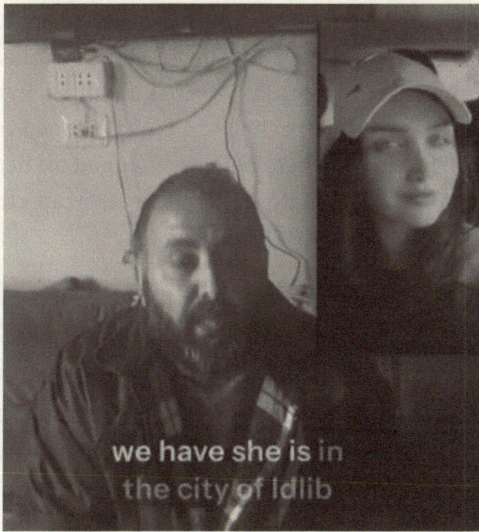

The HTS has kidnapped many people and has
targeted women. Here a husband
begs for return of his wife taken to Idlib.
(Kovalik, 2025)

As for the kidnappings of women—and it is mostly young, professional women—it is believed, as one Alawite friend on the coast explained, that these women are being brought to Idlib where they are being held as sex slaves. As my friend told me just this morning, "I document kidnappings. Yesterday, I received news of a girl who had been kidnapped. Her family knew that she was in Idlib and had been raped and tortured."

The online news service *21st Century Wire*, in an article reporting on the genocide against both Alawites and Christians, contained the following passage:

The fate of women

Between December 2024 and today, dozens of women have been targeted for kidnappings. Some were later found murdered and mutilated, including Professor Rasha al-Ali from Homs University. Videos show Alawite and Christian women being abducted.

One survivor reported 70 women taken from her village alone. Local media estimated over 100 professional women—including doctors, engineers, and teachers—were kidnapped in just two days. There are widespread fears that some of these women may have been trafficked to Idlib, where HTS has reigned for nearly a decade, and that a market for female slaves or organ trafficking may now exist, similar to practices under ISIS.[31]

When I visited Syria at the end of January of 2025, I met an Alawite woman living in Damascus. This individual, who I will call Elizabeth, was quite afraid for her safety, and quite reasonably so. Elizabeth's friend, a University Professor, had recently been kidnapped and killed. Tim Anderson, on Twitter, described what happened to this Professor:

Free Syria. Body of University Researcher Found After HTS Abduction.

Days after her abduction by HTS, the body of Dr. Rasha Al-Ali was discovered, bearing signs of brutal treatment, including the amputation of her fingers. Dr. Rasha, a respected university researcher and a member of the Arab Writers Union, was a prominent intellectual voice. Her crime ... criticism of wearing the Niqab on campus.

Her killing underscores the growing dangers faced by academics and intellectuals in the region, as well as the alarming rise in sectarian and targeted violence. This tragic loss highlights the need for immediate attention to the safety and protection of Syria's minority and intellectual communities.[32]

Shortly after this incident, Elizabeth herself just escaped being kidnapped. Elizabeth, a university instructor, was asked by a student to meet off-campus. Just before this meeting happened, however, other students warned her not to go, explaining that this was a ploy to kidnap her. While Elizabeth remains in Syria, she is considering leaving the country.

Elizabeth wrote to me later about another atrocity committed by extremists linked to the new HTS government. Thus, she wrote to me about a twenty-two-year-old woman named Nagam Issa who had been kidnapped in Homs while visiting a clinic for a pregnancy check-up. Her dead body, showing signs of torture, was found later, lying next to the body of another young woman. The kidnapping and death of Nagam were publicized on Facebook in a post which Elizabeth sent to me. According to this post, originally written in Arabic, "The primary suspect in the crime of kidnapping Mrs. 'Nagam Issa' is one of the terrorists and leaders of the armed sectarian factions belonging to the dirty Golani terrorist called Jassim Abu Moawya from Tklakh in the Homs countryside. This dirty sectarian terrorist continuously abducts and carries out armed attacks upon the people in the surrounding villages either to kill or to intimidate civilians, and he has documented and published these crimes. The last massacre committed by this sectarian savage was days ago . . .."[33]

The epicenter of the violence in Syria after Assad's ouster began in Homs. As *The Cradle* reported on January 29, 2025, "the western countryside of Homs has been gripped by a brutal security campaign marked by grave human rights violations, including field executions, looting, public humiliation, sectarian insults, and indiscriminate arrests. These atrocities were carried out by the interim government's Military Operations Department under the pretext of searching for wanted individuals and seizing weapons, but the campaign swiftly descended into lawlessness."[34]

According to one of my friends in Homs, "we are not happy with our lives. Our lives have been turned upside down. No work. No security. Kidnapping. Killing everywhere. The biggest problem is that what is happening is based on hatred for Alawites. We are being killed because we are Alawites." This is a common sentiment of Alawites throughout Syria. The new, self-proclaimed President of Syria, al-Jolani, seemed to publicly endorse the sectarian killings early on, stating in late January 2025, that the violence against certain minority groups such as Alawites and Christians—violence he initially tried to distance himself from—is "normal and may continue for two or three years."[35]

I visited Syria in the latter part of January 2025 to see for myself what Syria was like under the new regime. I had something to compare this to as I had visited Syria twice back in 2021 which it was still under the leadership of Basher al-Assad. In 2021, Syria was experiencing relative peace due to an uneasy ceasefire agreement between the Assad government and the anti-government forces allowed to continue existing and operating in the northwest province of Idlib under Turkish protection. I met and interviewed a number of people while in Syria. Of course, there was a diversity of opinion as there always would be in such a large and diverse society. Some people were hopeful that things could change for the better now, especially if the economic sanctions are lifted from Syria and the country is allowed to rebuild what was destroyed during the war—the prevention of such reconstruction being an intended goal of the sanctions.[36]

Indeed, almost everyone is unanimous that they are desperate to see the sanctions lifted and for economic life to return to the country. This makes eminent sense. The entire country remains devastated from the brutal war. Contamination from land mines and explosive remnants has killed at least 249 people, including 60 children, and injured another 379 since December 8, according to INSO, an international organization which coordinates safety for aid workers.[37] Center City Damascus, while spared the worst of the damage from the war, is still in bad shape, suffering as it is from dilapidated infrastructure and buildings. Other towns like Jobar, which I visited, resemble the bombed-out city of Dresden right after World War II. A recent article describes the devastation which remains in Syria after the war:

> Syria's infrastructure is so deteriorated that basic services are woefully insufficient for those who are there now—much less for a large influx of returning refugees. A decade and a half of warfare has damaged 23 percent of the total housing stock, especially where the fighting was most intense, and thus where many of the refugees lived. The education system is in shambles, with 2.4 million children not attending classes and heavily damaged school infra-

structure. Only slightly more than half of Syria's hospitals are fully functioning. And in addition to the refugees outside the country, more than 7 million Syrians are internally displaced.[38]

Meanwhile, an ever-growing number Syrians are not so hopeful for the future under HTS. One Christian cleric I interviewed, Monsignor Youhanna Jihad Battah of the Syrian Archevêque Syriac Catholic Church, spoke for a lot of people when he told me, "before, we had a dictatorship; now, we have something worse—a government run by extremists." He stated that "in my opinion, the U.S. brought us HTS, and they can take them back." His view was that what happened with the HTS takeover of Syria could not be termed a "revolution," for it was not an organic rising of the people. Rather, it was the triumph of a group funded and supported from the outside of Syria, made up in significant part of foreign fighters and based in only one part of the country—Idlib. This, in short, is not a group which can purport to represent the Syrian people.

Something must be said about Idlib here because it reflects on the very nature of Assad and his government. Assad made himself and his government vulnerable by allowing Idlib to exist for years as a hotbed of terrorists. Thus, as part of a 2020 agreement brokered between Russia and Turkey, which led to a ceasefire between the belligerents, but no lasting peace accord, a large portion of Idlib continued to be occupied by Turkey (which had taken this Syrian territory through force) and the terrorist groups within that territory that Turkey has been sponsoring.[39] The portion of Idlib controlled by Turkey became a state-within-a-state, controlled by groups like HTS which set up a mini-Caliphate there. As journalist Max Blumenthal commented, before HTS and other terrorist groups took over Idlib, the city was colorful, with the residents allowed to wear clothes of different hues. But once HTS and its allies set up its Caliphate, everyone was forced to wear black, and all of the women were forced to wear full burkas.

Meanwhile, HTS was allowed to grow in strength, re-arm, and recruit, and was finally able to capture Damascus in December of 2024 with little resistance. The point here is that few governments would have allowed such a situation—a veritable ticking time bomb—to exist in their own territory. Rather, a government like that of the U.S. or Israel, and many others for that matter, would have bombed the area to smithereens if it meant preserving the State and the country from an imminent terrorist threat. Assad never did that. Instead, far from being the blood-thirsty monster he has been portrayed to be, he showed great restraint and mercy—as he had done before by granting amnesties on at least three prior occasions.[40] In the end, though, this proved fatal to both his rule and to Syria itself.

What about Monsignor Battah's reference to the Assad government as a "dictatorship"? In some ways, this was true, and it indeed became more true *in response* to the extraordinary attempts of many nations, backing terrorist groups, to overthrow it. But this was to be expected, and indeed, it was one key tactic of the regime-change operations—to provoke state repression, which could then be pointed to as a justification for these very operations. But what might have happened if Assad had been allowed to govern unmolested? He may have been able to create a more open and democratic society as he seemed to be trying to do just before the war against him began. Indeed, as my Syrian American friend Johnny Achi, who led our trip to Syria in May of 2021, explained, Assad began loosening the reigns of the internal intelligence services in 2010, much to the joy of Syrian people. However, many Syrians, like himself, would soon come to regret this given what dark forces this allowed to emerge within the country.

Jean Bricmont, in his profound *Humanitarian Imperialism: Using Human Rights to Promote War*, makes this very point in regard to a number of nationalist and socialist movements in the Global South:

The same type of reflection applies to most formerly colonized countries. There is no telling what would have become of Algeria, Vietnam, Korea, China, the Middle East, without the destruction of war, the imposed opium trade, the occupation of Palestine, the

Sykes-Pico Accords, Suez, etc. Revolutionary violence can repeatedly be shown to the product rather than the cause of counter-revolutionary violence, as well as of long-standing oppression by traditional ruling classes and foreign invasions.

Moreover, if it is true, as often said, that most socialist regimes turn out to be dictatorships, that is largely because a dictatorship is much harder to overthrow or subvert than a democracy. It follows that the repeated assaults by the Western ruling classes against every form of socialism have provoked a sort of artificial selection that allows only dictatorial forms to survive.[41]

And indeed, Bricmont gives the example of Syria in the 1950s as compared to Iran under the rule of the very democratic and benign (indeed, it could be said, weak) Prime Minister Mohammad Mossadegh. As Bricmont explains, "[a]fter successfully ousting the democratically elected Mossadegh from power in Iran, the CIA agent Kermit Roosevelt tried to mount a similar putsch in Syria, but failed because Syria was already a dictatorship. Castro has survived in Cuba long after the fall of Allende in Chile."[42]

The colonial mindset underlying regime change operations is consistently judging foreign leaders by some idealized Western standard while presenting them to the public in caricatured terms. In reality, Assad like other leaders worldwide has many layers of complexity about him, both major accomplishments and deficiencies, but it is ultimately for Syrians to judge the degree to which he was a good or bad leader for their country. Monsignor Battah was among those to complain to us that he was disturbed how the misdeeds of the Assad government had been exaggerated, or even falsified, to provide *post hoc* justification for the takeover of HTS. The big lie he and others pointed to was that revolving around Sednaya Prison—the main focus of the mainstream press after the fall of Assad. As he and others explained, the media made up grotesque falsehoods about the prison—for example, claiming that tools used in the workshop there were in fact instruments of torture. One individual told me that they in fact knew someone who was imprisoned there, they believed quite wrongly. This person, upon being released thanks to a public campaign against his imprisonment, categorically denied that torture was happening in that prison.

As the great political thinker and philosopher, Michael Parenti, opined in 2013, after the first alleged chemical attack in Syria—the details of which he found quite suspect—it was precisely because of what Assad was doing for his people (rather than for Syria's would-be colonial masters), which led the West to want to get rid of him:

> Why do (some) U.S. leaders seek war against Syria? Like Yugoslavia, Iraq, Libya and dozens of other countries that have felt America's terrible swift sword—Syria has been committing economic nationalism, trying to chart its own course rather than putting itself in service to the western plutocracy. Like Iran, China, Russia and some other nations, Syria has currency controls and other restrictions on foreign investments. Like those other nations, Syria lacks the proper submissiveness. It is not a satellite to the U.S. imperium. And any nation that is not under the politico-economic sway of the U.S. global plutocracy is considered an enemy or a potential enemy.

> The Assad government had social programs for its people, far from perfect services but still better than what might be found in many U.S. satellite countries. When Iraqi refugees fled to Syria to escape U.S. military destruction, the Assad government gave them full benefits. So with the Libyan refugees who crossed over a few years later. Generally Damascus presided over a multi-ethnic society, relatively free of sectarian intolerance and violence.[43]

That is, the West disliked Assad precisely because of his positive attributes as a leader of Syria as opposed to his bad. However, as to the true, dark nature of those Assad was trying to keep out of Syria, Parenti had no doubt: "The 'Syrian freedom fighters' include men who are not even Syrian, much like the many mujahedeen who fought the Soviets in Afghanistan but who were not Afghani." As reported in the *Wall Street Journal* (September 19, 2013), the ISIS, an Iraqi Al Qaeda outfit operating in Syria, "has become a magnet for foreign jihadists" who view the war in Syria not primarily as a means to overthrow Assad "but rather as a historic battleground for a larger Sunni holy war. According to centuries-old Islamic prophecy they espouse, they must establish an Islamic state in Syria as a step to achieving a global one."[44]

The Islamic State is well on its way to being created. In addition to the genocide against the Alawite community, Christians are now under attack in Syria by the new regime, and Christians make up a portion of the tens of thousands of people killed by HTS and aligned armed groups in Syria. Indeed, the assault on Christians began swiftly. Thus, "[b]etween 8 and 25 December alone, the Salafi extremist groups attacked churches, raided Christian villages, fired on religious symbols, and killed shrine caretakers" throughout Syria.[45] In addition, some "Christian neighborhoods in Damascus have started paying money (jizya) to General Security (jihadi gangs) so that their neighborhoods are not exposed to their provocations and violations."[46]

One town which is not faring well after the HTS takeover is Maaloula—one of the last cities in the world where people still speak Aramaic, the language of Jesus. Maaloula has been home to many Christians and is the site of some of the oldest Christian Churches in the world. I visited Maaloula twice back in 2021, and I was awe-struck by the beauty and almost story-book nature of this town built into the stone mountains. I visited Maaloula for a third time on this recent trip to Syria. The first thing which struck me was that Maaloula seemed like a ghost town, with no cars on the street and nearly no visitors to the historic churches. This was contrasted with my first two trips in which the churches were teeming with pilgrims and the town seemed to be vibrant and full of activity.

Maaloula had been attacked back in 2013 by a number of terrorist groups, including the Al-Nusra Front—an Al Qaeda affiliate which was the predecessor of HTS and founded and led back then by none other than al-Jolani. These terrorists violently assaulted the churches and destroyed ancient religious icons and antiquities, including the tomb of Saint Thecla—the namesake of

The forerunners of the governing HTS attacked churches.
A Nun of the Convenant of Saint Thecla tells of her
kidnapping by terrorists. (Kovalik, 2021)

the historic Convent there. These same terrorists also kidnapped
the nuns of the Covenant of Saint Thecla. One of the nuns told
us of these events in my first trips to the Convent. Ultimately, it
was the Syrian Army, with the help of Hezbollah, which drove the
terrorists out of Maaloula.

The Christian residents of the town now live in fear as some of
the same people who terrorized the town are now in charge of the
country. As one priest who I interviewed there during my most
recent trip explained, over fifty Christian families (out of a total
of 325) have fled Maaloula for Damascus since the HTS takeover.
Other families have fled Syria altogether. This priest was uncertain
as to whether these families would ever return given the lack of a
sense of security in Maaloula. I talked to one individual who, when
they were alone with me for a moment, looked at me, shook their
head, and told me that things are terrible in Maaloula now. This
individual was obviously reluctant to talk to me in the presence
of the other individuals accompanying me. This individual too is
trying to get out of Maaloula, and out of Syria altogether.

An article by the Catholic News Agency (CNA) estimates that eighty Christian families (or about a quarter of the total) have fled Maaloula since HTS toppled the Assad government. As this article explained,

> A church source, speaking . . . on condition of anonymity, said that after former President Bashar al-Assad's regime regained control of Maaloula about 10 years ago, it prohibited some Muslims from entering the town due to their collaboration with the Al-Nusra Front in carrying out killings, kidnappings, and acts of vandalism targeting Christians and their churches. But following the regime's collapse, these individuals returned to the town, exerting pressure on Christians under the pretext that Christians had displaced them.

> "Some of those who had been expelled caused problems, and Christians were viewed as aligned with the previous regime," the source explained.[47]

As CNA further related, "Regarding the recent attacks on Christians, the source shared that threats began against five Christian families to seize their agricultural lands. Some Christians were also told to leave their homes and the town or they would face death. . . . These threats turned into action when the home and café of Bashar Shahin and his family were seized, despite some Muslims defending them. After mediation, Bashar was allowed to retrieve his belongings. Additionally, two homes were broken into and robbed. There were other forms of harassment as well, such as gunfire near a priest distributing Christmas gifts to children at a kindergarten, and reports from Christians about being spat on.'" As CNA further related, Christians in Maaloula have been left defenseless as the new HTS government took away all their weapons after gaining power.

* * *

While there are certainly reasons to despair over the fate of Syria which has been subjected to foreign takeover and Balkanization along sectarian lines—indeed, a number of Alawite leaders are expressing the view that an Alawite enclave within Syria may be their only option for survival—none of this is inevitable or preordained. Currently, there is a growing armed resistance, which is opposed to HTS and in favor of preserving Syria's national integrity as well as its religious and ethnic pluralism. This resistance is already busy defending the Syrian homeland.

As an article in the pro-Resistance source, the *Islamic World News*, explains, "[a]t the beginning of the year [2025], according to the Gregorian calendar, the 'Islamic Front of Syria' made itself felt when it claimed responsibility for the shelling of Zionist invaders near Deraa and Quneitra."[48] This same source predicts that the Islamic Front of Syria, a coalition of different Syrian and even Palestinian groups throughout Syria, will grow in response to the Israeli expansion in southern Syria. With Israel at the gates of Damascus, this Front, which has the potential of absorbing thousands of former members of the Syrian Arab Army who lay in wait in Syria and also Iraq, will not stand idly by and allow the takeover of Syria. And the Front will have the support of both Iran and Hezbollah to grow and fight. As the article concludes, "[r]egardless of the political future of Syria, the foundation of the anti-Zionist struggle has already been laid and it does not matter what kind of Syria will be (Takfiri dictatorship, democratic republic or fragmented quasi-state), the Islamic Resistance will gain momentum."

A question remains as to how the U.S. will respond to renewed outbreak of civil war in Syria and how much support the Trump administration will extend to an Islamist government that even the compliant U.S. media is having difficulty spinning as some kind of democratic beacon. Very likely, the U.S. will adopt the same model that it adopted during the regime-change campaign to topple Bashar-al-Assad chronicled in this book—covert operations, bombing, economic warfare and a propaganda offensive targeting Syria's liberators who will be branded as the next wave of terrorists the U.S. has to confront. The U.S. in turn will continue to supply arms and moral encouragement to its Israeli proxy as it brutalizes yet another of its neighbors. History, however, goes in cycles and the long-term likelihood of success of U.S. policy in Syria—as defined by the U.S. ruling elite—is extremely low. This is because the Syrian people will not tolerate a murderous government like the one that the U.S. has helped to install and because the age of colonialism is viewed widely as a relic of the past.

Epilogue

Hopefully readers of this book will have a better understanding of the complexities of Syrian politics and devastating consequences of U.S. and allied foreign intervention in Syria. Readers can further now be more alert to an ongoing regime-change operation and how propaganda and psychological warfare is crucial to carrying it out. The Syria case shows how a significant role is reserved in these operations for liberal and socialist intellectuals identified as being on the left who help cloak intervention under a humanitarian veneer and function as gatekeepers by ridiculing and helping to ostracize independent observers that puncture the mythological narrative underlying the regime change operation. The latter is crucial in preventing the growth of an effective opposition movement, which never emerged in the Syrian case.

The Syria case helps unravel the moral bankruptcy of the liberal human rights movement, which completely abandoned any commitment to the UN Charter and its emphasis on upholding nation's rights to self-determination and sovereignty under the belief that the U.S. state had to be mobilized against human rights violations and genocide. Progressives who subscribed to this view made the same mistake as their counterparts in World War I who naively believed that the state could be a moral agent and that military or covert intervention could yield democratic outcomes. The Syrian people now living under the grip of a brutal Islamic dictatorship that is allowing the country to be carved up by neighboring powers (notably Turkey and Israel) are the ones paying the ultimate price, including especially Alawites being targeted in ethnic pogroms.

Syria: Anatomy of Regime Change has detailed the real geo-strategic imperative underlying U.S. intervention in Syria dating back to the 1940s. This imperative has centered on a desire for construction of an oil pipeline running through Syria that can help enhance Western access to Middle Eastern oil and undercut the Russian oil industry. U.S imperial strategists have also long aimed to weaken and dismember a crucial Middle-Eastern nation at the heart of the Pan-Arabist movement since the Baath Party's triumph in the late 1950s. Additionally, Syria has been a staunch supporter of the Palestinian resistance, which the U.S. has long wanted to crush in order to allow for its regional pitbull, Israel, to expand its power. Syria under Assad was further a close ally of Iran, the final target of regime change in the post 9/11 neoconservative playbook. It is not surprising that a mere six months after Assad's removal, the U.S. and Israelis began bombing Tehran in an unprovoked aggression that threatens to draw the Russians and Chinese into World War III.

Because the real strategic designs underlying U.S. policy cannot be expressed publicly, the U.S. power elite relied heavily on the liberal intelligentsia to package the U.S. intervention in Syria as a humanitarian undertaking. The U.S. ruling elite at the same time had to carry out its dirty work covertly in a way that would distance the public from the brutality of the operations on the ground. If more U.S. personnel had been directly involved in Syria, then more Americans would have begun asking critical questions of what was really going on and may have started to raise hell about it, as they have done with other misbegotten policies.

Building off the precedent established with the secret war in Laos during the 1960s and 1970s, the Obama, Trump, and Biden administrations proved to be adept in adopting a light footprint approach that relied heavily on what the CIA used to call "Third Country Nationals" along with Special Forces and CIA operatives who coordinated the Timber Sycamore arms supply and terrorist training operation. This latter operation was comparable in many ways to Iran-Contra—including in the reliance on mafia liaisons who provided the weapons, and venality of the forces being supplied. However, there was no plane crash or whistleblower that spoke out to expose the criminal activity and very few journalistic investigations, ensuring that public attention was turned away.

Over the years, the U.S. ruling class has come to see the value not only of covert operations but also sanctions, which in the Syria case proved to be politically effective. This effectiveness was contingent on the horrific social and economic costs, which demoralized the Syrian population and reduced their willingness and ability to fight to save their country. The threat of protests breaking out within the U.S. against the cruel measures was mitigated by a reliance on the media and intellectual classes to spin it in a way that blamed Assad for the suffering of his own population.

In an article on the *World Socialist Website* in 2013, Alex Lantier wrote that Western intervention had thrust Syria back to the colonial era of the early twentieth century when French troops and proxy forces maintained French control of Syria by setting Christians, Druze, Sunni, Alawite, and other Syrians against each other. Now again, foreign powers seeking to plunder Syria's oil and take over its land are helping to inflame sectarian divisions and are pitting Syrians against one another as part of the game of divide and conquer.[1] When President Trump visited the Middle East in May 2025, he fittingly announced that in exchange for lifting sanctions, the al-Jolani government would offer Trump what the U.S. has wanted all along—Syria's oil and natural gas and the normalization of relations with Israel, along with the opportunity for U.S. companies to carry out the massive rebuilding needed as a result of the U.S.-led war against Syria.[2] As *Drop Site News* succinctly summarizes, "Syria would invite American companies to exploit the nation's oil and gas resources, and would work with American companies on reconstruction projects."[3] As a bonus, al-Jolani threw in an offer to build a Trump Tower in Damascus. The unholy deal was sealed in Riyadh with a handshake between Trump and al-Jolani, a man who was wanted by the U.S. for terrorism not long before.[4] As a downpayment, al-Jolani jailed leaders of the Palestinian resistance group, Islamic Jihad, in Syria shortly before the meeting with Trump.[5]

While the lifting of sanctions against Syria is certainly a humane and welcome act in many ways, the timing of this decision does not bode well for the Syrian minorities who continue to be attacked, killed, kidnapped, and raped by the new regime in Damascus. On April 20, 2025, *The New York Times* reported on the regime-backed violence against the Alawite community in the town of Baniyas in the governorate of Tartus on Syria's Mediterranean Coast. Journalist Christina Goldbaum wrote about armed men opening fire in the streets and going house to house, summarily executing civilians, 1,600 of whom were massacred. According to Goldbaum, "[m]any of those killed in Baniyas were buried in a mass grave under the supervision of government security personnel, according to residents who were at the burials as well as photographs and videos of the site verified by *The Times*. The new Syrian authorities effectively sealed off the region to foreign reporters as the violence unfolded, forcing us to leave the city."[6]

At the time of the massacre, the kidnapping of minority women and girls was continuing unabated. On April 18, 2025, the Syria Human Rights Observatory issued a report, entitled aptly "Absence of Law Deterrence," stating that at least fifty Alawite women had gone missing since the beginning of 2025. The most recent victims were from the village of Al-Mashrafa in eastern Homs countryside, where a young woman named Noor Kamal Khader (twenty-six years old) and her daughters, Naya (five years old) and Massa (three years old), went missing while walking to visit a friend's house. Evidence emerged to indicate that those Alawite women and girls were among those brought to Idlib and sold into sexual slavery.[7]

Despite the horrific nature of these crimes—which were on par if not far worse than those that Assad was accused of (Assad was never accused of taking child sex slaves)—the antiwar movement and progressive "left" did not mount any vociferous condemnations or protests directed against Trump's normalization policy with Syria or call for any new regime change operation, as they had done against Assad. When there is oil for the taking, such trifles as concerns about terrorism and human rights are generally thrown out the window. Al Qaeda, at one time the sworn enemy of the U.S., is now our friend. And indeed, the Western powers are currently using Al Qaeda in another theater—Burkina Faso—to try to engage in yet another coup operation against another government, that of revolutionary Ibrahim Traoré, who has incensed Western leaders by insisting on using his country's resources for his own people.[8] We pray that this will not be the subject of another study of regime change with as cataclysmic results as the one just consummated in Syria.

Notes

Introduction

1. Sawsan Madina, "The Carving Up of Syria," December 12, 2024, https://john-menadue.com/the-carving-up-of-syria/

2. Thomas L. Friedman, "Whatever Happens in Syria Will Not Stay in Syria," *The New York Times*, December 15, 2024, B4.

3. Mike Whitney, "Black Flag Over Damascus," *The Unz Review*, December 8, 2024; Jonathan Cook, "Syria's Assad Has Fallen—Just as the Pentagon Planned 23 Years Ago," jonathancook.substack.com. December 11, 2024.

4. Mostafa Salem, "How Syria's rebel leader went from radical jihadist to a blazer-wearing 'revolutionary'" *CNN*, December 8, 2024; Timour Azhari and Humeyra Pamuk, "Trump Tower Damascus? Syria Seeks to Charm US President for Sanctions Relief," *Reuters*, May 12, 2025.

5. https://en.wikipedia.org/wiki/Abu_Mohammad_al-Julani; https://www.winterwatch.net/2024/12/who-is-the-mossad-impostor-mole-mohammed-al-julani/. U.S. military prisons have a long history of torture and brainwashing. According to Wikipedia, Al-Jolani was "appreciative of the 9/11 attacks." He was a close associate of Abu Musab Al-Zarqawi, head of Al Qaeda in Iraq who was killed by U.S. forces in June 2006. Researcher Russ Winter raises questions as to where Jolani, just released from U.S. military prison, got the money to travel to Syria to support the uprising against Al-Assad. https://www.winterwatch.net/2024/12/who-is-the-mossad-impostor-mole-mohammed-al-julani/

6. Al-Jolani has admitted to being part of Al Qaeda but said that this was merely a "phase" in his career that he had outgrown. Salem, "How Syria's rebel leader went from radical jihadist to a blazer-wearing 'revolutionary.'"

7. Edward Hunt, "U.S. Officials Take Credit For Regime Change in Syria," *Foreign Policy in Focus*, December 17, 2024.

8. John Browden, "Biden Promises to Bring US Journalist Austin Tice Home as he calls fall of Assad a 'moment of historic opportunity for Syria,'" *The Independent*, December 8, 2024.

9. See as example, Jared Malsin, "'Executed, Executed, Dead From Sickness': The Grim Records From Syria's Notorious Prison; Search for loved ones in jail that hanged up to 50 people a day reopens wounds for families," *The Wall Street Journal*, December 12, 2024; Ed Caesar, "How Syria Became the Middle East's Drug Dealer," *The New Yorker*, November 4, 2024; Aryn Baker, "What is

Captagon, the Illegal Stimulant That Made al-Assad's Syria a Narco-State," *The New York Times*, December 13, 2024; Jared Downing, "Bashar Al-Assad's private fleet of luxury cars revealed as Syrians loot his palaces after dictator was forced to flee the country," *The New York Post*, December 8, 2024. The Post report is contradicted by the assessment of Trinity University professor David W. Lesch, who reported in his book *Syria: The Fall of the House of Assad* (New Haven: Yale University Press, 2012), 52 that there were no reports in Wikileaks about Assad's extravagant lifestyle—like other Arab leaders brought down in the Arab Spring such as Tunisia's Ben Ali.

10. "New Regime Forces in Syria Carry Out Summary Executions in Latakia," *Al Mayadeen*, December 10, 2024, https://english.almayadeen.net/news/politics/armed-groups-in-syria-carry-out-summary-executions-in-lataki; "HTS, Armed Groups, Assault Sayyeda Zeinab Shrine, St. Georges Church," *Al Mayadeen*, December 11, 2024, https://beeley.substack.com/p/safe-while-syria-burns; Hakan Ozal, "Mass Protests Against Jihadist HTS Rule in Syria," *World Socialist Website*, December 27, 2024; Jason Ditz, "Over 1,000 Reported Killed, Mostly Civilians, as HTS Syrian Forces Attack Alawites," *Antiwar.com*, March 8, 2025. Adam Rasgon, "Syria's New Government Ramps Up Its Campaign to Track Assad Loyalists," *The New York Times*, December 29, 2024, A6 did address the new Syrian government's efforts to hunt down and arrest Assad regime loyalists. The article specified that a leader of a "prominent human rights organization" had "raised alarm about the way the new government was going after Assad loyalists," saying it was carrying out "arbitrary arrests of supporters of the old regime." Eventually, other articles followed suit in the mainstream media in reporting on the escalating violence and oppression directed against Shia Alawites and other minority groups, though these articles characteristically provided no context that would explain the U.S. complicity in the slaughter.

11. These massacres included: the January 2012 al-Midan bombing, the 10 May 2012 Damascus bombings, the February 2013 Damascus bombings, the Hatla massacre, the Homs school bombing, the Qalb Loze massacre, the Zara'a massacre, the March 2017 Damascus bombings and the 2017 Aleppo suicide car bombing. https://www.winterwatch.net/2024/12/who-is-the-mossad-impostor-mole-mohammed-al-julani/. Colin P. Clarke, a counterterrorism analyst at a security consulting firm in New York was quoted in one *Times* article stating that under Jolani's rule, northwest Syria was "a harsh place where critics are silenced, tortured, jailed and disappeared." (Edward Wong, Michael Crowley and Helene Cooper, "U.S. Scrambles to Navigate Perils of a New Syria," *The New York Times*, December 9, 2024). *CNN* reported that in Idlib, "Al-Jolani embarked on a campaign to eliminate ISIS as well as potential threats to his influence, arresting former commanders and eliminating rivals. Human rights groups and local monitors have raised alarm about HTS' more recent treatment of dissidents in Idlib, alleging that the group conducted harsh crackdowns on protests and tortured and abused dissidents." Salem, "How Syria's rebel leader went from radical jihadist to a blazer-wearing 'revolutionary.'"

12. Neil McFarquhar, "The Assad Family's Legacy is One of Savage Oppression," *The New York Times*, December 8, 2024.

13. See Jeremy Kuzmarov, "Prestigious Weaponry Expert Censored After Demonstrating that a Deadly Poison Gas Attack—Blamed on the Syrian Government—Was Really a False-Flag Operation by U.S.-Funded Terrorists," *CovertAction Magazine*, November 22, 2021; Seymour M. Hersh, "The Red Line and the Rat Line," *London Review of Books*, April 17, 2014; Jeremy Kuzmarov, *Obama's Unending Wars: Fronting the Foreign Policy of the Permanent Warfare State* (Atlanta: Clarity Press, 2019), 268-274.

14. McFarquhar, "The Assad Family's Legacy is One of Savage Oppression."

15. Sune Engel Rasmussen, "Iran Suffers Blow of Historic Proportions With Assad's Fall." *The Wall Street Journal*, December 10, 2024.

16. Jeremy Kuzmarov, "Mainstream Media Colludes With U.S. Government to Conceal Source of Syria's Heartbreaking Humanitarian Crisis," *CovertAction Magazine*, June 30, 2023.

17. See flawed coverage in *Democracy Now*: https://www.democracynow.org/2024/12/10/syria_assad; https://www.democracynow.org/2024/12/13/syria_damascus

18. Caitlin Johnstone, "Syria is Absorbed Into the Empire," *Consortium News*, December 9, 2024.

19. Hunt, "U.S. Officials Take Credit For Regime Change in Syria."

20. https://www.youtube.com/watch?v=fAnNJW9_KYA

21. See Ben Cole, *The Syrian Information and Propaganda War: The Role of Cognitive Bias* (Switzerland: Palgrave Macmillan, 2022).

22. *The Wall Street Journal* disparaged Syria's supposedly stagnant "state dominated" economy for years. An oil contract signed by Gulfsands of Houston and Devon Energy of Oklahoma City in 2009 was reported to have been the first U.S. oil contract in 15 years. See e.g. Hugh Pope, "Hope Rises at Scene of Syrian Repression," *The Wall Street Journal*, June 19, 2000.

23. Robert F. Kennedy Jr., "Why the Arabs Don't Want Us in Syria," *Politico Magazine*, February 22, 2016; Christina Lin, "Syria in China's New Silk Road Strategy," *The Jamestown Foundation*, April 16, 2010. For analysis regarding the importance of undercutting Chinese influence to U.S. foreign policy in the Middle East, see James R. Norman, *The Oil Card: Global Economic Warfare in the 21stt Century* (Walterville, OR: Trine Day, 2008).

24. Vanessa Beeley, "Safe While Syria Burns," *Substack*, December 10, 2024.

25. Jeffrey Sachs, "How the U.S. and Israel Destroyed Syria and Called it Peace," *Common Dreams*, December 10, 2024. Curiously, *Democracy Now*, which has been very critical of Israel's conduct in Gaza and Lebanon, avoided discussion of Israeli aggression in Syria.

26. See e.g. "A Call to Defend Rojava," *New York Review of Books*, April 26, 2018.

27. Jeremy Kuzmarov, "Tulsi Gabbard Was Right to Question Official Narrative About Syrian Chemical Weapons Attack," *Substack*, December 9, 2024.

28. See Fred Branfman, *Voices From the Plain of Jars*, with new foreword by Alfred W. McCoy (Madison, WI: University of Wisconsin Press, 2013).

Chapter 1: The First U.S. Regime Change in Syria—The Early Cold War

1. Douglas Little, "Cold War and Covert Action: The U.S. and Syria, 1945-1958," *Middle East Journal*, 44, 1 (Winter 1990), 51-75.

2. Sami Moubayed, *Syria and the USA: Washington's Relation with Damascus From Wilson to Eisenhower* (London: I.B. Tauris, 2012), 77, 78; Patrick Seale, *The Struggle For Syria: A Study of Postwar Arab Politics, 1945-1958* (New Haven: Yale University Press, 1965), 43; Hugh Wilford, *America's Great Game: The CIA's Secret Arabists and the Shaping of the Modern Middle East* (New York: Basic Books, 2013), 97.

3. J.K. Gani, *The Role of Ideology in Syrian-U.S. Relations: Conflict and Cooperation* (New York: Palgrave Macmillan, 2014), 31, 34. Among other things, Al-Quwatli had requested that the U.S. provide police equipment and training to enable his government to maintain internal order.

4. Patrick Donovan Higgins, "Gunning for Damascus: The US War on the Syrian Arab Republic," *Middle East Critique:* 32:2 (2023), 217-241. George C. Marshall refused a request by the head of the U.S. Near East Department, Gordon P. Merriam, to finance Syria's police force and provide it with significant money for technical assistance. Gani, *The Role of Ideology in Syrian-U.S. Relations*, 31.

5. The make up of Truman's Cabinet and his hawkish foreign policies are discussed in Jeremy Kuzmarov and John Marciano, *The Russians Are Coming, Again: The First Cold War as Tragedy, the Second as Farce* (New York: Monthly Review, 2018), chapter 3. Forrestal—whose hands former Vice President Henry Wallace said were "stained with oil"—was actually weary of U.S. ties to Israel and the alienation of other Arab countries that would jeopardize U.S. ability to control Middle Eastern oil. He was murdered under suspicious circumstances.

6. Higgins, "Gunning for Damascus," Moubayed, *Syria and the USA*, 16.

7. Little, "Cold War and Covert Action;" Wilbur Crane Eveland, *Ropes of Sand: America's Failure in the Middle East* (New York: W.W. Norton, 1980), 178; Moubayed, *Syria and the USA*, 16. At the end of World War I, Al-Quwatli wrote in a letter to Charles Crane, an advisor to Woodrow Wilson, that "the Americans, according to what they say about themselves, can be considered as friends. But if they think of coming to these lands as occupiers, they will become enemies for sure. Reduction of sovereignty is non-negotiable. Tell President Wilson that our demand is to be free." Higgins, "Gunning for Damascus."

8. Higgins, "Gunning for Damascus," 222.

9. Little, "Cold War and Covert Action."

10. See Stephen Kinzer, *All the Shah's Men: An American Coup and the Roots of Middle Eastern Terror* (New York: John Wiley & Sons, 2003).

11. Wilford, *America's Great Game*, 99. Meade had also served with the Office of Strategic Services (OSS) during World War II. He participated in escape and evasion operations in Iran while disguised as a Kurdish tribesman and accompanied Archie Roosevelt on a mission to rescue some American missionaries who had been kidnapped by a German SS platoon. According to Wilford, Meade was a "highly coveted operative, lent out by the Army to the CIA whenever the need was felt for his peculiar combination of physical strength, language skills, and, to quote Miles Copeland Jr's *The Game Player,* 'earthly charm.'"

12. Little, "Cold War and Covert Action: The U.S. and Syria, 1945-1958."

13. Andrew Rathmell, *Secret War in the Middle East: The Covert Struggle for Syria, 1949-1961* (London: I.B. Tauris, 1995), 30.

14. Alford Carleton, "The Syrian Coups d'Etat of 1949," *Middle East Journal*, 4, 1 (January 1950), 7.

15. Rathmell, *Secret War in the Middle East*, 30; Moubayed, *Syria and the USA*, 70; Robert F. Kennedy Jr., "Why the Arabs Don't Want Us in Syria," *Politico Magazine*, February 22, 2016. Journalist Patrick Seale described Zaim as a "heavy thickly built man with broad cheeks, a fierce eye and the florid face of a Latin American dictator." Seale, *The Struggle for Syria*, 43.

16. Little, "Cold War and Covert Action: The U.S. and Syria, 1945-1958;" Wilford, *America's Great Game*, 125, 128; Rathmell, *Secret War in the Middle East*, 48. After the coup, Zaim declared that he "would unleash a war to the death against communism in Syria" and sent a squad of twelve boxers and wrestlers to execute speedy and clandestine arrests in Lebanon and Iraq.

17. Carleton, "The Syrian Coups d'Etat of 1949," 9.

18. Moubayed, *Syria and the USA*, 81. Moubayed wrote that "throughout the 137 days that he [Zaim] remained in power, the USA did not even once voice its displeasure at his human rights record, or criticize the lack of political freedom in Syria."

19. Seale, *The Struggle for Syria*, 118.

20. Little, "Cold War and Covert Action: The U.S. and Syria, 1945-1958." More on Shishakli can be found in *Al Jazeera's* documentary, "Al Shishakli: Syria's Master of Coups (2022)." Moubayed, *Syria and the USA*. Shishakli supported Zaim's coup.

21. Patrick Seale, *Asad of Syria: The Struggle for the Middle East*, with the assistance of Malcolm McConville (Berkeley: University of California Press, 1988), 46. "Al Shishakli: Syria's Master of Coups." Shishakli was enamored of the paramilitary aspects of the SSNP. His grandson cites as his major accomplishments his regime's providing women with the vote for the first time in Syrian history and investments in agriculture and industry along with the boosting of exports in wheat and cotton and achievement of overall economic growth. Known for his powerful oratory and effectiveness in harnessing the power of the radio, Shishakli was the first post-independence Arab leader to cultivate a cult of personality with his pictures appearing in every shop window and established a government ministry of information and propaganda when he was in power.

22. Albion Ross, "Twelve Lebanese Doomed as Rebels: Sentences After Mass Trial Follow Execution of Syria Popular Party's Leader," *The New York Times*, July 18, 1949.

23. "From Swastikas to Bullets: The SSNP's Disturbing Journey in Syrian Politics," *Levant24*, July 19, 2023.

24. "Al Shishakli: Syria's Master of Coups." In 1964, Nawaf al Ghazali, a Syrian expat living in Brazil where Shishakli was living in exile retaliated for the army attack in al Suwayda by shooting and killing Shishakli. This was a sorry end for a man who had been written up in Syrian newspapers for his exploits fighting against the French in the 1930s and who was considered one of the heroes of the 1948 Palestine War for his role in helping to take Samakh City and attacking Israeli positions on the Daughters of Jacob Bridge.

25. See David W. Lesch, *Syria and the United States: Eisenhower's Cold War in the Middle East* (New York: Routledge, 1992).

26. Maliki became a national hero. A statue of him was put up in Damascus and he was a great influence on Hafez al-Assad.

27. Jonathan Bloch and Patrick Fitzgerald, *British Intelligence and Covert Action*, with introduction by Philip Agee (London: Brandon Book Publishers, 1984), 120. Part of the plan was to have the Iraqis invade Syria. Journalist Tim Weiner reported that the CIA delivered half a million Syrian pounds to leaders of the coup plot. Tim Weiner, *Legacy of Ashes: The History of the CIA* (New York: Doubleday, 2007), 138.

28. Ben Fenton, "Macmillan Backed Syrian Assassination Plot," *The Guardian*, September 26.

29. Fenton, "Macmillan Backed Syrian Assassination Plot;" A.B. Abrams, *World War in Syria: Global Conflict on Middle Eastern Battlefields* (Atlanta: Clarity Press, 2021), 9.

30. Wilbur Crane Eveland, *Ropes of Sand: America's Failure in the Middle East* (New York: W.W. Norton, 1980), 253, 254.

31. Wilford, *America's Great Game*, 45. Wilford noted that the roots of Roosevelt's anticommunism dated to his school days. When he came across *The Daily Worker* in the Groton library, he said he "found its message of class hatred a calumny on the ideals of America." At the end of World War II, Roosevelt feared that Soviet Premier Joseph Stalin was intent on reestablishing the old Tsarist empire and pushing for domination of the "Straits of the Bosphorus and the Dardanelles, and a warm water port on the Persian Gulf."

32. Wilford, *America's Great Game*, 19, 44. Roosevelt befriended nationalist leaders like Mehdi Ben Barka in Morocco and Habib Bourguiba in Tunisia whom Roosevelt took to be a "visionary and modern prophet destined for greatness." Wilford suggests that Roosevelt had an Orientalist outlook similar to British imperialists that viewed the Middle East as a place of premodern simplicity that the U.S. could help to modernize and bring progress to. Roosevelt's second wife was a Lebanese woman named Selwa.

33. Abrams, *World War in Syria*, 9.

34. Rathmell, *Secret War in the Middle East*, 130; Bloch and Fitzgerald, *British Intelligence and Covert Action*, 124, 125. Stone lost much of his hearing after being exposed to too many explosives during his military training in World War II. Joe Holley, "Hearing-Impaired Activist and Spy, Rocky Stone Dies," *The Washington Post*, August 23, 2004.

35. Eveland, *Ropes of Sand*, 254; Weiner, *Legacy of Ashes*, 139; Seale, *The Struggle For Syria*, 293.

36. Abrams, *World War in Syria*, 10. U.S. ambassador to Syria, Charles Yost, called the CIA plot "clumsy."

37. Miles Copeland Jr., *The Game Player: The Confessions of the CIA's Original Political Operative* (London: Aurum Press, 1989). Previously, Copeland published *The Game of Nations: The Amorality of Power Politics* (London: Weidenfeld & Nicolson, 1969) and *Beyond Cloak and Dagger: Inside the CIA* (New York: Pinnacle Books, 1975).

38. Wilford, *America's Great Game*, 65, 67, 68, 69.

39. https://en.wikipedia.org/wiki/Miles_Copeland_Jr.

40. Deane R. Hinton, a political officer in the U.S. delegation in Syria, confirmed that Meade and Copeland Jr. had "conspired with Zaim in carrying out the coup." His statements undercut the claim of some scholars like Andrew Rathmell who believe that Copeland made up everything that he wrote in his book and that the U.S. was not involved in the 1949 Syrian coup or did not help coordinate it. Wilford, *America's Great Game*, 132.

41. Copeland tricked Barudi by having a Syrian intelligence agent he had paid off provide him with misinformation suggesting that Copeland had key secret documents in his home and would be away the weekend of the raid. Copeland had made like he was leaving for the weekend but hid out in his house so he was ready to expose and confront the raiders to make them look bad. For discussion of this incident, see also Wilford, *America's Great Game*, 103. Wilford notes corroboration of the incident by Copeland's son and an article in *The New York Times* describing how Syrian gunmen had fired into Copeland's residence.

42. Copeland Jr., *The Game Player*, 96.

43. Kennedy Jr., "Why the Arabs Don't Want Us in Syria."

44. Quoted in Wilford, *America's Great Game*, 128, 129.

Chapter 2: Back to the Future: Long-Term U.S. Regime-Change Strategy

1. Robert Reuel Naiman, "WikiLeaks Reveals How the US Aggressively Pursued Regime Change in Syria, Igniting a Bloodbath," *Truthout*, October 9, 2015.

2. Patrick Seale, *Asad of Syria: The Struggle for the Middle East*, with the assistance of Malcolm McConville (Berkeley: University of California Press, 1988); Magnus Seland Andersson and Hilde Henriksen Waage, "Stew in Their Own Juice: Reagan, Syria and Lebanon, 1981-1984," *Diplomatic History*, 44, 4 (2020), 664-691.

3. Seale, *Asad of Syria*.

4. Con Coughlin, *Assad: The Triumph of Tyranny* (London: Picador, 2023), 18.

5. Seale, *Asad of Syria*, 36.

6. A.B. Abrams, *World War in Syria: Global Conflict on Middle Eastern Battlefields* (Atlanta: Clarity Press, 2021), 17.

7. Atari had served as a doctor with Algerian revolutionary Houari Boumediene's forces during the Algerian War against France.

8. Patrick Donovan Higgins, "Gunning for Damascus: The US War on the Syrian Arab Republic," *Middle East Critique*: 32:2 (2023), 222. The U.S. government loathed Jadid. A CIA report shuddered at Syria's transformation under his rule into a "revolutionary base," labeling it a "center of instability" in which the "Syrian leadership was now largely of peasant stock, expressing a preference for irresponsible socialist policies that pushed many professional people and merchants to more stable environments outside the country."

9. Seale, *Asad of Syria*, 169, 171.

10. Abrams, *World War in Syria*. In 1972, the Syrian Communist Party chose to join the National Progressive Front set up by Assad and the Baath Party after it accepted the Arab nationalist and socialist orientation of the government. In the late 1970s, some communists broke with Assad over his deployment of Syrian troops into Lebanon. For much of the 1980s, the Syrian Communist Party operated

underground, with its newspaper banned, though the repression against it was lifted in 1986 as a concession to the Soviets.

11. James Kelly, "Syria: The Proud Lion and His Den," *Time*, September 5, 1983; Nikolas Van Dam, *The Struggle For Power in Syria: Politics and Society Under the Baath Party and Assad Dynasty* (London: I.B. Tauris, 1996), 61, 68. Baath Party member Ahmad Suwaidani was one of the longest political prisoners in the world, having been jailed from 1968, when he attempted a coup, until his release in 1994. *Time* reported on the adoption of electroshock torture at Mezzeh prison and beating of prisoners using steel cables. Salah ad-Din al-Bitar, one of the founders of the Baath Party, founded a journal in Paris, *Al-Ihya' al-'Arabi*, in which he denounced the misdeeds of the Assad regime. Bitar believed that the "situation in Syria has reached the limit: each day, the dictatorship grows more bloody and the international policies of Hafiz al-Asad are an insult to the Arab cause." In July 1980, after calling on Syrians to overthrow Asad, Bitar was killed in a Parisian garage. Although the French government did not make formal charges for this crime, Syrian opposition groups fingered the military attaché of the Syrian embassy in Paris, Colonel Nadim Umran, an Alawi. Daniel Pipes, "Terrorism: The Syrian Connection," *National Interest*, September 1989.

12. Reed, "Syria's Assad"; Stephen Gowans, *Washington's Long War on Syria* (Montreal: Baraka Books, 2017), 95. From 1980 through 1982, it was routine for the Defense Brigades and the Special Forces to seal off towns or quarters of cities and comb through the areas house by house; looting and rape were common. Anyone deemed suspect in the Brotherhood uprising could be put up against the wall and shot, along with his family. Rifaat's forces furthermore laid siege to Hama, which was turned into a giant ash heap, with 15 to 25 percent of the city's population being killed. The savage repression is detailed in Robert Fisk, *The Great War for Civilization: The Conquest of the Middle East* (New York: Vintage, 2007). Anderson in *The Dirty War in Syria* notes that most Syrians supported Assad's crushing of the Muslim Brotherhood uprising. However, afterwards, many "feared that the Syrian secret police were ever vigilant for Zionist spies and new Muslim Brotherhood conspiracies which led them to harass a wider range of government critics." (p. 40, 41). Robert Dreyfus, who has written about the West's collaboration with political Islam to undermine secular nationalists and communists in the Muslim world, argues that Western sources deliberately exaggerated the death toll in Hama in order to demonize the Baathists as ruthless killers, and that the Baathists went along with the deception in order to intimidate the Muslim Brotherhood.

13. Seale, *Asad of Syria*, 343, 452. According to Seale, Assad was more interested in power then its trappings.

14. Kelly, "Syria."

15. David W. Lesch, *Syria: The Fall of the House of Assad*, updated edition (New Haven: Yale University Press, 2012), 52.

16. Seale, *Asad of Syria*, 452.

17. Reuven Avi-Ran, *The Syrian Involvement in Lebanon Since 1975*, Translated from the Hebrew by David Maisel (Boulder, CO: Westview Press, 1991), 12.

18. Reed, "Syria's Assad."

19. "Syria Without Assad: Succession Politics," Central Intelligence Agency, National Assessment Center, November 7, 1978.

20. Ibid; Kelly, "Syria."

21. Paul Findley, *They Dare to Speak Out: People and Institutions Confront Israel's Lobby* (New York: Lawrence Hill Books, 1985), 304. Journalist Robert Azzi found in the 1970s that Damascus's mostly Sephardic Jewish population enjoyed freedom of worship and freedom of opportunity and were tolerantly embraced in the city. There were restrictions on travel and emigration but reprisals following the Six-Day and Yom Kippur War were rare and not supported by the government.

22. Seale, *Asad of Syria*, 441.

23. Seale, *Asad of Syria*, 441.

24. Kelly, "Syria." *Time* reported that even Hama, headquarters of the Muslim Brotherhood, experienced a building boom in the 1980s.

25. Oliver Boyd-Barrett, *Conflict Propaganda in Syria: Narrative Battles* (New York: Routledge, 2022), 125.

26. Seale, *Asad of Syria*, 441; "Syria's Assad;" Tim Anderson, *The Dirty War in Syria* (Montreal: Global Research, 2016), 40.

27. Mark Taliano, *Voices From Syria* (Montreal: Baraka Books, 2017); Anderson, *The Dirty War on Syria*. Even Free Syrian Army (FSA) leaders acknowledged that around 70% of the population supported Assad.

28. Anderson, *The Dirty War in Syria*, 45.

29. Kit Klarenberg, "Privatizing Syria: US Plans Post-Assad Sell-Off," *Global Delinquents*, December 22, 2024; Marta Teschendorff, "Loss of Access to Education Puts Well Being of Syrian Girls at Risk," *Our World*, September 17, 2015.

30. Boyd-Barrett, *Conflict Propaganda in Syria*, 125.

31. Klarenberg, "Privatizing Syria;" Report of the Special Rapporteur on the negative impact of unilateral coercive measures on the enjoyment of human rights on his mission to the Syrian Arab Republic, UNHRC, December 11, 2018; David W. Lesch, *Syria* points to increasing pay for teachers under Bashar and commitment to education though also notes some key problems such as inadequate regulations of certain industries, lack of a stock market, lack of transparency in government and a politicized judiciary.

32. Taliano, *Voices From Syria*, 28. Taliano also emphasizes the low unemployment rates under Assad.

33. Susan Spano, "Syria: a Bright Star in the Middle East," *LA Times*, December 26, 2010.

34. Noam Chomsky and Edward S. Herman, *The Political Economy of Human Rights: The Washington Connection and Third World Fascism* (Boston: South End Press, 1979).

35. Joe Stork, "The Carter Doctrine and US Bases in the Middle East," *Middle East Report*, 90 (September-October 1980); Lloyd C. Gardner, *The Road to Tahrir Square: Egypt and the United States From the Rise of Nasser to the Fall of Mubarak* (New York: The New Press, 2011). The Carter administration had begun supplying Egypt with pilotless drones. Joe Stork wrote of Sadat's "unabashed eagerness" to have Egypt serve as a "doormat for U.S. military incursions in the region"—which

Assad would not be. Stork, "The Carter Doctrine and US Bases in the Middle East."

36. Higgins, "Gunning for Damascus," 220; J.K. Gani, *The Role of Ideology in Syrian-U.S. Relations: Conflict and Cooperation* (New York: Palgrave Macmillan, 2014).

37. Lars Hasvoll Bakke and Hilde Henriksen Waage, "Facing Assad: American Diplomacy Towards Syria, 1973-1977," *The International History Review*, 40, 3 (2018), 562; Gowans, *Washington's Long War on Syria*. Kissinger said of Assad on April 11, 1989: "I rather like Hafez al-Assad. He is a cold analyst of the national interests of his country."

38. Seale, *Asad of Syria*, 141; Charles Glass, *Syria Civil War to Holy War?* (New York: OR Books, 2025), 96. Seale wrote that Damascus was viewed by the U.S. State Department in the 1970s as the enemy, the most militant of Israel's neighbors, the closest to Moscow, the only substantial obstacle to U.S. designs for the region." The following decade, Seale noted, "The Arab-Israeli dispute...became essentially a contest between Israel and Syria," as Assad had "proven himself the greatest single obstacle to Israel's aims in the Levant. Only if he were removed, or at least scared off the scene, could Israel proceed unchallenged. From Israel's point of view, Assad was a far more important target than either [Palestinian leader Yasser] Arafat or [Libyan leader Muammar] Gaddafi." Abrams, *World War in Syria*, 26, 27.

39. Seale, *Asad of Syria*, 141.

40. Bakke and Waage, "Facing Assad," 549. In 1974, Hafez met in Damascus with Illinois Congressman Paul Findley (R) who wanted to promote better U.S. relations with Syria. Hafez told Findley that he liked the Americans and had for years, but was bitter about the guns and ammunition the U.S. government was providing to Israel. Findley, *They Dare to Speak Out*, 4.

41. Seale, *Asad of Syria*, 169. Saddam Hussein viewed Assad as a sell-out to the Arab world, blaming him for a) surrendering Quneitra to the Israelis without a fight in 1967; b) cravenly asking for a ceasefire on the 2nd day of the 1973 Yom Kippur War; c) intervening in Lebanon in 1976 in collusion with Washington and Jerusalem; d) complicity in the massacre of Palestinians in that war; and e) conspiring to destroy the projected union between Syria and Iraq in 1979.

42. Higgins, "Gunning for Damascus," 220.

43. U.S. Central Intelligence Agency, "Syria: Assad and the Peace Process," November 11, 1988 (released October 17, 2012), at https://www.cia.gov/readingroom/docs/CIA-RDP89S01450R000600580001-8.pdf; Higgins, "Gunning for Damascus," 220. It is not surprising that when the Western-backed HTS took over after overthrowing Bashar al-Assad, they released a new map of Syria excluding the Golan Heights and therefore effectively ceding it to Israel. While Assad had found himself at odds with the leadership of the Palestine Liberation Organization (PLO), he supported a host of other Palestinian revolutionary organizations, including the Popular Front for the Liberation of Palestine (PFLP), the Popular Front for the Liberation of Palestine-General Command (PFLP-GC), and Sa'iqa, the Syrian Baath Party's own faction in the Palestine Liberation Organization (PLO). Assad also supported the "Fateh al Intifada, a splinter group" of the PLO.

U.S. officials accused Assad of attempting to "scuttle" negotiations between the PLO and Israel, stating that "there is no doubt that Syria is the only major frontline state dedicated to continuing strategic confrontation with Israel" and that Syria constituted "by far Israel's greatest problem."

44. Avi-Ran, *The Syrian Involvement in Lebanon Since 1975*.

45. Seale, *Asad of Syria*, 473; Andersson and Waage "Stew in Their Own Juice: Reagan, Syria and Lebanon, 1981-1984." Initially, Assad allied with Lebanon's Christians because he didn't want a radical adventurist Lebanon on his flank provoking and alarming the West by giving free reign to Palestinian militants. However, within a few years Syrian forces directly clashed with Christian Maronites functioning as U.S.-Israeli proxies, and allied more firmly with Shiite Muslims, the PLO, and leftist forces in Lebanon.

46. Seale, *Asad of Syria*, ch. 21 After the Ayatollah Khomeini took power, Assad sent him a gift. Syria was used as a land bridge for Iran's funneling weapons to Hezbollah.

47. For the domestic considerations driving aggressive U.S. imperial intervention around the world in the post-Vietnam era, see David N. Gibbs, *Revolt of the Rich: How the Politics of the 1970s Widened America's Class Divide* (New York: Columbia University Press, 2024).

48. Stork, "The Carter Doctrine and US Bases in the Middle East." In April 1979, in addition to the "floating base" constituted by the Sixth Fleet, the U.S. maintained 199 military facilities in active status in the Mediterranean.

49. Visit to the Syrian Arab Republic, Report of the Special Rapporteur on the negative impact of unilateral coercive measures on the enjoyment of human rights, Alena Douhan, UN HRC, July 3, 2023.

50. Anderson, *The Dirty War on Syria*, 2.

51. Seale, *Asad of Syria*, 336.

52. Seale, *Asad of Syria*, 336. Abrams notes that Saudi Arabia and Egypt were also accused of helping to support the Muslim Brotherhood insurrection. Egyptian president Anwar Sadat was accused directly of financing jihadists who massacred a group of Syrian cadets at the Aleppo Artillery School in July 1979. Abrams, *World War in Syria*, 24.

53. Seale, *Asad of Syria*, 336, 337; Anderson, *The Dirty War on Syria*, 25.

54. Gowans, *Washington's Long War on Syria*, 97.

55. Thomas L. Friedman, "U.S. Battleship Pounds Hills Held by Syrians in Lebanon," *The New York Times*, February 9, 1984; Micah Zenko, "When America Attacked Syria," *Council on Foreign Relations*, February 13, 2012; "Wars and Conflicts Between Syria and the U.S.," https://www.historyguy.com/u.s.-syria_conflicts.htm. Zenko notes that having received the latest Soviet infrared sensor technology, Syrian SAM capabilities were more advanced than Navy planners had assumed: "We didn't expect to encounter quite the level of defense we did," a member of the Reagan administration said.

56. Avi-Ran, *The Syrian Involvement in Lebanon Since 1975*, 174. See also Abrams, *World War in Syria*, 30.

57. David Wills, *The First War on Terrorism: Counter-Terrorism Policy During the Reagan Era* (New York: Rowman & Littlefield, 2003), 59.

58. Andersson and Waage, "Stew in Their Own Juice: Reagan, Syria and Lebanon, 1981-1984;" Avi-Ran, *The Syrian Involvement in Lebanon Since 1975*, 173; Wills, *The First War on Terrorism*. Secretary of State Alexander Haig was among the super-hawks in the Reagan administration who pushed for direct Israeli military attack on Syria.

59. Richard Gabriel, *Military Incompetence: Why the American Military Doesn't Win* (New York: Farrar, Strauss and Giroux, 1985), 146; Frank Greve, "Comeback of the Battleship is Making Political Waves," *Philadelphia Inquirer*, December 13, 1981, 14.

60. Bernard Weinraub, "President Accuses 5 Outlaw States of World Terror," *The New York Times*, July 9, 1985; Andersson and Waage, "Stew in Their Own Juice: Reagan, Syria and Lebanon, 1981-1984." Defense Secretary Caspar Weinberger stated after the U.S. Marine Barracks attacks "we have a pretty good idea of the general group from which they came and, as I said the first day, they are basically Iranians with sponsorship and knowledge and authority of the Syrian Government."

61. Weinraub, "President Accuses 5 Outlaw States of World Terror."

62. Wills, *The First War on Terrorism*; Zenko, "When America Attacked Syria;" Abrams, *World War in Syria*, 25.

63. Thomas Burrows, "Secret 1983 CIA intelligence report suggested America should encourage Saddam Hussein to attack Syria to secure oil pipeline to Med and Gulf," *The Daily Mail*, January 20, 2017; Abrams, *World War in Syria*, 24. Fuller believed that all of the Arab states except Libya would support an Iraqi invasion of Syria, though Iraq's leader, Saddam Hussein, refused to launch the attack. Referring to Assad as Israel's greatest problem, Fuller wrote that if the U.S. wanted to "rein in Syria" it needed to do so by showing "real muscle." Fuller felt that bringing in Iraq was the most challenging aspect of the plan. To do so could only be done by a "reorientation of U.S. policy towards Iraq" and might include "more active US participation in supplying high-tech items to Iraq's modernization efforts."

64. Wills, *The First War on Terrorism*, 171. The direct bombing of Syria was called off because of fear that it would spark a direct confrontation with the Soviets.

65. Brad Hoff, "Newly Declassified CIA Memo Presents Blueprint for Syrian Regime Collapse," *Third World Resurgence*, January-February 2017.

66. See Robert Dreyfuss, *Devil's Game: How the United States Helped to Unleash Fundamentalist Islam* (New York: Metropolitan Books, 2005).

67. Hoff, "Newly Declassified CIA Memo Presents Blueprint for Syrian Regime Collapse,"

68. Professor David N. Gibbs, "Brzezinski Interview: 1998 Interview with Zbigniew Brzezinski on Afghanistan in *Le Nouvel Observateur*, The University of Arizona.

69. Thierry Lalevee, "Syrian Drug Connection Indicted," *Executive Intelligence Review*, 4, 19, January 19, 1990; Daniele Ganser, *NATO's Secret Armies: Operation Gladio and Terrorism in Western Europe*, with foreword by john Prados (New York: Routledge, 2004).

70. Andersson and Waage, "Stew in Their Own Juice: Reagan, Syria and Lebanon, 1981-1984."

71. Edward S. Herman and Gerry O'Sullivan, *The 'Terrorism' Industry: The Experts and Institutions That Shape Our View of Terror* (New York: Pantheon Books, 1989), 63.

72. The Soviets had financed Palestinian Liberation Organization (PLO) training camps in Czechoslovakia in the late 1960s, though funding was cut thereafter and there was little actual evidence the Soviets officially backed any terrorist operations by the PLO or by left-wing groups such as the Baader Meinhof gang and Italian Red Brigades or FMLN.

73. Claire Sterling, *The Terror Network* (New York: Berkley Books, 1981), 236. Edward S. Herman wrote a rebuttal of Sterling's book, *The Real Terror Network: Terrorism in Fact and Propaganda* (Boston: South End Press, 1999). Herman called Sterling's book a "right wing fairy tale," showing how she ignored right wing terrorism supported by the CIA and overplayed the Soviet influence. Neoconservative writer Daniel Pipes called Syria under Assad the "international fulcrum for terrorism." Pipes, "Terrorism."

74. Seale, *Asad of Syria*, 471; Andersson and Waage, "Stew in Their Own Juice: Reagan, Syria and Lebanon, 1981-1984." Benjamin Netanyahu was especially valued in Washington because of his ability to manipulate public fears over terrorism in a way that lent support for heightened military aggression. Netanyahu consistently invoked the story of his brother Yonatan who was killed by Palestinian gunmen while trying to save passengers on a hijacked flight in Entebbe, Uganda in 1976 in what is known as the Entebbe raid.

75. Andersson and Waage, "Stew in Their Own Juice: Reagan, Syria and Lebanon, 1981-1984."

76. Greg Shupak, "Writing Out Empire: The Case of the Syria Sanctions," in *Sanctions as War: Anti-Imperialist Perspectives on American Geo-Economic Strategy*, ed. Stuart Davis and Immanuel Ness (London: Brill, 2022), 246.

77. Weinraub, "President Accuses 5 Outlaw States of World Terror."

78. Shupak, "Writing Out Empire," in *Sanctions as War*, ed. Davis and Ness, 246.

79. Hoff, "Newly Declassified CIA Memo Presents Blueprint for Syrian Regime Collapse."

80. Jeremy Kuzmarov, "Thirty Five Years Ago, 270 People Were Killed When Pan Am Flight 103 Crashed: Evidence Indicates that CIA Was Behind It," *CovertAction Magazine*, December 21, 2023, https://covertactionmagazine.com/2023/12/21/thirty-five-years-ago-270-people-were-killed-when-pan-am-flight-103-crashed-evidence-indicates-that-the-cia-was-behind-it/

81. Hoff, "Newly Declassified CIA Memo Presents Blueprint for Syrian Regime Collapse."

82. Jonathan V. Marshall, *The Lebanese Connection: Corruption, Civil War, and the International Drug Traffic* (Palo Alto: Stanford University Press, 2012), 118, 119, 123. An outstanding investigative journalist, Marshall makes clear that Rifaat al-Assad was no boy scout and appears to have been involved in illicit activity, however, he won several liberal suits and it is clear that his enemies (Muslim Brotherhood, Israel and the U.S.) were intent on blackening his reputation, and by association, that of his elder brother Hafez who was never directly implicated in any drug trafficking or mafia related activity. The allegations against Hafez were echoed a quarter century

later when Bashar and his brother Maher were accused of presiding over a drug empire in lurid stories that smacked of yellow journalism.

83. Schumer was one of Congress' strongest supporters of Israel who over the years received a fortune in campaign money from the American-Israeli Public Affairs Committee (AIPAC). This was in addition to support he received from Wall Street investment firms and military contractors who benefitted from U.S. imperial policies in the Middle East.

84. Jacques Baud, *Governing by Fake News: 30 Years of Fake News in the West.* (Paris: Max Milo, 2022), at 111-115.

Chapter 3: The Arab Spring and U.S. Interference in Syria

1. Richard Collett, "'Everything is better than before:' How Syria is reopening to tourists," *CNN,* February 11, 2025.

2. American Friends Service Committee, "The Iraqi Refugee Crisis," https://afsc. org/sites/default/files/documents/The%20Iraqi%20Refugee%20Crisis.pdf

3. American Friends Service Committee, "The Iraqi Refugee Crisis."

4. American Friends Service Committee, "The Iraqi Refugee Crisis."

5. Jacques Baud, *Governing by Fake News: 30 Years of Fake News in the West* (Paris: Max Milo 2022), 160-165. Baud served in the Swiss intelligence services and Swiss army.

6. Baud, *Governing by Fake News,* 163.

7. Baud, *Governing by Fake News,* 164. Baud quotes then Secretary of State John Kerry who admitted that the U.S. saw the rise and growth of ISIS as a bargaining chip against Assad, but that, instead of negotiating, Assad, much to Kerry's chagrin, turned to Russia for help.

8. Baud, *Governing by Fake News,* 111. Dumas stated "I was in England two years before the violence in Syria on other business—I met with top British officials, who confessed to me that they were preparing something in Syria. This was in Britain not in America. Britain was preparing gunmen to invade Syria."

9. Baud, *Governing by Fake News,* 112.

10. Baud, *Governing by Fake News,* 131-132. See also Patrick Donovan Higgins, "Gunning for Damascus: The US War on the Syrian Arab Republic," *Middle East Critique:* 32:2 (2023), 230. Donavan cites a study by William Van Wagenen of *The Libertarian Institute* who followed operatives moving into Syria in 2011 from nearby war zones, namely: the 2007 Nahr el-Bared conflict in Lebanon; the U.S.-run Camp Bucca prison in occupied Iraq; the 1990s U.S.-UK joint military ventures in Bosnia and Kosovo; and 2011 NATO campaign in Libya. Combining those research trails with reports that Ahrar al-Sham brigades were forming and mobilizing "well before March 2011," Van Wagenen's survey helps demolish the idea that sectarian armed insurgents only began to launch attacks in belated response to violent crackdowns on protests.

11. Ahmed Bensaada, *Arabesque Américaine: Le Rôle des États Unis dans les révoltes* (Montreal: Michel Brulé, 2011); Stuart Jeanne Bramhall, "The Arab Spring: Made in the USA," *Dissident Voice,* October 25, 2015.

12. A.B. Abrams, *World War in Syria: Global Conflict on Middle Eastern Battlefields* (Atlanta: Clarity Press, 2021).

13. Mostafa Salem, "How Syria's rebel leader went from radical jihadist to a blazer-wearing 'revolutionary,'" *CNN*, December 6, 2024.

14. Abrams, *World War in Syria*, 107-108.

15. Baud, *Governing by Fake News*, 131-132.; August, 2012 DIA document at https://www.judicialwatch.org/wp-content/uploads/2015/05/Pg.-291-Pgs.-287-293-JW-v-DOD-and-State-14-812-DOD-Release-2015-04-10-final-version11.pdf

16. David W. Lesch, *Syria: The Fall of the House of Assad,* updated edition (New Haven: Yale University Press, 2012); Charles Lister, *The Syrian Jihad: Al Qaeda, the Islamic State and the Evolution of an Insurgency* (New York: Oxford University Press, 2015). Lesch and Lister emphasize that the influx of refugees from Iraq—including numbers of radical jihadists who participated in the anti-U.S. insurgency—had helped destabilize Syria and intensified disaffection with Assad in the face of the decline of Syria's agricultural sector and widening inequality bred by economic liberalization policies. Drought conditions resulted in part from climate fluctuations and abnormally hot temperatures. Lesch pointed out that the huge influx of Iraqi refugees (ranging from 500,000-1.4 million) placed strain on an already brittle Syrian economy. Iraq refugees settled around Damascus, forcing up rents, reducing the availability of housing, overcrowding the schools and contributing to inflationary trends in the country.

17. Lesch, *Syria*, 51, 57.

18. Power quoted in Max Blumenthal, *The Management of Savagery: How America's National Security State Fueled the Rise of Al Qaeda, ISIS, and Donald Trump* (London: Verso, 2019), 184.

19. *Military Watch Magazine*, "Lessons From Damascus' Fall: Former British Ambassador to Syria Details How the West, Israel and Turkey Won," January 10, 2025. It is worth emphasizing that Assad sacked the local governor in the province where Daraa was based and freed the youth who had been arrested.

20. Anderson, *The Dirty War on Syria*, 24-27; Stephen Gowans, *Washington's Long War on Syria* (Montreal: Baraka Books, 2017), 126.

21. Anderson, *The Dirty War on Syria*; Charles Glass, "'Tell Me How This Ends:' America's Muddled Involvement With Syria," *Harper's Magazine*, February 2019; Gowans, *Washington's Long War on Syria*, 122. The slogan they chanted was "Alawites to the grave, and Christians to Beirut." Sunni fundamentalists viewed the Alawite sect as heretical to Islam. Some signs also called for banning of gender-mixed school and anti-feminist measures. Sunni businessmen's disaffection with the Assad regime and corruption are detailed in a Wikileaks cable as part of its Syria Files series. https://wikileaks.org/plusd/cables/06DAMASCUS3_a.html

22. Mark Taliano, *Voices from Syria* (Montreal: Global Research, 2017), 12; Gowans, *Washington's Long War on Syria*, 121.

23. Ben Cole, *The Syrian Information and Propaganda War: The Role of Cognitive Bias* (Switzerland: Palgrave Macmillan, 2022), 403. Cole points to a "halo effect" in western media surrounding the protesters, which distorted what was going on. In his judicious assessment, the Syrian government's claims of widespread violence from the outset of the "Arab Spring" was accurate. The uprising in Homs was particularly violent and sectarian from the outset. Assad in his propaganda

—which of course embellished or invented certain things—tried to claim that some protesters were "agitators" linked to his exiled uncle Rifaat, who had had a falling out with Hafez al-Assad.

24. Taliano, *Voices from Syria*, 7.

25. Anderson, *The Dirty War on Syria*, 23, 24. Anderson notes that the protests did not die down even when Assad displayed his intent of initiating political reforms demanded by some of the protesters such as easing media freedom and allowing for the registration of all political parties.

26. Anderson, *The Dirty War on Syria*, 26. David W. Lesch quotes a Daraa resident who said: "let Obama come and take Syria. Let Israel come and take Syria. Let the Jews come. Anything is better than Bashar Assad." This view was not shared by most Syrians, for good reason. Lesch, *Syria*, 97. After the Daraa protests, Assad announced a set of reforms, including salary raises for public workers and greater freedom for political parties and the media and releasing jihadists from prison—the latter being a key demand of many of the protesters.

27. Charles Glass, *Syria: Civil War to Holy War?* (New York: OR Books, 2025), 45, 57.

28. Oliver Boyd-Barrett, *Conflict Propaganda in Syria: Narrative Battles* (New York: Routledge, 2022), 135, 136.

29. Blumenthal, *The Management of Savagery*, 160. A Syrian youth characteristically told *Time*: "There is a lot of government help for the youth. They give us free books, free schools, free universities. Why should there be a revolution?"

30. Glass, *Syria: Civil War to Holy War?* 58.

31. Glass, "'Tell Me How This Ends.'"

32. CNN Wire Staff, "U.S. Pulls Envoy from Syria over Safety Concerns," *CNN*, October 24, 2011; Tara McKelvey, "Arming Syrian Rebels: Where the US Went Wrong," *BBC News*, October 9, 2015.

33. Boyd-Barrett, *Conflict Propaganda in Syria*, 80, 87, 111. Those refusing the offer of amnesty and dialogue included tech savvy youth who were western-oriented.

34. Cole, *The Syrian Information and Propaganda War*, 87.

35. Cole, *The Syrian Information and Propaganda War*, 87.

36. Anderson, *The Dirty War on Syria*, 26. Anderson notes that some protesters chanted the slogan "Alawites to the grave" which indicated support for ethnic cleansing and/or genocide which was carried out after the Islamic government took over in December 2024. Many of the protesters also began desecrating mosques.

37. Abrams, *World War in Syria*, 107; Gowans, *Washington's Long War on Syria*, 118, 119.

38. Benjamin Arthur Thomason, "Making Democracy Safe for Empire," Ph.D. Dissertation, Bowling Green University, 2024, 175, 176.

39. "Syrian Independent Media Outlet Celebrates Ten Years," *National Endowment For Democracy Communications*, November 1, 2022. *Enab Baludi* got some of its articles printed in Western publications like *The Guardian*. A June 2024 article in *Enab Baludi* promoted the State Department fiction that Al-Jolani was a pragmatic president. Omitting any discussion of ethnic pogroms targeting Shia Alawites, *Enab Baludi* further championed Syria's new openness to foreign investment under Al-Jolani's rule.

40. Craig Whitlock, "U.S. Secretly Backed Syrian Opposition Groups, Cables Released by Wikileaks Show," *The Washington Post*, May 21, 2023.

41. Scott Lucas, "Syria WikiLeaks Special: How the US Government «Supported Opposition Groups» (and for How Long?)," *EA Worldview*, April 20, 2011.

42. Thomason, "Making Democracy Safe for Empire," 176; Gowans, *Washington's Long War on Syria*, 111, 112.

43. See Jeremy Kuzmarov, *War Monger: How Clinton's Malign Foreign Policy Set the U.S. Trajectory From Bush II to Biden* (Atlanta: Clarity Press, 2024), ch. 4.

44. Patrick Cockburn, *The Rise of the Islamic State: ISIS and the New Sunni Revolution* (London: Verso, 2015), 112.

45. Cockburn, *The Rise of the Islamic State*, 88.

46. See Maximilian Forte, *Slouching Towards Sirte: NATO's War on Libya and Africa* (Montreal, Baraka Books, 2012). An investigation by *CovertAction Magazine* found that a network of CIA agents headed by Theodore Shackley were behind the downing of the Lockerbie Flight whose passengers included a team of DIA agents headed to Washington to expose criminal activities that Shackley's "secret team" was involved in. See Jeremy Kuzmarov, "Thirty Five Years Ago, 270 People Were Killed When Pan Am Flight 103 Crashed: Evidence Indicates that CIA Was Behind It," *CovertAction Magazine*, December 21, 2023.

47. Forte, *Slouching Towards Sirte*.

48. Daniel Kovalik, "Clinton Emails on Libya Expose The Lie of 'Humanitarian Intervention,'" *Huffington Post*, January 22, 2016.

49. Kovalik, "Clinton Emails on Libya Expose The Lie of 'Humanitarian Intervention.'"

50. Kovalik, "Clinton Emails on Libya Expose The Lie of 'Humanitarian Intervention.'"

51. "Barack Obama Says Libya was 'Worst Mistake' of his Presidency," *The Guardian* (April 11, 2016.

52. "'Slavery, Rape, Torture': Libya Threatened by Foreign Fighters," *Al Jazeera*, May 28, 2002.

53. "'Slavery, Rape, Torture': Libya Threatened by Foreign Fighters."

54. Forte, *Slouching Towards Sirte*.

55. Dr. Khaled Wazani, "The Socio-Economic Implications of Syrian Refugees in Jordan," *Konrad Adenauer Stiftung*, Chapter II, May 22, 2014, at https://www.kas.de/documents/252038/253252/The_Socio-Economic_Implications_of_Syrian_Refugees_on_Jordan-Chapter2.pdf/56abf0d9-c861-6a1a-c58d-520e7c19b485. Wazani considers the liberalization reforms to have been successful in contributing to economic growth and in dampening inflation, though other political analysts see them as fueling widening inequality and disaffection with the government that helped fuel the Arab Spring protests. i.e., Lesch, *Syria*.

56. "The Story of Maher Arar: Rendition to Torture," Center For Constitutional Rights, https://ccrjustice.org/files/rendition%20to%20torture%20report.pdf

57. Frederic C. Hof, "I almost negotiated Israel-Syria Peace. Here's How it Happened," *Atlantic Council*, May 26, 2022.

58. *The Cradle*, February 5, 2025

59. Elizabeth Tsurkov, "Inside Israel's Secret Program to Back Syrian Rebels," *Foreign Policy*, September 6, 2018. Israel was able to effectively extend its occupation of the Golan Heights under the new HTS government.

Chapter 4: Voices from Syria

1. This chapter, based upon travels to the Levant by Dan Kovalik, is written in the first person as they represent his observations and interviews with individuals there.
2. "Thousands reported killed in Syria as HTS-allied forces attack, execute Alawites," *The Grayzone*, March 11, 2025.
3. Paul Antonopoulos, "SYRIA: Turkey-backed jihadists massacre Greek Orthodox Christians and Alawites in latest bout of violence," *Greek City Times*, March 8, 2025.
4. See Paul Antonopoulos, "Breaking: 7,000 Christians and Alawites have been slaughtered in Syria," Twitter (X), March 10.
5. *Syrian Christians* post, March 15, 2025.
6. *Syrian Christians* post, March 15, 2025.
7. "Thousands reported killed in Syria as HTS-allied forces attack, execute Alawites."
8. Tom O'Connor, "Syria's Civil War Takes Another Deadly, Dramatic Turn," *Newsweek*, March 11, 2025.
9. Jared Malsin, Stephen Kalin and Nancy A. Youssef, "US Military Brokers Deals to Bring Syrian Factions Together," *The Wall Street Journal*, March 15, 2025.
10. "Counterterrorism Guide," US National Counterterrorism Center at https://www.odni.gov/nctc/terrorist_groups/hts.html
11. EEAS Press Team, "Spokesperson statement on latest developments in Syria," *European Union External Action*, March 8, 2025.
12. Javier Villamor, "Brussels Welcomes Syrian Terrorists Despite Massacre of Civilians," *European Conservative*, March 12, 2025.
13. Villamor, "Brussels Welcomes Syrian Terrorists Despite Massacre of Civilians."
14. Bassem Mroue and Sarah El Deeb, "2 Days of Clashes and Revenge Killings in Syria Leave More Than 1,000 people dead," *AP News*, March 8, 2025.
15. DD Geopolitics on X, March 8, 2025 at https://x.com/dd_geopolitics/status/1898446886627090740?s=46
16. "Satellite Imagery Reveals Seven New Israeli Army Outposts in Syria," *The Cradle*, February 19, 2025.
17. "Letters of the Permanent Mission of the Syrian Arab Republic to the UN," October 2, 2014, https://documents.un.org/doc/undoc/gen/n14/557/61/pdf/n1455761.pdf.
18. "Who is Inciting Against Christians in the Valley of the Christians?" *Syrian Christians*, February 17, 2025, https://t.me/syrianchristian/1240.
19. See *Syrian Christians*, March 17, 2025 at https://t.me/syrianchristian/2166.

Chapter 5: Charlie Wilson's War Redux? Operation Timber Sycamore and Other Covert Operations in Syria

1. Robin Wright, "Our High-Priced Mercenaries in Syria," *The New Yorker*, September 17, 2016. Charlie Wilson was a Texas Congressman (D) who championed the CIA operations in Afghanistan and was the focus of a blockbuster Hollywood movie starring Tom Hanks that was based on Charlie Crile's book, *Charlie Wilson's War: The Extraordinary Story of the Largest Covert Operation in History* (New York: Atlantic Monthly Press, 2003).

2. Mark Mazetti, Adam Goldman and Michael E. Schmidt, "Behind the Sudden Death of a $1 Billion Secret CIA War in Syria," *The New York Times*, August 2, 2017.

3. Charles Glass, *Syria: Civil War to Holy War?* (New York: OR Books, 2025), 210. In his 2006 book, *State of Denial* (New York: Simon & Schuster, 2006), journalist Bob Woodward recounted a 2003 conversation in which George J. Tenet, then the CIA director, told Condoleezza Rice, then the national security advisor, "We created the Jordanian intelligence service, and now we own it." Some fighters were also flown to Qatar to be equipped and trained there.

4. Ben Cole, *The Syrian Information and Propaganda War: The Role of Cognitive Bias* (Switzerland: Palgrave Macmillan, 2022), 365.

5. Eric McRoberts, *Timber Sycamore: Obama's War in Syria* (self-published, 2025). Some weapons were air dropped, others brought in through military convoys. The CIA also supplied critical communications equipment and basic necessities to the rebels. McRoberts points out that the lack of centralized control of the supply chain created huge opportunities for corruption.

6. "Operation Timber Sycamore Continues," *Voltaire Network*, December 14, 2018; Thierry Meyssan, "Billions of Dollars Worth of Arms Against Syria," *Voltaire Network*, July 18, 2017. As part of the quid pro quo, the U.S. supplied the corrupt Azerbaijani government with $100 billion in arms, despite its genocidal assault on the people of Artsak (Nagorno-Karabakh). See Jeremy Kuzmarov, "There is a Country That Receives $100 Million in Military Aid per Year from the Biden Administration While It Engages in Ethnic Cleansing and Literally Tries to Starve Another People to Death," *CovertAction Magazine*, January 23, 2023. Weapons were also purchased from Croatia, Ukraine and Belarus, which was under an EU arms embargo, among other countries. Dilyana Gaytandzhieva is a Bulgarian journalist who first helped break the story of the Timber Sycamore arms-terrorists pipeline and was in turn fired from her newspaper and interrogated by Bulgarian authorities as a potential national security threat. "Journalist Interrogated, Fired for Linking CIA Weapons Shipments to Syrian Jihadists," *Mint Press*, August 20, 2017.

7. "Bulgarian Killer Testified About PM Borisov's Mafia Ties," *Crime*, November 26, 2011; Obama White House Archives.

8. Simon Chase and Ralph Pezzullo, *Zero Footprint: The True Story of a Private Military Contractor's Covert Assignments in Syria, Libya, and the World's Most Dangerous Places* (Boston: Little, Brown & Co, 2016), 203, 204. Chase recounts procuring arms through a former member of the Bulgarian secret police whom he said was "now a member of the local mafia, which made its money from drug and sex trafficking, cigarette smuggling and extortion."

9. Ivan Angelovski, Lawrence Marzouk and Roberto Capocelli, "Pentagon Hires Scandal Hit Brokers For Syria Arms Buy-Up," *Balkan Insight*, September 15, 2017; Aram Roston, "The Pentagon's Shopping List of Weapons to Fight ISIS," *Buzz Feed News*, February 11, 2016; Aram Roston, "Mobbed Up: Arms Dealer in American Anti-ISIS Effort Linked to Organized Crime," *Buzz Feed News*, December 14, 2015.

10. Alex Lantier, "The petty-bourgeois 'left' promotes the CIA war in Syria," *World Socialist Website*, April 12, 2013.

11. "Azerbaijani Silk Way Airlines carries out 350 diplomatic flights transporting weapons for terrorists – scandalous investigation," Published by Armenpress, July 4, 2017. The cover on Bulgaria's involvement in Timber Sycamore was blown in June 2015 when Francis Norvello, a 41-year-old American employee of the Virginia-based private mercenary firm Purple Shovel, owned by former intelligence operative Benjamin Worrell, was killed in a blast when a rocket-propelled grenade malfunctioned at a military range near the village of Anevo in Bulgaria. Originally from Texas, Norvello was a former Navy Seal. Two other Americans and two Bulgarians were also injured. The U.S. Embassy to Bulgaria then released a statement announcing that the U.S. government contractors were working on a U.S. military program to train and equip moderate rebels in Syria.

12. Paul Malone, "Save Us From Today's Dr. Strangelove," *The Canberra Times*, July 6, 2016.

13. A.B. Abrams, *World War in Syria: Global Conflict on Middle Eastern Battlefields* (Atlanta: Clarity Press Inc., 2021), 384.

14. Jonathan Hackett, "Covert Action in Irregular Wars: Unraveling the Case of Timber Sycamore in Syria (2012-2017)" *Small Wars Journal*, March 4, 2025; Claire Bernish, "Ex-CIA Agent Comes Clean on Syria: Obama Allowed For the Creation of ISIS," *Mint Press*, April 5, 2016.

15. Charles Glass, "'Tell Me How This Ends:' America's Muddled Involvement With Syria," *Harper's Magazine*, February 2019. The Libya-Syria arms pipeline was confirmed in a "highly classified annex" to the Senate Intelligence Committee's report on the assault by a local militia in September 2012 on the American consulate and a nearby undercover CIA facility in Benghazi. The attack resulted in the death of ambassador Christopher Stevens, and three others, associated in the past with the illegal Iran-Contra arms pipeline.

16. Max Blumenthal, "The US Has Backed 21 of the 28 'Crazy' Militias Leading Turkey's Brutal Invasion of Northern Syria," *The Grayzone*, October 16, 2019. Clinton's longstanding hawkish views are profiled in Diana Johnstone's *Queen of Chaos: The Misadventures of Hillary Clinton* (Oakland, CA: Counterpunch, 2015).

17. Oystein H. Rolandsen and Kjetil Selvik, "Disposable Rebels: U.S. Military Assistance to Insurgents in the Syrian Civil War," *Mediterranean Politics*, March 2, 2023.

18. Vanessa Beeley, 'Syria: Consign Barrel Bombs to the Propaganda Graveyard," *The Alt World*, January 2017. The 11,000 figure was provided by Dr. Zahar Hajjo, the head of Forensics in Aleppo. Beeley detailed a horrific massacre carried out by U.S. supplied ISIS fighters in Sweida in northern Syria in July, 2018 in "The

ISIS Massacre in Sweida: A Story of Torment and Resilience For an Uninterested World," *Mint Press*, December 14, 2018.

19. Matt Powers, "Making Sense of SADAT, Turkey's Private Military Company," *War on the Rocks*, October 8, 2021. A UN report found that SADAT—which was nicknamed the "Turkish Wagner" after the Russian private military company—sent 5,000 Syrian mercenaries to fight in Libya's civil war, which erupted after the U.S.-NATO intervention in Libya. Matthew Petti noted in *Reason Magazine* that once the Trump administration cut funding for Timber Sycamore, many FSA soldiers rebranded themselves as the "Syrian National Army" and became soldiers of fortune for the Turkish government. These Syrian mercenaries acquired a reputation for pillaging, rape, and murder, especially against Kurds. Matthew Petti, "Outlaws With Pickup Trucks Accomplish What $1 Billion in CIA Money Couldn't," *Reason Magazine*, December 6, 2024.

20. Martin Berger, "Operation Timber Sycamore and Washington's Secret War on Syria," *Mint Press News*, December 1, 2016; Kanishka Singh, "Jury Finds US Defense Contractor Liable in Torture at Abu Ghraib Prison," *Reuters*, November 12, 2024; Aram Roston, "Meet the Obscure Company Behind America's Syria Fiasco," *Buzz Feed News*, October 11, 2015. On the importance of private military contractors to America's forever wars in the 21st century, see Jeremy Kuzmarov, " 'Distancing Acts': Private Mercenaries and the War on Terror in American Foreign Policy," *The Asia Pacific Journal*, December 21, 2014.

21. Mazetti, Goldman and Schmidt, "Behind the Sudden Death of a $1 Billion Secret CIA War in Syria;" Mark Mazetti and Ali Younes, "C.I.A. Arms for Syrian Rebels Supplied Black Market, Officials Say," *The New York Times*, June 26, 2016. The Jordanian officers who were part of the scheme reaped a windfall from the weapons sales, using the money to buy expensive SUVs, i-phones and other luxury items.

22. C.J. Chivers and Eric Schmitt, "Arms Airlift to Syria Rebels Expands, With Aid from C.I.A.," *The New York Times*, March 24, 2013. Soquor al Sham was further implicated in the torture and murder of detainees.

23. A.B. Abrams, *World War on Syria: Global Conflict on Middle Eastern Battlefields* (Atlanta: Clarity Press, 2021), at ps. 121-122. The irony was that Assad's forces also made us of Soviet era and Russian made weapons.

24. Chivers and Schmitt, "Arms Airlift to Syria Rebels Expands, With Aid from C.I.A."

25. "Behind the Sudden Death of a $1 Billion Secret CIA War in Syria."

26. Chivers and Schmitt, "Arms Airlift to Syria Rebels Expands, With Aid from C.I.A."

27. Mark Mazetti and Matt Apuzzo, "U.S. Relies Heavily on Saudi Money to Support Syrian Rebels," *The New York Times*, January 23, 2016.

28. Charles Lister, "Al Qaeda Reaps Rewards of U.S. Policy Failures in Syria," *The Daily Beast*, July 6, 2018; Glass, "'Tell Me How This Ends.'"

29. David Ignatius, "What the Demise of the CIA's Anti-Assad Program Means," *The Washington Post*, July 20, 2017.

30. Robin Wright, "Our High-Priced Mercenaries in Syria," *The New Yorker*, September 17, 2015.

31. Oliver Boyd-Barrett, *Conflict Propaganda in Syria: Narrative Battles* (New York: Routledge, 2022), 145.

32. Hackett, "Covert Action in Irregular Wars;" Aaron Maté, "In Syria Dirty War, 'Our Side' Has Won," Substack, December 12, 2024.

33. Dr. Christine Lin, "How the US Ends Up Training al-Qaeda and ISIS Collaborators," *ISPSW Strategy Series: Focus on Defense and International Security*, December 2016.

34. Tulsi Gabbard, "The Syrian People Desperately Want Peace," *Substack*, January 24, 2017. Gabbard started the Stop Arming the Terrorists Act in Congress.

35. Lin, "How the US Ends Up Training al-Qaeda and ISIS Collaborators."

36. Quoted in Boyd-Barrett, *Conflict Propaganda in Syria*, 111.

37. Boyd-Barrett, *Conflict Propaganda in Syria*, 91.

38. Matthew Petti, "U.S. Slap Sanctions on Formerly CIA-Backed Syrian Rebels," *Responsible Statecraft*, August 22, 2023. Abu Amsha, leader of the Suleiman Shah Brigade, was accused of raping one of his subordinates' wives. Petti reported further that another CIA-backed FSA offshoot, the Sultan Murad Division, which was also subjected to State Department sanctions, recruited child soldiers.

39. Glass, "'Tell Me How This Ends;'" Stephen Gowans, *Washington's Long War on Syria* (Montreal: Baraka Books, 2017), 145.

40. Abrams, *World War on Syria*, 120, viii. Ukraine sent 250 advisers to train jihadists in Idlib.

41. Abrams, *World War on Syria*, 123-124.

42. Blumenthal, "The US Has Backed 21 of the 28 'Crazy' Militias Leading Turkey's Brutal Invasion of Northern Syria." One fighter promised mass ethnic cleansing if Kurds in the area refused to convert to his Wahhabi strain of Sunni Islam. "By Allah," the fighter declared, "if you repent and come back to Allah, then know that you are our brothers. But if you refuse, then we see that your heads are ripe, and that it's time for us to pluck them."

43. Abrams, *World War on Syria*, 123-124; Danny Gold, "Chatting About Game of Thrones with Syria's Most Feared Islamic Militants," *Vice*, May 7, 2013.

44. Abrams, *World War on Syria*, 123-124. The FSA worked hand-in-glove with Al Qaeda's Al Nusra Front, now rebranded HTS, with an FSA spokesman stating that Al-Nusra supplied the "elite commando troops" for the revolution FSA was purporting to lead.

45. Max Blumenthal, *The Management of Savagery: How America's National Security State Fueled the Rise of Al Qaeda, ISIS, and Donald Trump* (London: Verso, 2019), 193, 194.

46. Blumenthal, *The Management of Savagery*, 197.

47. Nabih Bulos, W.J. Hennigan, Brian Bennett "In Syria, militias armed by the Pentagon fight those armed by the CIA," *LA Times*, March 27, 2016; Boyd-Barrett, *Conflict Propaganda in Syria*, 91.

48. Tom O'Connor, "U.S. Military Battles Syrian Rebels Once Supported by CIA, Now Backed by Turkey," *Newsweek*, August 29, 2017.

49. Glass, "'Tell Me How This Ends;'" Barbara Plett Usher, "Joe Biden Apologized Over IS Remarks, But Was He Right?" *BBC*, October 7, 2016. Douglas Laux, a key CIA point man for Timber Sycamore also stated explicitly that there were "no moderates." Blumenthal, *The Management of Savagery*, 173.

50. Boyd-Barrett, *Conflict Propaganda in Syria*, 91.

51. Glass, *Syria: Civil War to Holy War?* 175; Kevin Maurer, "Special Forces Soldiers Reveal First Details of Battle With Russian Mercenaries in Syria," *Military.com*, May 12, 2023. Palmyra's historic monuments and ruin were tragically destroyed by these IS terrorists backed by the U.S.

52. Wright, "Our High-Priced Mercenaries in Syria." Canada assisted the coalition by providing intelligence aircraft and air-to-air refueling for U.S. jets that bombed Syria. Yves Engler, *House of Mirrors: Justin Trudeau's Foreign Policy* (Montreal: Black Rose Books, 2020), 93.

53. Bauer, "Behind the Lines;" Dave Phillips and Eric Schmitt, "How the U.S. Hid an Air Strike That Killed Dozens of Civilians in Syria," *The New York Times*, November 15, 2021. *The New York Times* reported on a March 2019 bombing attack in Baghuz that struck a crowd of women and children, killing at least 60.

54. Boyd-Barrett, *Conflict Propaganda in Syria*, 92.

55. Anand Gopal, "America's War on Syrian Civilians," *The New Yorker*, December 14, 2020.

56. Jeffrey D. Sachs and Sybil Fares, "How the US and Israel Destroyed Syria and Called it Peace," *Common Dreams*, December 12, 2024. This is a role the U.S., always opting for war, has played many times, for example in the former Yugoslavia where it blocked two peace agreements in the 1990's which could have ended hostilities, and also in Ukraine where it blocked a peace deal which had been agreed to in principle back in March of 2022, just a month after the war between Russia and Ukraine had begun.

57. "Operation Timber Sycamore Continues," December 14, 2018, *Voltaire.net*. A top government official told *The New York Times* in 2013 that Petraeus, the CIA director until November 2013, was "instrumental" in "helping to get this aviation network [for arms supplies under Timber Sycamore] moving and had prodded various countries to work together on it." KKR's website touts its growing investment in the Middle East.

58. Benjamin Arthur Thomason, "Making Democracy Safe for Empire," Ph.D. Dissertation, Bowling Green University, 2024, 205.

59. Thomason, "Making Democracy Safe for Empire," 203.

60. Boyd-Barrett, *Conflict Propaganda in Syria*, 79.

61. " $9 Million USAID aid Channeled To Al-Qaeda Via Fraud Scheme in Syria," *Turkey Today*, November 21, 2024; "DOJ Investigation Reveals Massive USAID Fraud, $9 Million Diverted To Al-Qaeda Affiliate," *The Commons*, February 6, 2025.

62. Thomason, "Making Democracy Safe for Empire," 203.

63. "Soros Gives $1 Million to Syria Humanitarian Aid," *AP News*, November 7, 2013. Incidentally, the IRC paid $6.9 million to settle allegations that its staff participated in a kickback scheme using USAID and U.S. government money.

64. Thomason, "Making Democracy Safe for Empire," 203.

65. Glass, "'Tell Me How This Ends.'" See also Blumenthal, *The Management of Savagery*.

66. Cole, *The Syrian Information and Propaganda War*, 97.

67. See Marilyn B. Young, *The Vietnam Wars* (New York: Harper Perennial, 1991); *Laos: War and Revolution*, ed. Alfred W. McCoy and Nina Adams (New York: Harper & Row, 1970); Jeremy Kuzmarov, *Modernizing Repression: Police Training*

and Nation Building in the American Century (Amherst, MA: University of Massachusetts Press, 2012), ch. 7.

68. Calling for Assad to be tried in a Nuremburg-style court, Roth sent out 200 tweets alone in a short period accusing Assad of deploying thousands of barrel bombs of Hiroshima level intensity, which was an impossibility. He also joined the chorus in accusing Assad of carrying out chemical weapons attacks and advanced myths about the Caesar photos (discussed in subsequent chapters), ignoring any evidence that proved otherwise. See e.g. "Remarks of Kenneth Roth at the 2017 Nuremburg International Human Rights Award," September 24, 2017.

69. Boyd-Barrett, *Conflict Propaganda in Syria*, 79, 80. This assessment fits well with the critique of human rights NGO's put forward by Alfred de Zayas, former senior lawyer with the Office of the UN High Commissioner for Human Rights, in his book, *The Human Rights Industry* (Atlanta: Clarity Press, 2023).

70. "Lessons From Damascus," *Military Watch Magazine*, January 10, 2025.

71. Dave Phillips, Eric Schmitt, and Mark Mazetti, "Civilian Deaths Mounted as Secret Unit Pounded ISIS," *The New York Times*, December 12, 2021. One former task force member said that Talon Anvil operators who rotated through roughly every four months were trained as elite commandos and had little experience running a strike cell. In addition, he said, the daily demands of overseeing strike after strike seemed to erode operators' perspective and "fray their humanity." Phillips, Eric Schmitt, and Mark Mazetti, "Civilian Deaths Mounted as Secret Unit Pounded ISIS."

72. Phillips, Eric Schmitt, and Mark Mazetti, "Civilian Deaths Mounted as Secret Unit Pounded ISIS." The Talon Anvil Special Forces operated from an abandoned cement factory on the Iraqi border. They would use first names and no rank or uniforms. Many had bushy beards and went to work in shorts and footwear that included Crocs and Birkenstocks, though they "controlled a fleet of Predator and Reaper drones that bristled with precision Hellfire missiles and laser-guided bombs."

73. Jeremy Kuzmarov, "Why is Joe Biden Discreetly Looking the Other Way as His AFRICOM Commander Commits War Crimes for Which He Would Have Been Hanged at Nuremburg," *CovertAction Magazine*, January 13, 2022.

74. Kuzmarov, "Why is Joe Biden Discreetly Looking the Other Way as His AFRICOM Commander Commits War Crimes for Which He Would Have Been Hanged at Nuremburg."

Chapter 6: Strange Bedfellows: The Multi-National Alliance Against Syria

1. Christopher Davidson, *Shadow Wars: The Secret Struggle for the Middle East* (London: One World Publishing, 2016), 461.

2. https://transcripts.cnn.com/show/cnr/date/2015-02-11/segment/09

3. Davidson, *Shadow Wars*, 461-462.

4. Davidson, *Shadow Wars*, 463.

5. Davidson, *Shadow Wars*, 464-465.

6. Mark Modalek, "Remembering American Journalist Killed in Suspicious Car Crash in turkey After Entering Erdoğan's Crosshairs," *Mint Press*, August 5, 2016.

7. Foundation for Defense of Democracies, "10 Things to Know about Turkey's Interventions and Influence in Syria," February 24, 2025.

8. Foundation For the Defense of Democracies, "10 Things to Know about Turkey's Interventions and Influence in Syria."

9. "Turkish-Backed Jihadist Groups and Their Commanders Accused of Civilian Deaths in Syria," *Nordic Monitor*, March 11, 2025.

10. Stephen Gowans, *Washington's Long War on Syria* (Montreal: Baraka Books, 2017), 175.

11. Gowans, *Washington's Long War on Syria*, 175.

12. Patrick Cockburn, *The Rise of Islamic State: ISIS and the New Sunni Revolution* (London: Verso, 2015), 100. In the early 1970s, the Nixon administration signed a key deal with the Saudis that exchanged security guarantees for Saudis promise to trade its oil in U.S. dollars, guaranteeing the world supremacy of the U.S. dollar in the face of the OPEC oil embargo. The U.S. Saudi alliance was originated in the 1940s under the FDR administration.

13. Cockburn, *The Rise of Islamic State*, 101.

14. Cockburn, *The Rise of Islamic State*, 101

15. Gowans, *Washington's Long War on Syria*, 170-173.

16. Gowans, *Washington's Long War on Syria*, 158.

17. Gowans, *Washington's Long War on Syria*,158-159.

18. Davidson, *Shadow Wars*, 458-459.

19. Davidson, *Shadow Wars*, 458-459.

20. Davidson, *Shadow Wars*, 460-461.

21. Noam Chomsky, *Failed States: The Abuse of Power and the Assault on Democracy* (New York: Holt Paperbacks, 2006), 170.

22. *Al Jazeera* was equally bad for Libya, advancing a demonized view of Gaddafi and lending support for the U.S.-NATO regime-change operation and bombing that plunged Libya into a new dark age. See Maximilian Forte, *Slouching Towards Sirte: NATO's War on Libya and Africa* (Montreal: Baraka Books, 2012), 13, 105.

23. A.B. Abrams, *World War in Syria: Global Conflict on Middle Eastern Battlefields* (Atlanta: Clarity Press, 2021),103.

24. Abrams, *World War in Syria*.

25. Abrams, *World War in Syria*, 104.

26. Abrams, *World War in Syria*, 104.

27. Abrams, *World War in Syria*, 104.

28. @RedStreamNet, Twitter (X), December 25, 2024, at https://x.com/redstreamnet/status/1906307934553780548?s=46

29. @RedStreamNet, Twitter (X), December 25, 2024, at https://x.com/redstreamnet/status/1906307934553780548?s=46

30. @RedStreamNet, Twitter (X), December 25, 2024, at https://x.com/redstreamnet/status/1906307934553780548?s=46

31. Emanuel Fabien, "Israel Participating in Joint Air Force Drills in Greece with 11 other countries, including Qatar," *Times of Israel*, March 31, 2025.

32. TOI Staff, Netanyahu aides reportedly suspected of recently receiving six-figure sums from Qatar," *Times of Israel*, March 8, 2025.

33. Jimmy Dore, "THIS Is Why The Irish Are Passionate About Gaza! w/ Tadhg Hickey," *The Jimmy Dore Show*, March 23, 2025.

34. Dore, "THIS Is Why The Irish Are Passionate About Gaza! w/ Tadhg Hickey."

35. Jeremy Kuzmarov, "U.S. Exposed as 'Secret Partner' in Israeli Air Strikes Against Syria That Violate International Law," *CovertAction Magazine*, June 29, 2022.

36. Judah Ari Gross, "IDF Chief Acknowledges Long-Claimed Weapons Supply to Syrian Rebels," *Times of Israel*, January 14, 2019.

37. Gross, "IDF Chief Acknowledges Long-Claimed Weapons Supply to Syrian Rebels."

38. Gross, "IDF Chief Acknowledges Long-Claimed Weapons Supply to Syrian Rebels."

39. Gross, "IDF Chief Acknowledges Long-Claimed Weapons Supply to Syrian Rebels."

40. Abrams, *World War in Syria*, 128-129.

41. Abrams, *World War in Syria*, 128-129.

42. Kuzmarov, "U.S. Exposed as 'Secret Partner' in Israeli Air Strikes Against Syria That Violate International Law."

43. Kuzmarov, "U.S. Exposed as 'Secret Partner' in Israeli Air Strikes Against Syria That Violate International Law."

44. Dore, "THIS Is Why The Irish Are Passionate About Gaza! w/ Tadhg Hickey."

45. Mostafa Salem, "In Netanyahu's New Middle East, Syria Could Become Israel's Biggest Strategic Gain," *CNN*, March 14, 2025. Walid Jumblatt, a Lebanese Druze leader who is widely respected by Druze outside Lebanon, warned about Israel's ambitions when he said that "Israel wants to use tribes, sects and religions for its own benefit. It wants to fragment the region." The Druze "should be careful," he added. Israel gets 30% of its water supply from the Golan Heights.

46. Shir Peretz, "Israel Approves Plans to Expand Communities in the Golan Heights," *The Jerusalem Post*, December 16, 2024; Jason Ditz, "Israel Demolishes South Syria Homes, Detains Civilians," *antiwar.com*, June 18, 2025. Netanyahu said that "strengthening the Golan is strengthening the State of Israel." The IDF was sent to fire at protesters opposed to Israeli expansionism, including ironically in Daraa where the Arab Spring first started.

47. Vanessa Beeley, "The Zionist 'loot unit' strips Gaza, south Lebanon and Syria of weapons and valuables," *The Alt World*, March 2, 2025; "Report Reveals Vast Loot Israeli Soldiers Took From Gaza, Lebanon, Syria," *Middle East Eye*, February 28, 2025. Israeli soldiers joked that their backs hurt from carrying so much stolen goods. Some Israeli troops were filmed holding a drunken passover seder in one of the Syrian homes that they took over.

48. Jason Ditz, "IDF Chief Tours Occupied Syria, Says Long-Term Control 'Vital,'" *antiwar.com*, April 21, 2025. Israeli Prime Minister Benjamin Netanyahu for his part claimed credit for starting the chain of events that led to the fall of Assad's regime, presenting the day of Assad's downfall as a "historic day in the history of the Middle East. The Assad regime is a central link in Iran's axis of evil—this regime has fallen." Lazar Berman, "Netanyahu Claims Credit For Starting 'Historic' Process That Led to Fall of Assad Regime," *The Times of Israel*, December 8, 2024.

49. Salem, "In Netanyahu's New Middle East, Syria Could Become Israel's Biggest Strategic Gain."

50. Dore, "THIS Is Why The Irish Are Passionate About Gaza! w/ Tadhg Hickey."

Chapter 7: Shades of the Gulf of Tonkin: Chemical Weapons False Flag

1. Romain Houeix, "A History of the Syrian Chemical Weapons 'Red Line,'" *France24*, April 16, 2018.

2. In Jeremy Kuzmarov, *Obama's Unending Wars: Fronting the Foreign Policy of the Permanent Warfare State* (Atlanta: Clarity Press, 2012), 272. Obama's attack plan involved a "monster strike." Two wings of B-52 bombers were shifted to airbases close to Syria and navy submarines and ships equipped with Tomahawk missiles were deployed in preparation. In June 2013, Deputy National Security adviser Ben Rhodes issued a statement saying the intelligence community had determined that the Assad regime had used chemical weapons, including the nerve agent sarin, "on a small scale against the opposition multiple times in the last year," killing an estimated 100 to 150 people. The Obama administration, which had already committed $250 million in nonlethal aid to the Syrian opposition, including food, medical supplies, body armor, and night vision goggles, said it would expand its support for anti-Assad forces. The following month, congressional intelligence committees approved sending CIA weapons to the Syrian opposition. Shane Bauer, "Behind the Lines," *Mother Jones*, May/June 2020.

3. Seymour Hersh, "Trump's Red Line," *Welt*, June 25, 2017.

4. Jeremy Kuzmarov, "Prestigious Weaponry Expert Censored After Demonstrating that a Deadly Poison Gas Attack—Blamed on the Syrian Government—Was Really a False-Flag Operation by U.S.-Funded Terrorists," *CovertAction Magazine*, November 22, 2021.

5. Hersh, "Trump's Red Line."

6. See A.B. Abrams, *Atrocity Fabrication and Its Consequences: How Fake News Shapes World Order* (Atlanta: Clarity Press, 2023); Tim Anderson, *The Dirty War in Syria* (Montreal, CA: Global Research 2016).

7. Kuzmarov, *Obama's Unending Wars*, 272.

8. See Fred A. Wilcox, "Dying Forests, Dying People: Agent Orange and Chemical Warfare in Vietnam," *The Asia Pacific Journal*, December 11, 2011.

9. Peter Byrne, "The Use of Deadly Sarin Nerve Gas During the Secret War on Laos," *The Edge*, February 19, 2005.

10. Aaron Maté, "Despite smear campaign, Tulsi Gabbard is not at odds with US intel on Syria," *Substack*, January 28, 2025.

11. Daniele Ganser, "Who Used Poison Gas in Syria?" *Free 21*, October 29, 2017; Anderson, *The Dirty War in Syria*, 143; Max Blumenthal, *The Management of Savagery: How America's National Security State Fueled the Rise of Al Qaeda, ISIS, and Donald Trump* (London: Verso, 2019), 186. A Russian investigation determined that the chemical agent allegedly used at Khan al-Assal was carried by a "Bashair-3 unguided projectile," which was produced by the Basha'ir al-Nasr Brigade, a rebel group affiliated with the CIA-backed Free Syrian Army (FSA).

12. Anderson, *The Dirty War in Syria*, 147; Abrams, *Atrocity Fabrication and Its Consequences*, 419. The only other explanation is that Assad and his military commanders were ridiculously incompetent, constantly attacked their own soldiers with chemical weapons, killing their own men and giving the West a pretext to attack Syria.

13. Ben Cole, *The Syrian Information and Propaganda War: The Role of Cognitive Bias* (Switzerland: Palgrave Macmillan, 2022), 202.

14. Seymour Hersh, "The Red Line and the Rat Line," *The London Review of Books*, April 17, 2014. Hersh wrote that "the White House's misrepresentation of what it knew about the attack, and when, was matched by its readiness to ignore intelligence that could undermine the narrative. That information concerned al Nusra."

15. Hersh, "The Red Line and the Rat Line."

16. Hersh, "The Red Line and the Rat Line."

17. Hersh, "The Red Line and the Rat Line."

18. Anderson, *The Dirty War in Syria*, 145. The father of a rebel said that his son had asked him what he thought the weapon he was asked to carry from Saudi Arabia was and the father said he thought it was chemical weapons. The son then died in a tunnel used to store weapons provided by Saudi militants known as Abu Ayesha.

19. Hersh, "The Red Line and the Rat Line."

20. Hersh, "The Red Line and the Rat Line."

21. Hersh, "The Red Line and the Rat Line." Qassag self-identified as a member of the al-Nusra Front.

22. Ganser, "Who Used Poison Gas in Syria?"

23. Hersh, "The Red Line and the Rat Line."

24. Anderson, *The Dirty War in Syria*, 145, 146. Even Human Rights Watch reported on the abduction of children in Northern Latakia.

25. Oliver Boyd-Barrett, *Conflict Propaganda in Syria: Competing Narratives* (New York: Routledge, 2022), 220.

26. Eva Bartlett, "Douma: Three Years On: How independent media shot down the false 'chemical attack' narrative," *Off-Guardian*, May 25, 2021.

27. Maté, "Despite smear campaign, Tulsi Gabbard is not at odds with US intel on Syria."

28. Maté, "Despite smear campaign, Tulsi Gabbard is not at odds with US intel on Syria."

29. Theodore Postol and Richard Lloyd, letter to the editor, *London Review of Books*, April 17, 2014; Theodore Postol and Richard Lloyd, "Possible Implications of Faulty US Technical Intelligence in the Damascus Nerve Agent Attack of August 21, 2013," Washington, D.C., January 14, 2014. An athlete who had been drafted by the LA. Dodgers, Lloyd was also a former UN weapons inspector.

30. Postol and Lloyd, letter to the editor, *London Review of Books*, April 17, 2014.

31. Cole, *The Syrian Information and Propaganda War*, 371. Around 100 protesters gathered in Chicago at the Trump Tower there before marching along Michigan Avenue chanting. "Hey, Hey, Donald J, how many kids have you killed today?"

32. *ABC News*, "Strike on Syria gets mixed reactions for Lawmakers," April 6, 2017. *Military History Fandom.com*. "House Majority Leader Kevin McCarthy (R–CA) said, 'Assad has made his disregard for innocent human life and long-standing norms against chemical weapons use crystal clear. Tonight's strikes show these evil actions carry consequences.'" Even those congressmen who questioned the air strikes pointed to Assad's being guilty of carrying out a chemical weapons attack.

33. This section is drawn from Kuzmarov, *CovertAction Magazine*, November 25, 2021. "Prestigious Weaponry Expert Censored After Demonstrating that a Deadly Poison Gas Attack—Blamed on the Syrian Government—Was Really a False-Flag Operation by U.S.-Funded Terrorists."

34. Kuzmarov, "Prestigious Weaponry Expert Censored..."

35. Boyd-Barrett, *Conflict Propaganda in Syria*, 232

36. Tareq Haddad, "MIT expert claims latest chemical weapons attack in Syria was staged," *International Business Times*, April 17, 2017.

37. Inspector A, *The Syria Scam: An Insider Look into Chemical Weapons, Geopolitics and the Fog of War* (Green Hill Publishing, 2025), 191, 192. Trump had claimed in launching the strikes: "Tonight, I ordered a targeted military strike on the air base in Syria from where the chemical attack was launched. It is in this vital national security intereset of the United States to prevent and deter the spread and use of deadly chemical weapons."

38. Cole, *The Syrian Information and Propaganda War*, 206. Trump finished his tweet by stating: "Another humanitarian disaster for no reason whatsoever. SICK!"

39. James Harkin and Lauren Freeney, "What Happened in Douma? Searching For Facts in the Fog of Syria's Propaganda," *The Intercept*, February 9, 2019. The timing of the alleged chemical gas attack was very convenient as Trump had previously discussed potentially removing U.S. troops from Syria. The "rebel" group controlling Douma at the time, Jaysh al-Islam, part of the Islamist opposition to Assad that includes the Syrian branch of Al Qaeda as well as the remnants of ISIS, had been credibly accused of using chlorine gas in the course of fighting against Kurdish forces and civilians in Aleppo in 2016. That charge, made by the Kurds, was given extensive publicity by Voice of America, the propaganda arm of the U.S. government. Patrick Martin, "CIA Stages Gas Attack Pretext for Syria Escalation," *The World Socialist Website*, April 9, 2018.

40. Inspector A, *The Syria Scam*. 254. The original report that Henderson helped draft was doctored to fit the conclusion that Assad had likely carried out a chemical weapon attack at Douma. A senior staffer told him that "we've been told that we've got to make it sound like we found something." Henderson was subsequently blacklisted, and then ignored by U.S. and UK diplomats when he testified before the UN Security Council. The U.S. also voted to block the testimony of former OPCW Director Jose Bustani when he tried to testify in support of Henderson and the other OPCW whistleblower.

41. Inspector A, *The Syria Scam*. 345-375. Henderson notes that witnesses who reported on a chemical attack were anti-Assad Syrian refugees living in Turkey whereas those living in Douma did not report on any chemical weapons attacks. Henderson's interview with doctors in Douma confirmed what Robert Fisk had reported about respiratory symptoms related to bombings but no chemical weapons attack. Henderson additionally knew the photos were staged because they showed bodies allegedly piled on top of each other in a building, which the people would have in reality tried to escape. Their deaths would have been from asphyxiation and more gradual so they would not have all fallen in one spot on top of each other. Toxicologists had found that symptoms documented were inconsistent with

those derived from chlorine gas. Also, the cylinder allegedly carrying the chemical weapons was not in any way deformed, which is scientifically impossible, and was not found to have caused the crater that was photographed (which Henderson found to have been formed by some kind of explosive). The helicopters alleged to have dropped the weapons would have had to have flown at a low altitude, and yet no witnesses observed low flying helicopters dropping anything in Douma at the time of the alleged attack.

42. Aaron Maté, "Syria scandal: New whistleblower claims chemical weapons watchdog OPCW suppressed Douma evidence," *The Grayzone Project*, November 16, 2019; Niles Niemuth, "New Wikileaks Documents Expose Phony Claims of 2018 Syria Chemical Weapons Attack," *The World Socialist Website*, December 16, 2018; Abrams, *Atrocity Fabrication and Its Consequences*, 433; No evidence was found to actually indicate that sarin gas was used in Douma. Colonel Lawrence Wilkerson stated that the claims regarding Assad and the chemical weapons attacks were "preposterous. When you see a man standing beside a crater, for example, and allege VX or Sarin was used, you know it's preposterous. The man would be dead."

43. Mark Taliano, "Crimes Against Syria," 2023, https://marktanliano.net/crimes-against-syria/. See also Bartlett, "Douma: Three Years On." Ahmed Toumeh, a 42 year-old from Hamouriya told journalist Vanessa Beeley that "when the chemicals were used, they had hospitals ready always two days before—they had information in advance of the supposed attacks. How could they know unless they were involved?" Mahmoud Al Khaled, a 28-year old from Douma said that "the armed groups or the White Helmets would visit us in the basements and tell us we were going to be hit with chemical weapons. They would tell us to be careful and to go outside to avoid injury. They always told us two or three days beforehand. They planned all the chemical operations in Eastern Ghouta." Vanessa Beeley, "Eastern Ghouta: Syrian Voices Raised in Condemnation of White Helmets," *21st Century Wire*, May 31, 2018.

44. Boyd-Barrett, *Conflict Propaganda in Syria*, 235. Admiral Lord West had asked: "Why would Assad use chemical weapons at this time? He's won the war. That's not just my opinion, it is shared by senior commanders in the US military. There is no rationale behind Assad's involvement whatsoever . . . .The jihadists and the various opposition groups who've been fighting against Assad have much greater motivation to launch a chemical weapons attack and make it look like Assad was responsible." In Cole, *The Syrian Information and Propaganda War*, 207.

45. Aaron Maté, "Leaked OPCW report suggests Syria gas attack was 'staged,' MIT scientist says," *The Grayzone*, May 25, 2019. A member of the BBC production team, Riam Dalati broke ranks with his UK Government-aligned media, on Twitter, to announce that "after almost 6 months of investigation, I can prove, without a doubt, that the Douma hospital scene was staged." Almost immediately after the alleged incident in Douma, he tweeted out his frustration that "activists and rebels" had used "corpses of dead children to stage emotive scenes for Western consumption." Vanessa Beeley, "Real 'Obscene Masquerade:' How BBC Depicted Staged Hospital Scenes as Proof of Douma Chemical Attacks," *RT*, February 18,

2019. A third former OPCW official who worked in a senior role, blamed external pressure and potential threats to their family for their failure to speak out about the corruption of the Douma investigation.

46. Robert Burns and AP National Security Writer, "US Has No Evidence of Syrian Use of Sarin Gas, Mattis Says," *Associated Press*, February 2, 2018.

47. Martin, "CIA Stages Gas Attack Pretext for Syria Escalation." The sole on-the-spot accounts of the alleged Douma chemical weapons attack came from the White Helmets, celebrated by the media as a rescue organization, but affiliated with the anti-Assad "rebels" and largely funded by the U.S., Britain, Germany and other imperialist powers. This includes $23 million from USAID, a longtime front for the CIA.

48. Niemuth, "New Wikileaks Documents Expose Phony Claims of 2018 Syria Chemical Weapons Attack." Patrick Martin wrote that "the brazen lies of the media are accompanied by breathtaking hypocrisy. The *Times*, the *Washington Post*, NBC, ABC, CBS, CNN and company downplay and cover up the atrocities carried out by American forces and their allies—the incineration of Mosul and Raqqa, the gunning down of demonstrators in Gaza by the Israeli military, the mass killings in Yemen carried out with U.S. support by Saudi Arabia, even as its crown prince is feted by the U.S. ruling elite, and the ongoing slaughter in Afghanistan." Martin, "CIA Stages Gas Attack Pretext for Syria Escalation."

49. Isaac Stanley-Becker, "How a Contrarian MIT Professor Fueled Tulsi Gabbard's Doubts About Syrian Gas Attacks," *The Washington Post*, January 28, 2025; Maté, "Despite smear campaign, Tulsi Gabbard is not at odds with US intel on Syria." Bellingcat's funding from NED is detailed in Kit Klarenberg, "Bellingcat funded by US and UK intelligence contractors that aided extremists in Syria," *The Grayzone*, October 9, 2021.

50. Kuzmarov, "Prestigious Weaponry Expert Censored..." Despite his lack of proper credentials, Higgins was often a main media source for the allegations of chemical weapons attacks by Assad and even used as a main source for an investigation carried out by Human Rights Watch of the 2013 Eastern Ghouta attacks, which Human rights Watch blamed on Assad.

51. https://worldview.stratfor.com/article/gauging-syrian-conflict

52. The supposedly alternative program *Democracy Now* was among those to report incorrectly on Houla and to blame the Assad government for a crime committed by U.S.-backed rebels.

53. Abrams, *Atrocity Fabrication and Its Consequences*, 410, 411; Anderson, *The Dirty War in Syria*; Robert Fisk, "Inside Duraya—How a Failed Prisoner Swap Turned Into a Massacre," *The Independent*, August 30, 2012; Alex Thompson, "Was There a Massacre in the Syrian Town of Aqrab?" Channel 4, December 14, 2012. There are strong parallels with the Ukraine conflict, where the U.S. government and media blamed Russians for atrocities like at Bucha that independent investigators found were carried out by the Ukrainian military and its neo-Nazi adjuncts and that the crime scene was subsequently staged to make it look like the Russians did it. See Jeremy Kuzmarov, "Remember the Maine: The Alleged Russian Atrocity at Bucha Looks Like Another in a Long Line of False Pretexts for War," *CovertAction Magazine*, May 13, 2022.

54. Jeffrey Lewis, "Buzz Bomb: Why Everyone's Wrong About Assad's Zombie Gas," *Foreign Policy*, January 25, 2013.

55. Vanessa Beeley, 'Syria: Consign Barrel Bombs to the Propaganda Graveyard," *The Alt World*, January, 2017; Craig Murray, "The Barrel Bomb Conundrum," *CraigMurray.org*, September 18, 2016. Murray notes that barrel bombs are a crude version of a conventional weapon, a point obscured in the U.S. media. Murray wrote that "the blanket media use of 'barrel bomb' as though it represents something uniquely inhumane is a fascinating example of propaganda, especially set beside the repeated ludicrous claims that British bombs do not kill civilians."

56. Boyd-Barrett, *Conflict Propaganda in Syria*. *Democracy Now's* Syria coverage cane be followed at https://www.democracynow.org/topics/syria/91?oldest_first=true. From the outbreak of the Dara protests, the show's coverage routinely featured human rights activists who were against the Assad regime and that presented the anti-Assad struggle as a valiant pro-democracy one while blaming Assad exclusively for committing horrific atrocities. Little was mentioned of the violent character of the opposition and its dominance by Islamic fundamentalists. The Ghouta attack segment can be found here. https://www.democracynow.org/2013/8/23/syrian_activist_on_ghouta_attack_i. To its credit, *Democracy Now* did include some skeptics such as Patrick Cockburn and reporters who had visited the alleged contaminated site.

57. Spencer Ackerman, "Meet the Assadosphere, the Online Defenders of Syria's Butcher," *Wired*, December 11, 2012.

58. "Sanders Statement on U.S. Missile Strike on Syria," April 7, 2017.

59. William S. Kiser, *The Business of Killing Indians: Scalp Warfare and the Violent Conquest of North America* (New Haven: Yale University Press, 2025), 202; Abrams, *Atrocity Fabrication and Its Consequences*; Peter Dale Scott, *The War Conspiracy* (Indianapolis: Bobbs-Merrill, 1972) among many other works. California settler William Jarboe and others claimed that the Yuki Indians had been killing white settlers' livestock for years. Eyewitnesses insisted, however, that almost every account of Yuki wrongdoing had been either totally fabricated or egregiously exaggerated in order to justify deadly operations against them in the 1860s that led to their decimation.

Chapter 8: A War by Other Means: Sanctions and the U.S. Regime-Change Operation

1. The website *Sanctions Kill* noted that "sanctions are imposed by the U.S. and its junior partners against countries that resist their agendas. They are a weapon of economic war, resulting in chronic shortages of basic necessities, economic dislocation, chaotic hyperinflation, artificial famines, disease and poverty. In every country, the poorest and the weakest—the infants, children, the chronically ill and the elderly—suffer the worst impact of sanctions."

2. Quoted in Mark Taliano, *Voices From Syria* (Montreal: Global Research, 2017), 95.

3. Greg Shupak, "Writing Out Empire: The Case of the Syria Sanctions," in *Sanctions as War: Anti-Imperialist Perspectives on American Geo-Economic Strategy*, ed. Stuart Davis and Immanuel Ness (London: Brill, 2022), 253.

4. Hekmat Aboutkhater, "I crashed an anti-Syria lobby meeting where they pushed for a new Caliphate and more starvation sanctions," *The Grayzone*, August 21, 2023; "Jordanian Figures: Caesar Act a Crime Against Humanity," *Sana*, June 15, 2020.

5. Karin Strohecker and Libby George, "Syria's Economy: The Devastating Impact of War and Sanctions," *Reuters*, January 6, 2025.

6. Max Blumenthal, *The Management of Savagery: How America's National Security State Fueled the Rise of Al Qaeda, ISIS, and Donald Trump* (London: Verso, 2019), 223.

7. Jeremy Kuzmarov, "Mainstream Media Colludes with U.S. Government To Conceal Source of Syria's Heartbreaking Humanitarian Crisis," *CovertAction Magazine*, June 30, 2023.

8. Charles Glass, *Syria: Civil War or Holy War?* foreword by Aaron Maté (New York: OR Books, 2025), 257; Tim Anderson, *The Dirty War on Syria* (Montreal, Canada: Global Research, 2016); A.B. Abrams, *World War in Syria: Global Conflict on Middle Eastern Battlefields* (Atlanta: Clarity Press, 2021), 338; Taliano, *Voices From Syria*.

9. Kuzmarov, "Mainstream Media Colludes with U.S. Government To Conceal Source of Syria's Heartbreaking Humanitarian Crisis." Rebel shelling of hospitals is also discussed in Anderson, *The Dirty War on Syria*, 165. On the horrifying effects of U.S. sanctions in the 1990s in Iraq, see *Iraq Under Siege: The Deadly Impact of Sanctions and War*, ed. Anthony Arnove (Boston: South End Press, 2000).

10. Kuzmarov, "Mainstream Media Colludes with U.S. Government To Conceal Source of Syria's Heartbreaking Humanitarian Crisis."

11. Glass, *Syria: Civil War or Holy War?* xiii; Zhang Chungyue, "US Forces Continue Blatant Looting of Syrian Oil, 'Exposing Gangster Nature,'" *Global Times*, September 6, 2022. Data released by Syria's Ministry of Oil and Mineral Resources showed that in the first half of 2022, U.S. forces allegedly stole more than 80 percent of Syria's oil resources every day as the country's average daily oil production can reach 80,000 barrels and 66,000 barrels were taken by the U.S. and U.S.-backed opposition armed groups. Zhu pointed out that that "such barefaced robbery in Syria" was "not much different from colonial plunder." He added that "there is no greater injustice than the world's wealthiest country robbing one of the poorest."

12. Chungyue, "US Forces Continue Blatant Looting of Syrian Oil, 'Exposing Gangster Nature."

13. "Lessons From Damascus' Fall: Former British Ambassador to Syria Details How the West, Israel and Turkey Won," *Military Watch Magazine*, January 10, 2025.

14. Patrick Donovan Higgins, "Gunning for Damascus: The US War on the Syrian Arab Republic," *Middle East Critique:* 32:2 (2023), 217-241.

15. David W. Lesch, *Syria: The Fall of the House of Assad*, updated edition (New Haven: Yale University Press, 2012), 17. Another Democrat supportive of the sanctions, Gary Ackerman (D-NY), stated: "This is not too big a nut to crack.

Syria is a small, decrepit little terror state that has been yanking our diplomatic chain for years." Shelley Berkley (D-NV) referred to Assad as a "kinder, gentler terrorist" from his father "and we don't need another one of those."

16. Shupak, "Writing Out Empire," in *Sanctions as War*, ed. Davis and Ness, 246; Sean Matthews, "US Sanctions on Syria: How They Work and What They Mean," *Middle East Eye*, December 26, 2024; Stephen Gowans, *Washington's Long War on Syria* (Montreal: Baraka Books, 2017), 110.

17. Shupak, "Writing Out Empire," in *Sanctions as War*, ed. Davis and Ness, 249, 250; Blumenthal, *The Management of Savagery*, 223.

18. Dr. Khaled Wazani, "The Socio-Economic Implications of Syrian Refugees in Jordan," *Konrad Adenauer Stiftung*, Chapter II, May 22, 2014, at https://www.kas.de/documents/252038/253252/The_Socio-Economic_Implications_of_Syrian_Refugees_on_Jordan-Chapter2.pdf/56abf0d9-c861-6a1a-c58d-520e7c19b485

19. https://www.state.gov/syria-sanctions/

20. John Dagge and Ghalia Lababidi, "Sanctioning Syria," https://search.wikileaks.org/syria-files/emailid/1104909

21. "Statement by President Obama on the Situation in Syria," August 16, 2011.

22. Shupak, "Writing Out Empire," in *Sanctions as War*, ed. Davis and Ness, 248; Gowans, *Washington's Long War on Syria*, 110.

23. Shupak, "Writing Out Empire," in *Sanctions as War*, ed. Davis and Ness, 250.

24. Taliano, *Voices From Syria*, 20.

25. https://docs.un.org/en/A/HRC/54/23/ADD.1

26. Shupak, "Writing Out Empire," in *Sanctions as War*, ed. Davis and Ness, 251.

27. Shupak, "Writing Out Empire," in *Sanctions as War*, ed. Davis and Ness, 251.

28. https://docs.un.org/en/A/HRC/54/23/ADD.1; Anderson, *The Dirty War on Syria*, 169; Patrick Cockburn, "US and EU sanctions are ruining ordinary Syrians' lives, yet Bashar al-Assad hangs on to power," *The Independent*, October 7, 2016, https://www.independent.co.uk/voices/syria-syrian-war-us-eu-sanctions-bashar-alassad-patrick-cockburn-a7350751.html Syria's literacy rate declined from 91 to 80 percent over a decade of war and sanctions.

29. Shupak, "Writing Out Empire," in *Sanctions as War*, ed. Davis and Ness, 252; Blumenthal, *The Management of Savagery*, 223.

30. Taliano, *Voices From Syria*, 33. See also https://docs.un.org/en/A/HRC/54/23/ADD.1

31. Eva Bartlett, "The Caesar Act: The Latest Western Attack on Syria Didn't Drop From a Plane," *Mint Press*, June 19, 2020, https://www.mintpressnews.com/caesar-act-latest-western-attack-syria-didnt-drop-from-plane/268697/

32. "The Toll of War: The Economic and Social Consequences of the Conflict in Syria," *World Bank*, July 10, 2017, at https://reliefweb.int/report/syrian-arab-republic/toll-war-economic-and-social-consequences-conflict-syria

33. Between 2019 and 2021, as one example, the price of basic foods in Syria increased by 800 percent, according to the UN World Food Program. Aida Chavez, "Keeping Sanctions in Force Would 'Pull the Rug Out From Under Syria,'" *The Intercept*, December 13, 2024, https://theintercept.com/2024/12/13/assad-syria-sanctions-congress/

34. In 2017, Donald Trump signed the Countering America's Adversaries Through Sanctions Act (CAATSA) which sanctioned governments (i.e., Russia and Iran) that sold arms to Syria.

35. Oliver Boyd-Barrett, *Conflict Propaganda in Syria: Narrative Battles* (New York: Routledge, 2022), 176, 261.

36. Lara Seligsman and Ben Lefebvre, "Little Known Firm Secures Deal for Syrian Oil," *Politico*, July 3, 2020, Bill Van Auken, "U.S. Stages Military Buildup to Enforce Deal to Steal Syria's Oil," *The World Socialist Website*, August 25, 2020. The U.S. military trucked in components for two modular refineries to assist the company in exploiting and marketing Syrian oil. The principals in Delta Crescent Energy included James Cain, a North Carolina Republican Party official and former U.S. ambassador to Denmark who gained brief notoriety by calling for the execution of Chelsea Manning. Also on the company's board was James Reese, a former Delta Force officer who became a private security consultant and *Fox News* contributor after retiring from the military.

37. On the Syrian American Council, see Ben Norton, "Syria war lobby that hosted genocide advocate campaigns to censor book exposing its operations," *The Grayzone*, April 4, 2019. The Syrian American Council advocated for U.S. bombing of Syria and other aggressive actions to more quickly facilitate regime change. In 2015, the lobby group hosted Maher Sharafeddine who publicly incited mass violence and ethnic cleansing against Syria's Alawite minority.

38. Ben Cole, *The Syrian Information and Propaganda War: The Role of Cognitive Bias* (Switzerland: Palgrave Macmillan, 2022), 12; Rick Sterling, "The Caesar Photo Fraud That Undermined Syrian Negotiations. "A Pattern of Sensational But Untrue Reports That Lead to Public Acceptance of Western Military Intervention," *Dissident Voice*, March 3, 2016. During his trip to Washington, Caesar also appeared at the Holocaust Memorial Museum, visited the White House and met with Samantha Power, the American ambassador to the United Nations, and a zealous proponent of "humanitarian intervention" in Syria. Human Rights Watch published a report, *If The Dead Could Speak*, supposedly corroborating Caesar's claims though the report's research methods were slipshod and it was clearly a politicized document. Cole notes in his judicious study that of the remainder of photos that were not Syrian government soldiers killed, the circumstances of the deaths were unclear.

39. Ian Black, "Syrian regime document trove shows evidence of 'industrial scale' killing of detainees," *The London Guardian*, January 27, 2014.

40. Michael R. Gordon, "Syrian Opposition to Post Dead Detainees Photos," *The New York Times*, March 4, 2015. Gordon laments in the piece that Caesar's revelations had not led to that point to an escalation of U.S. military operations in Syria. He quotes from then Secretary of State John Kerry telling a UN human rights group that "anyone who has seen the images will never forget them. Maimed bodies, people with their eyes gouged out, emaciated prisoners. It defies anybody's sense of humanity." Gordon's fake news story on the chemical weapons attack in Khan Shaykhoun was co-written with Anne Barnard and titled "Worst Chemical Attack in Syria in Years; U.S. Blames Assad," *The New York Times*, April 4, 2017. The evidence presented in a previous chapter shows that it is unlikely any chemical attack took place in

Khan Shaykhoun, so what does this say about Gordon's integrity as a reporter and methodologies? Gordon presented this chemical attack as part of a wider pattern, repeating State Department and CIA disinformation. Gordon also wrote about chemical attacks by Assad supposedly confirmed by U.S. intelligence in *The Wall Stret Journal*. Gordon's role in the Iraq War is detailed in Peter, Hart, "Looking Back at Iraq With . . ..Michael Gordon," *Fairness and Accuracy in Reporting*, March 20, 2013. In September 2002, Gordon co-wrote an article with Judith Miller claiming, based on unnamed Bush administration sources, that Saddam Hussein was on a worldwide "hunt" to acquire aluminum tubes for uranium enrichment. The article seemingly validated Bush administration charges about Saddam's attempt to acquire weapons of mass destruction, though was later discredited. Gordon subsequently championed the U.S. bombing of Iraq.

41. Shupak, "Writing Out Empire," in *Sanctions as War*, ed. Davis and Ness, 256.

42. *New York Times* editorial writer Farah Stockman characteristically claimed that the U.S. sanctions in Syria were instituted "with the best of intentions." Farah Stockman, "What Syria Needs in Order to Rebuild," *The New York Times*, December 9, 2024.

43. The latter was an explicit purpose of the sanctions. In a CovertAction Magazine webinar on July 14, 2025 Vanessa Beeley emphasized Russian frustration with Assad and alliance with Turkey as a reason why Russian troops did not do enough to try and prevent the HTS takeover in December 2024.

44. Bartlett, "The Caesar Act."

45. " Lessons From Damascus' Fall."

46. Rick Sterling, "How the West Destroyed Syria," *Orinoco Tribune*, January 19, 2025.

47. See Holly Sklar, *Washington's War on Nicaragua* (Boston: South End Press, 1988). In the election, Nicaraguans chose a candidate, Violetta Chamorro, whose family had been financed by the National Endowment for Democracy (NED), a CIA front. The U.S. financed the Sandinista opposition and spent $50 million on the election, according to a report compiled by peace activist S. Brian Willson. (S. Brian Willson, talk before Nicaraguan Solidarity Committee, March 2, 2025).

48. Sklar, *Washington's War on Nicaragua*, 265.

49. "Engel Statement on Syria Caesar Sanctions Act," June 17, 2020, https://democrats-foreignaffairs.house.gov/2020/6/engel-statement-on-syria-caesar-act-sanctions

50. Hekmat Aboukhater, "Inside the anti-Syria lobby's Capitol Hill push for more starvation sanctions," *The Grayzone*, March 20, 2024.

Chapter 9: The White Helmets: Al Qaeda's Partner in Crime

1. Writing in the neoconservative journal *Commentary*, Bruce Bawer went so far as to claim that the White Helmets saved over 100,000 lives. Bruce Bawer, "Useful Idiots," *Commentary*, September 2019.

2. Jacques Baud, *Governing by Fake News: 30 Years of Fake News in the West* (Paris: Max Milo, 2022), at p. 173.

3. Baud, *Governing by Fake News*.

4. Andrei Popoviciu, "Syria's White Helmets continue to help people in devastated Aleppo," *Al Jazeera*, March 2, 2025.

5. Andrew Waller, "After Years in exile the White Helmets return to Aleppo after Assad's fall ready to rebuild the city," *The New Arab*, January 9, 2025.

6. Mariia Ulianovska, "Syrian White Helmets co-founder: 'No perpetrator or criminal will live forever,'" *Voice of America*, December 13, 2024.

7. Benjamin Arthur Thomason, "Making Democracy Safe for Empire: History and Political Economy of the National Endowment for Democracy, United States Agency for International Development, and Twenty-First Century Media," April, 2024, 198-199.

8. A.B. Abrams, *World War on Syria: Global Conflict on Middle Eastern Battlefields* (Clarity Press, Atlanta, 2021), 289.

9. Abrams, *World War on Syria*, 289.

10. Thomason, "Making Democracy Safe For Empire," 199.

11. Thomason, "Making Democracy Safe For Empire," 199.

12. Yves Engler, *House of Mirrors: Justin Trudeau's Foreign Policy* (Montreal: Black Rose Books, 2020), 96. Canadian Foreign Minister Crystia Freeland characterized the White Helmets as "heroes." Former Canadian Justice Minister Irwin Cotler nominated them for the Nobel Peace Prize.

13. "Dutch Accountant Uncovers Fraud Behind Syria Resue Organization," *NL Times*, July 17, 2020.

14. Baud, *Governing by Fake News*, 175.

15. Baud, *Governing by Fake News*, 175.

16. Baud, *Governing By Fake News*, 870.

17. "Widow Blames Financial Problems for ex-UK officer's Death," *Hürriyet Daily News*, December 20, 2020.

18. "Why no-one could save the man who co-founded the White Helmets," *BBC*.

19. Abrams, *World War in Syria*, 289.

20. Baud, *Governing By Fake News*, 172.

21. Baud, *Governing By Fake News*, 173-174, 855.

22. "Syria's White Helmets: War By Way of Deception," *21st Century Wire*, October 23, 2015.

23. Baud, *Governing By Fake News*, 174.

24. Tim Anderson, *Axis of Resistance, Towards an Independent Middle East* (Atlanta: Clarity Press, 2019), 185.

25. Tom O'Connor, "Syria's White Helmets, Subject of Oscar-Winning Film, Caught Dumping Dead Soldiers, Fire Volunteer," *Newsweek*, September 22, 2017.

26. Abrams, *World War in Syria*, 288.

27. Anderson, *Axis of Resistance*, 183.

28. Anderson, *Axis of Resistance*, 183.

29. Anderson, *Axis of Resistance*, 183-184.

30. Anderson, *Axis of Resistance*, 182.

31. Anderson, *Axis of Resistance*, 182.

32. Baud, *Governing By Fake News*, 174.

33. Pedro Garcia, "The White Helmets Fraud in Syria," *Monthly* Review (reprinted from *Prensa Latina*), December 22, 2020.

34. Wesley Dockery, "Germany offers asylum to selected Syrian White Helmets," *DW*, July 24, 2018.

35. Abrams, *World War in Syria*, 288.

36. Abrams, *World War in Syria*, 288.

37. Abrams, *World War in Syria*, 288,290.

38. Abrams, *World War in Syria*, 288.

39. Abrams, *World War in Syria*, 305-306.

40. Abrams, *World War in Syria*, 305.

41. Abrams, *World War in Syria*, 305.

42. Abrams, *World War in Syria*, 305.

43. Anderson, *Axis of Resistance, 145-146.*

44. "White Helmets Director Raed Al-Saleh Addresses UN," *Levant24*, December 5, 2024. Al Saleh had a history of being refused entry into the U.S. because of his ties to extremist and terrorist organizations.

45. Christopher Davidson, *Shadow Wars: The Secret Struggle for the Middle East* (One World, London, 2016), 347.

46. Laith Marouf, "What is Really Happening in Syria: Testimonies from Survivors. 40 thousand Killed in HTS Genocide," *Free Palestine TV*, March 23, 2025.

47. "White Helmets Response Report in Latakia and Tartus—March 13," *WhiteHelmets*.org.

Chapter 10: The Liberal Intelligentsia Plays Its Role

1. Jeremy Kuzmarov, Roger Peace and Charles Howlett, "United States Participation in World War One," https://peacehistory-usfp.org/ww1/; Philip Knightly, *The First Casualty: The War Correspondent as Hero and Myth-Maker* (New York: Harcourt, Brace Jovanovich, 1975), 120. Groups like the Industrial Workers of the World (IWW) who opposed U.S. intervention in World War I while supporting class war at home were branded as agents of the German Kaiser.

2. See A.B. Abrams, *Atrocity Fabrication and Its Consequences: How Fake News Shapes World Order* (Atlanta: Clarity Press, 2023).

3. See Randolph Bourne, "The Responsibility of Intellectuals" and "Twilight of the Idols," in Carl Resek, ed., *War and the Intellectuals: Collected Essays 1915-1919* (New York: Harper Torch Books, 1964; reprinted, Indianapolis: Hackett Publishing Co., 1999).

4. See Frances Stonor Saunders, *The Cultural Cold War: The CIA and the World of Arts and Letters* (New York: The New Press, 2013); Hugh Wilford, *The Mighty Wurlitzer: How the CIA Played America* (Cambridge, MA: Harvard University Press, 2009).

5. Mark Taliano estimated in his 2017 book *Voices From Syria* (Global Research) that the terrorists killed an estimated 150,000 civilians and another 260,000 fighters and kidnapped thousands more, some of whom were used for illegal organ harvesting.

6. On the latter, see Robert Dreyfuss, *Devil's Game: How the U.S. Helped to Unleash Fundamentalist Islam* (New York: Metropolitan Books, 2005).

7. See Maximilian Forte, *Slouching Towards Sirte: NATO's War on Libya and Africa* (Montreal: Baraka Books, 2012).

8. Bhaskar Sunkara, "Syria: What Comes Next After the Despot? An Interview with Anand Gopal," *Jacobin Magazine*, December 11, 2024. Gopal admitted later

in the interview to Islamist support for the resistance to Assad, however, claimed that the Islamist rebels were "a mixed bag; some are truly reactionary, while others have moderated themselves and are meaningful vehicles for national liberation." This is an overly sympathetic and naïve view disproved by the events of early 2025.

9. Sunkara, "Syria." Gopal stated that he could not predict the future, but that "whatever comes next will be better than what came before," which has proven to be wrong. Gopal stated in another embarrassing claim: "Now for the first time, there's a real chance the suffering will end." In July 2017, *Jacobin* ran an article by Stephen R Shalom, a leftist who had written in the past for *Z Magazine*, which claimed that Seymour Hersh's reporting on the "fake chemical gas attack" in Khan Sheykhoun "should not be taken seriously." (Stephen R. Shalom, "The Chemical Attack at Khan Sheikhoun") If *Jacobin* had intellectual integrity, it would have updated readers by reporting on MIT scientist Theodor Postol's findings regarding Khan Sheykhoun that indeed validated Hersh's reporting. Amazingly, Shalom—who has written impressive books in the past on U.S. neocolonialism in the Philippines—cited Eliot Higgins of the intelligence front Bellingcat as a credible scientific expert when Higgins does not even possess a college degree and has admitted he knows nothing about science.

10. Mark Townsend, "Network of Syria Conspiracy Theorists Identified—Study," *The Guardian*, June 19, 2022.

11. *The Syria Dilemma*, ed. Nader Hashemi and Danny Postel (Cambridge, MA: The MIT Press, 2013).

12. Nader Hashemi, "Syria, Savagery, and Self-Determination: What the Anti-Interventionists Are Missing," in *The Syria Dilemma*, ed. Hashemi and Postel.

13. See Jeremy Kuzmarov, "The Responsibility of Intellectuals Redux: Humanitarian Intervention and the Liberal Embrace of War in the Age of Clinton, Bush and Obama," *The Asia-Pacific Journal*, Vol. 11, Issue 24, No. 1, June 16, 2014.

14. Michael Ignatieff, "Bosnia and Syria: Intervention Then and Now," in *The Syrian Dilemma*, ed. Hashemi and Postel, 45-58.

15. Ignatieff, "Bosnia and Syria," in *The Syrian Dilemma*, ed. Hashemi and Postel, 46.

16. Ignatieff, "Bosnia and Syria," in *The Syrian Dilemma*, ed. Hashemi and Postel, 48.

17. Ignatieff, "Bosnia and Syria," in *The Syrian Dilemma*, ed. Hashemi and Postel, 47.

18. Jeremy Kuzmarov, *War Monger: How Clinton's Malign Foreign Policy Shaped the U.S. Trajectory from Bush II to Biden* (Atlanta: Clarity Press, 2024), ch. 4; Alija Izetbegovic, *The Islamic Declaration* (Sarajevo, 1990). A 1980 follow-up book by Izetbegovic was entitled: *Islam: Between East and West*.

19. Cees Wiebes, *Intelligence and the War in Bosnia 1992-1995* (Hamburg and London: Lit Verlag Munster, 2003), 68; 125, 126; Kit Klarenberg and Tom Secker, "Declassified Intelligence Files Expose Inconvenient Truths of Bosnian War," *The Grayzone Project*, December 30, 2022. The Srebrenica massacre was also presented misleadingly. See *The Srebrenica Massacre: Evidence, Context and Politics*, ed. Edward S. Herman and Philip Corwin. A Canadian intelligence report specified that "the Muslims are not above firing on their own people or UN areas and then

claiming the Serbs are the guilty party in order to gain further Western sympathy. The Muslims often site their artillery extremely close to UN buildings and sensitive areas such as hospitals in the hope that Serb counter-bombardment fire will hit these sites under the gaze of the international media."

20. David N. Gibbs, *First Do No Harm: Humanitarian Intervention and the Destruction of Yugoslavia* (Nashville: TN: Vanderbilt University Press, 2009),143, 144, 146.

21. See Michael Chossudovsky, "Dismantling Yugoslavia, Colonizing the Bosnia," *Covert Action Quarterly*, Spring 1996; Carol Shaffer, "The West's Charming Lies: How the Dayton accords, and privatization have kept Bosnia in tragic limbo," *The Nation*, January 9/16, 2023, 27-31. The U.S. sustained heavy military training programs and economic policies were controlled by the European Bank of Reconstruction and Development and International Monetary Fund (IMF), which imposed privatization and austerity measures that came to trap the people in poverty.

22. Ignatieff, "Bosnia and Syria," in *The Syrian Dilemma*, ed. Hashemi and Postel, 50.

23. Ignatieff, "Bosnia and Syria," in *The Syrian Dilemma*, ed. Hashemi and Postel, 55.

24. Ignatieff, "Bosnia and Syria," in *The Syrian Dilemma*, ed. Hashemi and Postel, 56.

25. See William Blum, *Killing Hope: U.S. Military and CIA Interventions Since World War II* (Monroe, ME: Common Courage Press, 1998).

26. Pilar Melendez, "Trump: 'We Left Troops Behind in Syria Only for the Oil,'" *The Daily Beast*, November 13, 2019. A lot of Western journalists and academics present the viewpoint of anti-Assad Syrian refugees as if it was representative of all Syrians. See ie. Wendy Pearlman, *We Crossed a Bridge and It Trembled: Voices From Syria* (New York: HarperCollins, 2017); *The Home I Worked to Make: Voices From the New Syrian Diaspora* (New York: W.W. Norton, 2024). Pearlman is a professor of political science at Northwestern University. She claims that the Arab Spring protests were entirely peaceful and spread through Facebook and repeats many distorted claims such as that Assad used chemical weapons against his people.

27. Shadi Hamid, "Syria is Not Iraq," in *The Syrian Dilemma*, ed. Hashemi and Postel, 19-29.

28. Mary Kaldor, "A Humanitarian Strategy Focused on Syrian Civilians," in *The Syrian Dilemma*, ed. Hashemi and Postel, 156. Kaldor was listed as a professor of global governance at the London School of Economics. Human Rights Watch director Kenneth Roth called for a tightening of sanctions on Syria.

29. An essay by Charles Glass called for a halt to all arms supplies, and a rather enlightening essay by CNN host Fareed Zakaria explained some of the regional political dynamic and warned of the pitfalls of U.S. and other foreign intervention in Syria.

30. One of the essays actually invoked a dated Orientalist text, Karl Wittfogel's book *Oriental Despotism: A Comparative Study of Total Power* (New Haven: Yale University Press, 1957) to try and explain Assad.

31. See Samantha Power, *'A Problem From Hell:' America in the Age of Genocide* (New York: Basic Books, 2002); and for a detailed critique of this book, see

Kuzmarov, "The Responsibility of Intellectuals Redux." Power in her book presents misleading history and cartoonish narratives of various conflicts to make it seem like the U.S. did nothing to intervene to stop genocides. However, in many cases, it had in fact intervened and triggered the wars that resulted in genocides. Failing to discuss the real geopolitical and economic imperatives driving U.S. foreign interventions and class-based rule in the U.S., the book characteristically ignored any cases where the U.S. directly supported genocide or supported it through proxy. Power overall makes it appear that the problem is that the U.S. does not intervene enough to halt genocide when the drive for empire results in repeated genocides.

32. Slaughter was then the Director of the Woodrow Wilson School of International Affairs at Princeton University.

33. Anne Marie Slaughter, "Syria is Not a Problem From Hell—But if We Don't Act Quickly it Will Be," in *The Syrian Dilemma*, ed. Hashemi and Postel, 93-99.

34. See Kuzmarov, *War Monger;* Robin Philpot, *Rwanda and the New Scramble For Africa: From Tragedy to Useful Imperial Fiction* (Montreal: Baraka Books, 2013).

35. Joe Emersberger argued that Slaughter's assessment would be tantamount to accusing Abraham Lincoln of being responsible for all of the deaths that took place during the U.S. Civil War, including the hundreds of thousands of Union troops. Emersberger notes that: "by a slave owner's reading of history, Abraham Lincoln butchered 260,000 to 400,000 of his 'own people' in the South to keep the Confederate States from seceding from the USA. Lincoln was actually a perpetrator of genocide against the indigenous peoples of North America like the all the US presidents who established the USA. He also wanted to expel the Black population to Haiti after the Civil War. But taken in isolation, his military victory over the Confederate States—even if you know that the plight of slaves was not actually Lincoln's priority—cannot be used by any reasonable person to depict him as a monster. There is no 'freedom' to establish a giant confederation of slave owners that anyone should respect. Waging a civil war to prevent it was fully justified." According to Emersberger, "President Bashar al-Assad of Syria also fought, but in his case ultimately lost, a civil war that he was fully justified in waging. Since 2011 until his ouster weeks ago, Assad fought to prevent his country from being conquered and partitioned by the greatest evil in the world today: the US Empire. Assad fought armed rebels backed by the US and its top clients in the region: Turkey, Israel and Saudi Arabia. The case for depicting Assad as a monster is based on the premise that Assad had no right to defend his country against the US and its allies." The Anti Empire Project and Joe Emersberger, "Evaluating Bashar al-Assad's Human Rights Record in Syria: Can Resisting the Genocidal US Empire Be a Stain on Your human Rights Record?" *Medium*, December 15, 2024.

36. Gilbert Achcar, "How to Avoid the Anti-Imperialism of Fools," *The Nation Magazine*, April 5, 2021.

37. For a critique of Achcar's hawkish position on Syria and Libya, see Alex Lantier, "New Anti-Capitalist Party Demands Military Escalation Against Turkey in Syria," *World Socialist Website*, October 13, 2019. Lantier wrote that "as NATO carpet-bombed Libyan cities, Achcar insisted that the NATO war had to be

supported as a humanitarian act to protect anti-government protesters in Libya. Claiming that he was regretfully compelled to support war, Achcar declared that in 'the absence of any alternative means of achieving the protection goal, no one can reasonably oppose it... You can't in the name of anti-imperialist principles oppose an action that will prevent the massacre of civilians.'"

38. Gilbert Achcar and Noam Chomsky, *Perilous Power: The Middle East and U.S. Foreign Policy* (New York: Routledge, 2015). Achcar also wrote a well-researched book on Arabs and the Nazi Holocaust.

39. Dave DeCamp, "US Plans to Relocate Troops in Kurdish-Controlled Syria to Two New Military Bases," *Antiwar.com*, April 22, 2025.

40. See Matthew Petti, "U.S. Slap Sanctions on Formerly CIA-Backed Syrian Rebels," *Responsible Statecraft*, August 22, 2023. The Suleiman Shah Brigade, which had been supported by the CIA under Operation Timber Sycamore, was, according to the Biden administration, "directed to forcibly displace Kurdish residents and seize their property, providing vacated homes for Syrians from outside the region who [were] often related to fighters in the brigade." According to Matthew Petti, the Suleiman Shah Brigade and others like it earned a particular reputation for brutality against Kurdish civilians.

41. Layla Maghribi, "Liberation in Syria is a Victory Worth Embracing," *New Lines Magazine*, reprinted on Portside, December 10, 2024.

42. Joseph Daher, "Understanding the Rebellion in Syria," *Counterpunch*, December 10, 2024; Daniel Falcone-Stephen Zunes, "The Ousting of the Brutal Assad Regime Brings Euphoria and More Questions," *Counterpunch*, December 11, 2024. The term "tankie" was a pejorative term used to criticize North American communists who supported the Soviet Union's sending of tanks to crush an uprising led by social democrats in Hungary in 1956 and again in Czechoslovakia in 1968. Ironically, newly released government documents from the JFK assassination files show that the CIA supported the Hungarian uprising as the Soviets had alleged.

43. Daher, "Understanding the Rebellion in Syria."

44. Daher, "Understanding the Rebellion in Syria."

45. Falcone-Zunes, "The Ousting of the Brutal Assad Regime Brings Euphoria and More Questions."

46. Stephen Zunes, "Lessons and False Lessons From Libya," *Truthout*, August 30, 2011.

47. Falcone-Zunes, "The Ousting of the Brutal Assad Regime Brings Euphoria and More Questions."
Zunes said that "President Obama had been subjected to unfair criticism both for providing some support for the resistance as well as for not doing enough."

48. Shireen Akram-Boshar, "As Assad Regime Falls, Syrians Celebrate—and Brace for an Uncertain Future," *Truthout*, December 11, 2024. Akram-Boshar was involved with the Students For Justice in Palestine group at Brown University and was attacked by the fascistic Canary Mission website for supporting Palestinian rights.

49. https://www.democracynow.org/2024/12/13/syria_damascus. Another *Democracy Now* segment featured a search for Assad mass graves while nothing

was said about mass graves from atrocities directed by rebel forces that long targeted Shia Alawites in violent ethnic cleansing operations. https://www.democracynow.org/2024/12/19/syria_mass_graves

50. Shane Bauer, "Behind the Lines," *Mother Jones*, May/June 2020; https://www.democracynow.org/2019/8/8/behind_the_lines_shane_bauer_travels; Alexander Rubinstein and Max Blumenthal, "US Judge Awards Pro Regime Change Journo Shane Bauer $113 Million Seized From Iran," *The Grayzone*, January 1, 2025. Bauer, who also attacked Tulsi Gabbard, accused Putin and Assad of waging a disinformation campaign that helped obscure the wide scope of Syrian atrocities. It escapes him that the U.S. or CIA could have waged a far more expansive disinformation operation than Putin or Assad, which he appears to be part of. Bauer gained fame as an investigative journalist for working undercover as a guard at a private prison to expose its abuses and won a huge financial settlement after being detained in an Iranian prison after being accused of being an American spy along with two other Americans. Named after a legendary labor activist, *Mother Jones* was founded by Adam Hochschild, the son of Harold Hochschild, a wealthy mining tycoon who made a fortune off the plunder of Africa and was a financier of the Africa-America Institute, a CIA front that brought African leaders to the U.S. and promoted U.S. propaganda in Africa.

51. Bauer repeats the false mainstream media and Obama administration claim that Seymour Hersh's articles exposing the Obama administration's lies about the chemical gas attacks and prevalence of a new Gulf of Tonkin, "had been widely discredited." Chapter 7 in this book shows quite the opposite. Predictably, Bauer never actually engages with the evidence that Hersh's presents, showing his suspect nature or at best lack of intellectual rigor or professionalism. Bauer tellingly cites a report put out by a pro-NATO-pro-humanitarian intervention think-tank and that cites intelligence linked sources like Bellingcat as authoritative alleging that there were over 330 chemical attacks in Syria, 98 percent of which were carried out by Assad. While some aspects of his reporting are valuable because he is interviewing first-hand participants, Bauer's work is further misleading because he makes it seem like the Kurds main fight was against ISIS, obscuring the fact that they were also being used as part of a regime change operation targeting Assad. Additionally, he appears to be partisan towards the Democratic Party, criticizing aspects of Trump's policy in Syria, but rarely Obama's

52. See David W. Conde, *CIA—Core of the Cancer* (New Delhi: Entente Private Limited, 1970); David Price, *Cold War Deceptions: The Asia Foundation and the CIA* (Seattle: University of Washington Press, 2024).

53. Quoted in Jeremy Kuzmarov, "JFK's Lover Was Among Victims of CIA Murder Machine, According to Son of Former High-Level CIA Official," *CovertAction Magazine*, November 22, 2024.

54. See Mark Lause, *Counterfeiting Labor's Voice: William A.A. Carsey and the Shaping of American Reform Politics* (Urbana: University of Illinois Press, 2024).

55. Kirkpatrick Sale, "The Rise of Ugly Socialism in the Democratic Party," *Counterpunch*, December 13, 2024.

56. Some have suggested that this was by the design of the CIA, which supported intellectuals like Herbert Marcuse who helped influence the turn away from

working class solidarity and towards the embrace of identity politics. See e.g. Gabriel Rockhill, "The CIA and the Frankfurt School's Anti-Communism," *The Philosophical Salon*, June 27, 2022.

57. See James Peck, *Ideal Illusions: How the U.S. Government Coopted Human Rights* (New York: Metropolitan Books, 2011).

58. See Kuzmarov, *War Monger.*

59. See Statement of the High Commissioner, April 30, 1999, at https://www. ohchr.org/en/press-releases/2009/10/high-commissioner-human-rights-calls-immediate-end-ethnic-cleansing-kosovo

60. See Jeremy Kuzmarov, *Obama's Unending Wars: Fronting the Foreign Policy of the Permanent Warfare State* (Atlanta: Clarity Press, 2019).

61. Arvind Dilawar, "Homage to Rojava: An American Fighter in ISIS Territory," *L.A. Review of Books*, January 11, 2020.

62. See e.g. Shane Bauer, "I Went to Syria to Meet the People Trump Just Gave Turkey Permission to Kill," *Mother Jones*, October 8, 2019. In this piece, Bauer profiles an antifa activist named "Barry" who wore a black anarcho-syndicalist patch on the arm of his uniform. Bauer acknowledges that "Barry," whose commanders called in aerial strikes from American jets, fought side by side with other mercenaries who went to Syria because they "wanted to kill sand n____" At the end of the piece, Bauer wrote: "they are soldiers, projecting fantasies onto Syria to find meaning in their war."

63. *Revolution in Rojava: Democratic Autonomy and Women's Liberation in Syrian Kurdistan*, ed. Michael Knapp et al., with foreword by David Graeber (London: Pluto Press, 2016); "Pete Dolack, "Why Are Leftists Cheering the Potential Demise of Rojava's Socialist Experiment," *Counterpunch*, January 4, 2019; Alex De Jong, "The Rojava Project," *Jacobin*, November 30, 2016; Bauer, "I Went to Syria to Meet the People Trump Just Gave Turkey Permission to Kill;" Meredith Tax, *A Road Unforeseen: Women Fight the Islamic State* (Bellevue Literary Press, 2016). The latter book argues that the left should support the Kurdish struggle.

64. Thomas Jefrey Miley, "The Kurdish Freedom Movement, Rojava and the Left," August 1, 2020, https://popularresistance.org/the-kurdish-freedom-movement-rojava-and-the-left/

65. David Graeber, foreword to *Revolution in Rojava*, xiv.

66. Lantier, "New Anti-capitalist Party demands military escalation against Turkey in Syria."

67. "Under Kurdish Rule: Abuses in PYD-Run Enclaves of Syria," *Human Rights Watch*, June 19, 2014; Wes Enzinna, "A Dream of Secular Utopia in ISIS' Backyard," *The New York Times*, November 24, 2015. A 36-year-old Kurdish man was reportedly beaten to death by police in Rojava for criticizing Ocalan and numbers of protesters were killed by security forces.

68. "Syria: US Ally's Razing of Villages Amounts to War Crimes," *Amnesty International*, October 13, 2015; Enzinna, "A Dream of Secular Utopia in ISIS' Backyard." The Amnesty report specified that thousands of civilians were deliberately displaced by the U.S. supported Kurdish militias. One witness told the Amnesty researcher: "they pulled us out of our homes and began burning the home... they brought the bulldozers... They demolished home after home until

the entire village was destroyed." Another resident in a village south of the town of Suluk said that "they told us we had to leave or they would tell the US coalition that we were terrorists and their planes would hit us and our families."

69. "In Rojava: People's War is not Class War," October 30, 2014, https://www.leftcom.org/en/articles/2014-10-30/in-rojava-people%E2%80%99s-war-is-not-class-war; "PYD Asayish arrests Hassan Saleh, deputy secretary of Kurdish Yekiti Party in Syria (P.Y.K.S)," August 15, 2018, https://en.yekiti-media.org/pyd-asayish-arrests-hassan-saleh-deputy-secretary-kurdish-yekiti-party-syria-p-y-k-s/; "Hunger strike in solidarity with the political detainees in the prisons of PYD," September 16, 2016, https://syriafreedomforever.wordpress.com/2016/09/16/hunger-strike-in-solidarity-with-the-political-detainees-in-the-prisons-of-pyd. Journalist Matt Broomfield, co-founder of the Rojava Information Center, wrote in a 2023 essay that some anarchist volunteers who went to Rojava "left despondent, their idealized view of the 'Rojava revolution' foundering on the reality of mass poverty, limited political engagement and an increasingly prominent security apparatus." Matt Broomfield, "Is Rojava a Socialist Utopia?" *Unherd*, March 28, 2023. The "devolution of decision-making authority" in Rojava was also said to be "partial and inconsistent...directing an economy or a war requires centralized policy, and most locals are content to leave these issues to their leaders, visiting the commune only to collect the chits for their subsidized bread and oil." The PKK was put on the State Department's terrorist watchlist in 1997.

70. Andrea Giloti, "Rojava: A Libertarian Myth under Scrutiny," *Al Jazeera*, August 5, 2016. Giloti wrote that when she was living in Rojava with a Syrian Kurdish family in 2013, most of the people she met were "busy dealing with the rising cost of living and had no idea of the difference between federalism and libertarian municipalism [Bookchin vision]."

71. Lantier, "New Anti-capitalist Party demands military escalation against Turkey in Syria." Later in the same article, Lantier wrote that "attempts to portray Rojava as a revolutionary, democratic way forward for the Kurds and other peoples of the world were a shameless fraud." He continued: "Rojava operated under the diktat of the Pentagon, the decisive counterrevolutionary force in the Middle East. As such, its population was subordinated to the relentless war scheming of American imperialism and its European allies, and their accelerating preparations for war with Iran and an all-out military conflagration across the Middle East."

72. "In Rojava: People's War is not Class War."

73. Bill Rood, letter to the editor, https://popularresistance.org/the-kurdish-freedom-movement-rojava-and-the-left/. Rood referenced the Oded Yinon Plan by which the Western Powers and Israel wanted to balkanize the Middle-East so they could dominate it. Assad incidentally had granted 22,000 Kurds Syrian citizenship in April 2011.

74. Jeremy Kuzmarov, *Modernizing Repression: Police Training and Nation Building in the American Century* (Amherst, MA: University of Massachusetts Press, 2012) discusses the strategy of arming tribal minorities and its pitfalls.

75. Zhang Chungyue, "US Forces Continuing Blatant Looting of Syrian Oil, 'Exposing Gangster Nature,'" *Global Times*, September 6, 2022. For historical

precedents, see Alfred W. McCoy, *The Politics of Heroin: CIA Complicity in the Global Drugs Trade*, rev ed. (New York: Lawrence Hill Books, 2001).

76. A.B. Abrams, *World War in Syria: Global Conflict on Middle Eastern Battlefields* (Atlanta: Clarity Press, 2021), 268.

77. Adam Entous, "The Partnership: America's Hidden Role in the Ukraine War," *The New York Times*, March 30, 2025, 14. Donahue was from Wilkes Barre, Pennsylvania and helped oversee the U.S. withdrawal from Afghanistan. General Christopher Cavoli, who also played a key role running the Ukraine War, said of him: "He is without a doubt, the most experienced war fighter we have in the U.S. Army, more than 20 deployments covering literally every single named operation, combat or otherwise, that we have been busy (with) in the last 30 years. It's almost like a comic book action hero." John Vandiver, "'Almost Like a Comic Book Action Hero'": Donahue Takes Up Army Leadership of Army's Europe Mission," *Stars and Stripes*, December 10, 2024.

78. "Former Syrian Detainee Recounts Indiscriminate PKK/YPG Torture," *Daily Sabbah*, December 23, 2024; Abrams, *World War in Syria*, 273.

79. Oliver Boyd-Barrett, *Conflict Propaganda in Syria: Narrative Battles* (New York: Routledge, 2022), 260.

80. On the later, see e.g. Jennifer Pearcy, "Meet the American Vigilantes Who Are fighting ISIS," *The New York Times*, September 30, 2015; Michael McCanne, "Fighting For Rojava: A Jewish American anarchist who fought alongside the Kurds against ISIS reflects on his experiences and the current state of the region." *Jewish Currents*, October 29, 2019. Many of the volunteer mercenaries quickly realized there was nothing heroic about the Kurdish militias they were fighting with. One told *New York Times* reporter Jennifer Percy that "this is the Twilight Zone," and another said. "lovely fairy tale."

81. Abrams, *World War in Syria*, 274.

82. Jeremy Kuzmarov, "Tulsi Gabbard Was Right to Question Official Narrative About Syrian Chemical Weapons Attacks," *CovertAction Magazine*, December 16, 2024.

83. Kuzmarov, "Tulsi Gabbard Was Right to Question Official Narrative About Syrian Chemical Weapons Attacks;" Jeremy Kuzmarov, "Prestigious Weaponry Expert Censored After Demonstrating that a Deadly Poison Gas Attack—Blamed on the Syrian Government—Was Really a False-Flag Operation by U.S.-Funded Terrorists," *CovertAction Magazine*, November 22, 2021.

Chapter 11: Syria After the Western-backed Al Qaeda Triumph—As Witnessed by Dan Kovalik

1. "New U.S. Intel Chief Slams Obama Era Policy of Supporting Al Qaeda in Syria: What Was CIA Operation Timber Sycamore?" *Military Watch Magazine*, February 1, 2025.

2. Seymour Hersh, "The Redirection," *New Yorker Magazine*, February 27, 2007.

3. See Robert Dreyfuss, *Devils Game: How the U.S. Helped to Unleash Fundamentalist Islam* (New York: Metropolitan Books, 2005). Another Muslim Brotherhood offshoot is Hamas, which grew out of the Muslim Brotherhood's Palestinian branch in 1987, with no small amount of help from Israel which wanted

to use Hamas as a counterweight to the PLO and Yasser Arafat. See Mehdi Hasan, Dina Sayedahmed, "Blowback: How Israel went from Helping Create Hamas to Bombing it," *The Intercept*, Feb. 19, 2018. Syria too provided much support to Hamas in the 1990's, but for the purpose of supporting the Palestinian struggle. Giorgio Cafiero, "Why Syria is So Silent About Hamas," *Stimson*, March 19, 2024. Syria would even give Hamas its base of operations in Damascus in 2001. Tragically, Hamas, following the lead of the Muslim Brotherhood of Syria, joined the armed struggle against Bashar al-Assad from 2011 to 2017, even helping build the tunnels that the terrorist groups used to enter Syria. Hamas would later apologize to Assad for this treachery, but the damage was done, and its efforts in fighting Assad would later come back on the Palestinians themselves, and upon Hamas in particular.

4. Stephen Gowans, *Washington's War on Syria* (Montreal: Baraka Books, 2017), 147.
5. Gowans, *Washington's War on Syria*. Evidence one of the author's has been privy to indicates that CIA operative Robert Booth Nichols oversaw military training of Bin Laden in Australia.
6. Christopher Davidson, *Shadow Wars: The Secret Struggle for the Middle East* (One World Publications Ltd., London, 2016), 13-19.
7. Maya Gebeily and Timour Azhari in Beirut; Menna Alaa El-Din and Muhammed Al Gebaly in Cairo, "Syria's Sharaa says it will take 4-5 years to hold Presidential Elections," *US News & World Reports* (reprinted from *Reuters*), February 3, 2025.
8. Nidal Betare, "A New Opportunity for Palestinians in Syria," Arab Center, Washington D.C., March 21, 2025. The Arab Center concludes that the HTS quickly "dismantled the traditional Palestinian political structure developed over many decades under the Assad regimes, with the goals of reducing the presence of these groups in Syria and transforming them into community-based organizations."
9. The Cradle's Palestinian Correspondent, "How Syria's HTS is Quietly Dismantling the Palestinian Cause," *The Cradle*, March 25, 2025.
10. The Cradle's Palestinian Correspondent, "How Syria's HTS is Quietly Dismantling the Palestinian Cause."
11. The Cradle's Palestinian Correspondent, "How Syria's HTS is Quietly Dismantling the Palestinian Cause."
12. Ibid. In late April, British journalist Richard Medhurst reported that senior leaders of Palestinian Islamic Jihad (PIJ) were arrested by Jolani's men. Under Assad, PIJ was headquartered in Damascus. Jolani spent the last months dismantling their presence. https://x.com/richimedhurst/status/1914613354917732669?s=46
13. https://x.com/richimedhurst/status/1914613354917732669?s=46
14. Betare, "A New Opportunity for Palestinians in Syria."
15. Betare, "A New Opportunity for Palestinians in Syria."
16. Betare, "A New Opportunity for Palestinians in Syria."
17. Betare, "A New Opportunity for Palestinians in Syria."
18. Yaniv Kubovich and Avi Scharf, "Satellite Images Reveal Seven New IDF Outposts in Syria along the Border with Israel," *Haaretz*, February 18, 2025.
19. "Syrian Interior Ministry Releases New Map Without the Golan Heights and Alexandretta," *The Cradle*, February 5, 2025

20. "Syrian Interior Ministry Releases New Map Without the Golan Heights and Alexandretta."
21. Laith Marouf, "HTS Attacks North Lebanon, Israel Provides Air Cover," *Palestine TV*, February 10, 2025.
22. Christina Goldbaum, "As Other Arab States Condemn Israeli Attacks on Iran, Syria is Notably Silent," *The New York Times*, June 17, 2025.
23. Ali Haj Suleiman, "Syria's New Rulers Face Unprecedented Criticism as Israel Uses Air Space to Attack Iran," *Middle East Eye*, June 17, 2025.
24. "Statement on Outlawing of the Syrian Communist Party (Bakdash), *Struggle La Lucha*, February 4, 2025, https://www.struggle-la-lucha.org/2025/02/04/statement-on-outlawing-of-the-syrian-communist-party-bakdash/
25. See Declassified 2012 DDI Document, as posted by Judicial Watch: https://www.judicialwatch.org/wp-content/uploads/2015/0
26. "Annual Threat Assessment of the US Intelligence Community," Office of the Director of National Intelligence, March 18, 2025, https://www.dni.gov/files/ODNI/documents/assessments/ATA-2025-Unclassified-Report.pdf
27. Jennifer Hansler, "Trump admin has terminated majority of its funding for key Syrian humanitarian organization," *CNN*, March 27, 2025.
28. Pamela Geller, "Syria Now Controlled by Isis: Mass Slaughter Continues, Upwards of 50,000 Killed," *Geller Report*, March 30, 2025; Jason Ditz, "14 Alawites Killed in Central Syria as Sectarian Purge Continues," *antiwar.com*, April 27, 2025. Ditz reported on civilians being dragged out of their homes and summarily executed.
29. Mostafa Salem, "In Netanyahu's New Middle East, Syria Could Become Israel's Biggest Strategic Gain," *CNN*, March 14, 2025.
30. Geller, "Syria Now Controlled by Isis: Mass Slaughter Continues, Upwards of 50,000 Killed." One of Jolani's advisers, Matin Abu Ahmed, was photographed holding the head of a Palestinian boy that he had chopped off during the war.
31. "HTS Murder of Alawites and Christians: Details of Syria's Silent, Sectarian Slaughter Emerge," *21st Century Wire*, March 28, 2025,
32. Tim Anderson, Twitter (X), January 25, 2025, https://x.com/timand2037/status/1883217970199167212?s=46
33. Adib Hawala, *Facebook*, February 5, 2025, https://www.facebook.com/story.php?story_fbid=1686487478890733&id=61559790864015&mibextid=wwXIfr&rdid=kIuo8SJbVjbjzZ4f
34. The Cradle's Syria Correspondent, "Sectarian Murder in Syria: Rogue Militias or Policy from Damascus," *The Cradle*, January 29, 2025.
35. Ibid.
36. Matthew Petti, "US has no plans to aid Civilians, Reconstruction in Syria," *Responsible Statecraft*, December 11, 2020.
37. Ghaith Alsayed and Sally Aljoud, "I thought I'd Died: How Land Mines Are Continuing to Claim Lives in Post-Assad Syria," *Associated Press*, April 21, 2025.
38. Shelly Culbertson and Louay Constant, "After the Assad Regime's Fall will Syrian Refugees Return," *Rand Corporation* (reprinted from the *LA Times*), February 4, 2025.
39. Andrew Roth, "Russia and Turkey agree to ceasefire in Syria's Idlib province," *The Guardian*, March 5, 2020.

40. Francesco Santioianni, *Syrian Fake News: 13 Years of Lies That Have Destroyed Syria* (Naples: LAD Ezizioni, 2025), 17.

41. Jean Bricmont, *Humanitarian Imperialism: Using Human Rights to Promote War* (Monthly Review Press, New York, 2006), 46-47

42. Bricmont, *Humanitarian Imperialism*, 47.

43. Michael Parenti, "The Sarin Mysteries," *Znet*, October 2, 2013.

44. Parenti, "The Sarin Mysteries."

45. "HTS Murder of Alawites and Christians: Details of Syria's Silent, Sectarian Slaughter Emerge," *21ˢᵗ Century Wire*.

46. @Burano25, Twitter (X), March 25, 2025, https://x.com/burano2025/status/1904581651176251687?s=46

47. Souhail Lawand, "Safety Concerns Escalate for Christians in Historic Syrian Town of Maaloula," *Catholic New* Agency, December 31, 2024.

48. Damir Nazarov, "Strength Amid Struggles: Syria's Foundation of Resistance Takes Shape," *Islamic World News*, March 27, 2025.

Epilogue

1. Alex Lantier, "The petty-bourgeois 'left' promotes the CIA war in Syria," *World Socialist Website*, April 12, 2013.

2. Murtaza Hussain and Ryan Grim, "Syria's New President Has an Offer For Trump," *Drop Site News*, May 9, 2025; "Jolani proposes Trump Tower in Damascus, peace with Israel for sanctions relief: Report," *Press TV*, May 12, 2025.

3. Hussain and Grim, "Syria's New President Has an Offer For Trump."

4. Selina Sykes, "Trump meets Syrian leader in Saudi Arabia ahead of Qatar visit," *France 24*, May 15, 2024.

5. Hussain and Grim, "Syria's New President Has an Offer For Trump."

6. Christina Goldbaum, "Inside a City Swept by Roving Gunmen, Deadly Grudges and Fear," *The New York Times*, April 20, 2025.

7. "Absence of law deterrence: 50 Alawite women missing since beginning of 2025," Syria Human Rights Observatory, April 20, 2025; Joshua Landis, "Young Alawite Women Kidnapped in #Syria," Twitter (X), April 21, 2025, https://x.com/joshua_landis/status/1914364522820985195?s=46

8. "Burkina Faso Violence: Al-Qaeda-linked Group Kills 100+ But President In Russia For Putin's Event," *Times Now*, May 14, 2025; Alan McLeod, "Burkina Faso's 37-Year Old Leader Draws U.S. Ire," *Consortium News*, May 13, 2025.

FSC MIX Paper FSC® C100212 www.fsc.org

Printed by Imprimerie Gauvin
Gatineau, Québec